DISCARDED

Income Distribution Policies and Economic Growth in Semiindustrialized Countries

Robert E. Looney

The Praeger Special Studies program—utilizing the most modern and efficient book production techniques and a selective worldwide distribution network—makes available to the academic, government, and business communities significant, timely research in U.S. and international economic, social, and political development.

Income Distribution Policies and Economic Growth in Semiindustrialized Countries

A Comparative Study of Iran, Mexico, Brazil, and South Korea

PRAEGER SPECIAL STUDIES IN INTERNATIONAL ECONOMICS AND DEVELOPMENT

Praeger Publishers   New York   Washington   London

Library of Congress Cataloging in Publication Data

Looney, Robert E
   Income distribution policies and economic growth in simiindustrialized countries.

   (Praeger special studies in international economics and development)
   Bibliography: p.
   1. Income distribution—Iran. 2. Income distribution—Mexico. 3. Income distribution—Brazil.
4. Income distribution—Korea. I. Title.
HC79.I5L65   339.2   74-33036
ISBN 0-275-05380-6

PRAEGER PUBLISHERS
111 Fourth Avenue, New York, N.Y. 10003, U.S.A.

Published in the United States of America in 1975
by Praeger Publishers, Inc.

All rights reserved

© 1975 by Praeger Publishers, Inc.

Printed in the United States of America

PREFACE

Several books have been written on the subject of income distribution in developing countries.[1] It may therefore be pertinent to ask "Why another one?" The answer is that the previous books have limited their analyses to only one segment of the economy—for example, the effect of taxes on the rural distribution of income.[2] It is my contention that since all segments of the economy are interrelated, all must be considered in any study of the subject.

Only those with a superficial knowledge of economic forces look for a rapid solution to the profoundly serious problems of social justice and inequality that often arise in the course of economic development. The first task of any new investigation into these problems is therefore clearly to define the appropriate historical or dynamic frame of reference for examining actual conditions and policies and for designing alternative approaches. Such a frame of reference is conspicuously absent, not only in the reports of such prestigious missions as those carried out by the World Bank or the International Labor Organization,[3] but also in the modern development literature.[4]

The significance of a new study on income distribution is that interest in the subject has been suddenly forced upon us by a series of disasters in countries where development seemed to be vigorously underway. The civil war in Nigeria, the bloody falling apart of Pakistan, and the violent death of Salvador Allende in Chile can be traced directly to the growing inequalities of income in these respective countries.

One study could not of course cover the multitude of emerging countries. Four countries have been selected here, and though not typical of all, the four—Mexico, Iran, Brazil, and South Korea—have exhibited the capacity for rapid advancement. They are examined with the aim of determining if increasing income disparities can be prevented while high rates of economic growth are at the same time sustained.

With the emergence of many developing countries after World War II, the governments of those countries selected one of two broad strategies for growth. The first of these strategies emphasized production, particularly of manufactured goods, for the domestic market, and was associated with various government policies such as tariffs, exchange controls, overvalued exchange rates, subsidized credit, and low taxes. This was the approach taken toward development by Mexico, Iran, and Brazil, and by most of the other semiindustrialized countries.[5]

v

The second strategy, which was followed in South Korea, emphasized production for the world market; in this case tariff protection was slight, subsidies for industrial production directed to the home market were slight, and free market forces were the primary device used to allocate resources.

Both strategies resulted in high rates of growth for the four countries studied here, yet evidence from the 1960s and early 1970s suggests that as much as a 20 percent drop in the per capita income of the poorest 40 percent of households occurred in Brazil, with lower declines for Mexico and Iran. On the other hand, in Korea the income levels did not decline for those income groups, but rather grew at more or less the same rate as national income, and thus the income distribution for the country remained fairly stable.

This suggests that alternative development strategies may have different impacts on the incomes of different groups, even in a period as short as a decade. Thus it is important and worthwhile to examine which variables and government policies affect income distribution and to what extent. The intent of the framework presented here is to provide a basis for which the implications can be examined for the distribution of income resulting from strategies of economic growth as followed by Brazil, Iran, and Mexico on the one hand and by Korea on the other.

I have determined that the distribution of income in those economies is primarily the by-product of their production and consumption activities, and that any government decision to use a particular policy to influence the pattern of income distribution must be formulated in a framework that traces the circular flow of income and product in a mutually consistent and interrelated fashion. Given this context income distribution can play an important role in the economic development of the countries. Far from being of interest only in terms of some vague notion of equity or social justice, the distribution of income itself can provide a major contributing force to the growth process.

This work is the culmination of several years of field work and study on the process of development in emerging countries. I am indebted to more individuals than can be conveniently identified within the confines of this Preface. However, I would like to thank Robert Davenport of Stanford Research Institute; Sheldon Simon and Halder Fisher of Battelle Memorial Institute, Columbus, Ohio; Max Borlin of the Battelle Memorial Institute, Geneva; Mamoud Tajdar and Ahmed Kooros of the Bank Markazi Iran; Mario Belotti and Daniel Dick of the University of Santa Clara; Harry Oshima of the University of Hawaii; Frank Child, Tom Mayer, and Bruce Glassburner of the University of California, Davis; Earle Orr, Graham Smith, Derish Wolff, Raoul Auzmendi, Frank Ryan, and particularly Peter Gajewski, all of Louis Berger International; and Alexis Andolenko of the Bureau Central d' Etudes, Paris. Special thanks are given to Christine Tapley for her invaluable assistance in conceptualizing and organizing the final draft.

NOTES

1. *Income Distribution in Latin America* (New York: The United Nations, 1971); Nancy Baster, *Distribution of Income and Economic Growth* (Geneva: United Nations Research Institute for Social Development, 1970); Hollis Chenery et al., *Redistribution with Growth* (London: Oxford University Press, 1974); and Irma Adelman and C.T. Morris, *An Anatomy of Patterns of Income Distribution in Developing Countries* (Stanford: Stanford University Press, 1971).

2. Cf. Richard Bird, *Taxing Agricultural Land in Developing Countries* (Cambridge: Harvard University Press, 1974).

3. *The Current Economic Position and Prospects of Ecuador* (Washington: International Bank for Reconstruction and Development, 1973); *The Current Economic Position and Prospects of Peru* (Washington: International Bank for Reconstruction and Development, 1973); *Economic Growth of Colombia* (Washington: International Bank for Reconstruction and Development, 1972); *Nigeria: Options for Long Term Development* (Washington: International Bank for Reconstruction and Development, 1974); *Towards Full Employment: A Programme for Colombia* (Geneva: International Labor Office, 1970); *Employment, Incomes and Equality: A Report on Kenya* (Geneva: International Labor Office, 1972); *Matching Employment Opportunities and Expectations: A Programme of Action for Ceylon* (Geneva: International Labor Office, 1971); *Employment and Income Policies for Iran* (Geneva: International Labor Office, 1973); and *Intraregional Trade Projections, Effective Protection and Income Distribution* (Bangkok: United Nations Economic Commission for Asia and the Far East, 1972).

4. For a detailed bibliography see D. Morawetz, "Employment Implications of Industrialization in Developing Countries," *The Economic Journal* (September 1974).

5. For a detailed description of the characteristics of semi-industrialized countries see Carlos F. Diaz-Alejandro, *Exchange Rate Devaluation in a Semi-Industrialized Country: The Experience of Argentina, 1955-1961* (Cambridge: MIT Press, 1965).

CONTENTS

	Page
PREFACE	v
LIST OF TABLES AND FIGURE	xi

Chapter

1 DEVELOPMENT OF INCOME AND GROWTH PATTERNS IN FOUR SELECTED COUNTRIES — 1

    Iran — 1
    Mexico — 5
    Brazil — 10
    South Korea — 14
    A Relatively Similar Sequence of Development in the Four Countries — 18
    Strategies for Future Growth — 19
    Notes — 20

2 CREDIT, CAPITAL MARKET POLICIES, AND INCOME DISTRIBUTION — 23

    Nature of the Financial Structure — 23
    Use of Monetary Controls — 26
    Problems of Controlling Credit Allocation — 27
    Agricultural Credit in Mexico — 28
    Agricultural Credit in Brazil — 30
    Agricultural Credit in Iran — 32
    Agricultural Credit in South Korea — 33
    Problems of Industrial Credit — 35
    Summary of Credit and Financial Policies — 37
    Notes — 38

3 THE EFFECT OF GOVERNMENT TAX POLICIES ON INCOME DISTRIBUTION — 40

    Iran — 40
    Mexico — 50
    Brazil — 53

Chapter		Page
	South Korea	57
	The Impact of Taxes on Income Distribution for the Four Countries	59
	Notes	61
4	THE EFFECT OF EDUCATION ON INCOME DISTRIBUTION	63
	Iran	64
	Mexico	70
	Brazil	74
	South Korea	77
	Conclusions about Educational Planning in the Four Countries	80
	Notes	81
5	THE EFFECT OF GOVERNMENT AGRICULTURAL POLICIES ON INCOME DISTRIBUTION	82
	Mexico	83
	Brazil	89
	Iran	94
	South Korea	103
	Conclusions for the Four Countries	108
	Notes	109
6	THE EFFECT OF GOVERNMENT INDUSTRIAL POLICIES ON INCOME DISTRIBUTION	113
	Mexico	114
	Brazil	122
	Iran	127
	South Korea	139
	Conclusions for the Four Countries	143
	Notes	145
7	THE TOTAL EFFECT OF GOVERNMENT POLICIES ON INCOME DISTRIBUTION	149
	Major Deficiencies in Government Policy toward Income Distribution	150
	A New Framework for Policy Making	156
	Conclusions	161

Chapter	Page
Notes	163

APPENDIX

A	INCOME DISTRIBUTION AND ECONOMIC GROWTH	164
B	DISTRIBUTION AND EMPLOYMENT	179
BIBLIOGRAPHY		182
ABOUT THE AUTHOR		195

LIST OF TABLES AND FIGURE

Table		Page
3.1	Brazil: Estimated Effective Tax Rates, by Income Class	56
4.1	Iran: Private Rate of Return for Five Fields of Education	67
4.2	Mexico: Estimated Rates of Return per Years of Education	72
4.3	Korea: Rates of Return on Education	79
5.1	Iran: Size Classification of Agricultural Units, End of 4th Plan (1972-73)	98
5.2	Yields per Acre for Foodgrains, 1948-50 and 1968-70	105
6.1	Iran: Material Inputs and Spatial Variations, 1965	131
6.2	Iran: Cost Structure of Production, 1965	132
7.1	Sources of Mexican Growth: Three Studies	155
7.2	Long-Run Impact of Economic Policy Instruments on Goals	159
A.1	Iran: Regional and Sectoral 1977 Output Levels Based on Plan Organization Fifth Plan Targets	170
A.2	Iran: Regional and Sectoral 1977 Output Targets for the Regionalization of the Fifth Plan	172
A.3	Iran: Regional and Sectoral Investment Implied by Plan Organization National Fifth Plan Targets	174
A.4	Iran: Regional Fifth Plan Investment Requirements	175

Figure

| 7.1 | Analytical Schema for Income Distribution | 157 |

CHAPTER

1

DEVELOPMENT OF INCOME AND GROWTH PATTERNS IN FOUR SELECTED COUNTRIES

IRAN

The aim of the economic policy in Iran since the mid-1950s has been to improve rapidly the welfare of the population through an accelerated expansion of the country's productive capacity. The shah and other high government officials have recognized that only within an expanding economy is it possible to solve the problems arising from the efforts of different social groups to obtain a larger share of the national product.[1]

Growth of the Economy

The Iranian economy, particularly since the mid-1960s, has recorded remarkable growth, averaging over 11 percent annually in real terms.[2] The gross national product (GNP) at constant (1959) market prices increased by 59 percent during Iran's Third Plan period (1963-67) and by a further 54 percent during the first four years of the Fourth Plan period (1968-72). An additional boost was given to the economy in 1971 as a result of a series of new financial arrangements with the major consortium of oil operating companies and in 1973 by the sharp rises in oil prices. By the beginning of the Fifth Development Plan in March 1973, per capita annual income was approximately $600, compared with only $250 in 1959.

Production has expanded more or less evenly in Iran among the various sectors except for agriculture, which has lagged behind the development of all other major areas of economic activity, and the oil sector, which has shown by far the most rapid growth. In real terms industrial output, as well as transportation and other services, is currently (1975) from three to five times higher than in 1959. The average productivity of capital, equipment, and other tangible assets has risen.

There has been an overall improvement in production techniques as well as rapid growth in communication, electric power capacity, land under irrigation, and many other installations that have represented large investment efforts. This expansion and interaction of the basic economic structure undoubtedly has benefited all branches of activity and has contributed to raising both productivity and income.

The nature of Iran's industrial development since the mid-1960s also indicates that the country is attempting to establish a solid base for an improved standard of living. For example steel production capacity has been increased by the construction of the Aryamehr steel mill in Isfahan, capable of producing 1.9 million tons per year; electric power capacity is now five times greater than in 1959; and the chemical industry can now produce several times more than in the mid-1960s. The output of petroleum derivatives also has risen tremendously. The manufacture of equipment and machinery has expanded to an extent that is not yet adequately recorded by statistics. The first steps have been taken toward the production of vehicles; and the overall variety of consumer goods now made available in Iran is impressive.

Growth and transformation have been accompanied by broader education and by better sanitation conditions that are reflected in lower mortality rates. Social services also have been widely extended and have given the worker more security in his job and income. Undeniably, Iran has made great strides both culturally and socially. The country's progress has been achieved in the absence, until the 1970s, of appreciable rates of inflation and has been attributable largely to high rates of investment approaching 23 percent per annum.

The development of the Iranian economy can in part be traced to the 1920s and 1930s when many public works programs were initiated; these have helped to integrate the national market and increase production. During those years some industrial expansion was already evident. But the economy as a whole, because of slow internal changes, was in spite of increasing oil revenues almost stagnant in the twenty years before 1959. In fact agricultural production was apparently quite static—barely keeping pace with the rise in population. The "miracle" of Iran's economic development has thus been brought about for the most part since the mid-1960s.

The manufacturing industry in Iran, despite dramatic development, is still of relatively minor importance, contributing (together with mining) around 14 percent of gross domestic product (GDP). This compares with 30 to 35 percent for such highly industrialized nations as England, Belgium, the United States, Denmark, and Italy, and—among the less industrialized countries—with 14.4 percent for Turkey, 16.5 percent for Colombia, and 20.0 percent for Argentina. Nevertheless, considerable structural change is taking place as the result of the industrial sector's growing at a somewhat faster rate than the national average. As a consequence, the share of primary activity, that is, agriculture, fell from 30.4 percent to 18.1 percent between 1959 and 1970, while secondary activity (manufacturing) and oil correspondingly increased their share of production.

Distribution of Income

Iran's rapid growth in national income during the 1960s is questionable in view of the large and increasing disparities in consumption by region and class. Urban and rural household expenditures compiled by the Iranian Statistical Center indicate the expenditure distribution of households to be highly unequal. The lowest 10 percent of families in the income scale account for 2.5 percent of the total consumption; the highest 10 percent account for 32.5 percent.

In general, therefore, the Iranian economy, despite a reasonably high level of per capita income (mainly a result simply of oil revenues) still displays characteristic signs of economic backwardness. There is still a considerable lack of integration between sectors, a wide discrepancy between the income of the upper-level urban households and other households (a ratio of 6:1 on a per capita basis for lower urban households, and 11:1 for rural households).

There is also a strong regional imbalance in Iranian economic development, which must be considered in projecting future growth. In addition to the industrial concentration in Teheran, per capita income in the capital city is 45 percent higher than in other large provincial cities and 70 percent higher than in small towns. Modernization has not reached into every corner of Iran, nor is the resource base evenly divided. There are considerable educational and cultural differences, and some areas are either inaccessible or have not yet been penetrated by efficient commercial transportation. As a result, the great majority of the Iranian population has not been incorporated into the purchasing power brackets needed to sustain the extensive and dynamic industry that is now manufacturing consumer durable goods. Furthermore, the rural zones, particularly in the agricultural-based west and south of the country, where half the population lives, show the lowest average family income. The problem of economic development is therefore centered in agriculture, where both productivity and income must be raised.

Indeed, there may be an extended slowdown in industrial output unless the incomes and purchasing power of the great majority of the population, especially in rural areas, is increased. Through increased purchasing power, many consumer goods industries currently with excess capacity could operate at full capacity with reduced production costs and therefore better export prospects. Moreover, a wider market would make possible the local manufacture of industrial parts and even of the equipment necessary for future expansion. Industries producing farm machinery and equipment for processing primary materials would also be aided by measures directed toward achieving a more equitable distribution of income.

On the other hand, if income distribution is not improved, consumer durable goods industries will gradually saturate their limited urban markets and then grow at a rate only slightly above that of the population.

Government Economic Policies

Unfortunately, the Iranian public sector, although not poor in resources (because of oil revenues), is slow and complicated in procedure, uncoordinated in operation, and frequently inefficient in the execution of its programs. Government administration seems to be organized in a way more appropriate to the past—when economic development was altogether unplanned. Consequently, the task of coordinating the policy of development must be carefully evaluated in economic terms; it cannot and should not be left to partial arrangements, emergencies, or the impromptu solutions of politicians or experts. The government, although it has realized that its problems of growth have become more complex and difficult for solution, has not sufficiently applied itself to formulating an integrated development policy expressed in attainable quantitative objectives that anyone could understand. There is little public discussion of the alternative courses of action open to the government. There is certainly talk of planning, sometimes dealing with one sector of the economy, sometimes with a region. But it appears to be no more than a physical planning of projects without any clear economic content. A nationwide concept of the country's development potential is lacking, as are adequate studies on which to examine possible alternative national strategies.

INCOME AND GROWTH PATTERNS

Conclusions

If Iran has in the past carried out a reasonably effective combination of policies, the policies have not always been well coordinated. The policies—in view of population growth, of uncertainties as to expansion of oil exports at a sufficient rate, and of the new and complex issues arising from growth itself and from changing social and political aspirations among the people—require to be updated and in some cases thoroughly revised. To move in the direction of a sustained growth rate of about 12 percent—perhaps the minimum rate necessary to absorb an expanding young population into productive employment—agricultural and industrial growth will have to be redressed.

Government (particularly the Plan Organization, the official planning agency) must face the issues and work out the necessary planning machinery to ensure optimum utilization of Iran's many positive trends and experiences in development. A mere continuation of the policies of the past is bound to fail in spite of the successful overall growth rates since the mid-1960s.

MEXICO

The main problems of modern Mexico are the continued existence of large and small firms in industry, the agricultural sector, poor distribution of income, and unemployment—a result of a series of historical and cultural factors, particularly those stemming from the revolution of 1910-16.

At that time the conspicuous way of living of the upper classes—830 families owning 100 percent of industry and 97 percent of the productive land on the one hand and the "lack of freedom, land, bread, and justice" on the other—pushed the Mexican peasantry into a revolution, the immediate result of which was a change in the ruling class, as well as in the government power structure and its working philosophy.[3] The new government pursued two main targets: the creation of a minimum of socioeconomic infrastructure mainly through a program of extensive land distribution, mass education, and penetration of road networks; and the formation of various institutions designed to attack the urgent problems, which has led to the creation of the Central Bank, the Irrigation Commission, the Agricultural Credit Bank, the Ruling Party Organization, the Federal Labor Legislation, and the National Bank for Infrastructure and Industrial Investment.

The new policies have resulted in the following:

1. A politically mature and independent government, which has reached a clear compromise and division of responsibilities with the private sector.
2. The popular acceptance of economic intervention of the government along with the maintaining of private ownership (this would release the public funds for other more urgent projects, while channeling private investment into a socially necessary activity).
3. An entrepreneur class, which has developed real dynamism and ingenuity as well as its share of responsibility for the country's welfare.
4. An international consensus of a semiindustrialized country, with the reputation of stability and dynamism, which may attract many more joint ventures than would other countries, without the granting of numerous concessions.[4]

In order to illustrate the working environment and traditions of the country, an analysis of some of the structural elements comprising the Mexican economy is necessary. Identification of these dynamic interrelationships helps to provide some insights into the country's current economic problems, particularly that of income distribution.

Growth of the Economy

The growth rate of GDP has been high in Mexico. During the 1960s GDP increased by 46 percent, in comparison with 26 percent in the 1950s and 38 percent in the 1940s. In the three decades after 1940, therefore, the Mexican economy grew at an annual rate of more than 6 percent. On a per capita basis the rate exceeded 3 percent in real terms.[5]

Sectoral shifts in both output and employment over the three decades illustrate the fundamental nature of the changes which the Mexican economy has experienced. The agricultural sector in 1940 employed 65 percent of Mexico's work force and constituted over 23 percent of the GDP; three decades later it employed less than half the work force and accounted for 16 percent of aggregate domestic product. In contrast, manufacturing activity raised its share of the total domestic product from 17.8 percent to 26 percent, and by 1970 employed more than 16 percent of the labor force. Except for mining, the industrial sectors have annually registered the highest rates of growth; from 1965 through 1968, for example, the manufacturing, construction, and electrical energy sectors all grew at average annual rates of 9 percent or better. Furthermore, by 1970, Mexico had become largely

INCOME AND GROWTH PATTERNS

self-sufficient in the production of foodstuffs, basic petroleum products, steel, and most consumer goods.

While overall growth rates have been impressive, the growth rate of the agricultural sector declined significantly during the second half of the 1960s, when it reached an average of 1.3 percent per annum, in contrast to growth rates of 3.8 percent and 4.7 percent respectively during the 1950s and the first part of the 1960s. There was a close relationship between annual growth rates for domestic farm products and farm exports during the 1960-70 period. From 1960 to 1965 the agricultural GDP at current prices rose to 10.9 percent, while farm exports expanded by 7.5 percent. In contrast, these rates totaled 4.1 percent and 1 percent respectively in 1966-70, as a result of the fact that a sizable share of farm exports represented surplus production in this sector. In this connection, recovery of the growth rate in the agrarian sector is very important because of the contribution it can make to improving the national balance of payments.

The country's accelerated growth rate in the 1960s, therefore, caused an unbalanced growth of different sectors of the economy, some of which were highly developed and productive and others admittedly underdeveloped—a situation which until the 1970s was not a serious obstacle to development. Then, however, it became evident that the unbalanced growth had resulted in (1) the small size of Mexico's domestic market, especially in the rural market; (2) the lack of integration of agriculture and industry and of efficiency in certain industrial sectors; and (3) the long-run worsening of the balance of payments.

By 1971 in fact the Mexican economy was experiencing severe internal and external strains that adversely affected its customary industrial growth rates. In that year the GDP expanded by 3.1 percent compared with an average annual rate of more than 6 percent in the 1960s.

Income Distribution

Rapid economic growth in Mexico has taken place in an environment of widespread rural and urban poverty. There is even some indication that the gap between the very poor and those benefiting from economic progress has widened so that overall income inequality has increased during the post-World War II period.

The average income for the top half of the families in Mexico is still some five-and-one-half times the average income of the poorer half of the population. Thus it is very largely those in the top half who have benefited from the rapid economic growth. The great bulk of the poorer half is still engaged in traditional farming and related activities, and although the situation of many in this group has improved somewhat, it is apparent that the great bulk of the gain has gone to those who have been incorporated into the modern urban sector.

These trends become more apparent if the income of the population of the country is broken down into ten deciles (the top decile contains the richest 10 percent of the households, and so on). Between 1963 and 1970 there was a drop in the share of income going to those families in the lowest income decile. The next three deciles (from the bottom) recorded no marked change in their relative participation. In contrast, the average levels of the population, in deciles five to eight, increased their participation in total family income more rapidly. Little change took place in the relative position of families in the highest two deciles.

These figures indicate that families in the middle-income strata have received the most benefits, in terms of relative income, during the process of rapid growth experienced by Mexico in the 1960s.[6] These developments are a result of increased education among the middle classes; the country's growing capitalization, which has been concentrated in urban areas and has led to rapid gains in productivity of labor in industry and some services; and finally redistributive measures adopted by the government.

Since middle-income classes are confined largely to urban rather than rural families, the problems of family income distribution in Mexico are largely a manifestation of regional imbalances between rural and urban areas and between regions more favored and those less favored in terms of natural resources and location.

These developments have occurred in spite of the fact that the distribution of income (particularly that going to the low-income households) has been a subject of great concern to the Mexican government, particularly since the Cardenas regime in the 1930s.

Government Economic Policies

Direct and indirect action by the government is behind every aspect of the Mexican development—ranging from intangible factors such as monetary and political stability to the direct ownership and operation of steel and oil companies. The government has concentrated its efforts in infrastructural investments (transport networks, electricity, and irrigation) and in basic or strategic industries (steel mills, petroleum, and heavy capital equipment), leaving a very small and decreasing share of its budget to direct agricultural promotion.

Government has also facilitated private industrial growth both directly and indirectly. Directly, it has assisted the private sector

INCOME AND GROWTH PATTERNS

through its policies on social security, tax exemptions, and tariff protection; and by placing quantitative controls and tariffs on imports it has promoted production of domestic substitutes for imports. Indirectly, it has aided development through social and political stability; through stable exchange rates; and through improvements in the public financial institutions, the tax system, and the administration of public expenditure.[7]

But for all the government's continued high-minded statements, actual living standards for the majority of Mexicans have not improved significantly, despite increased productivity, minimum wage levels, and government social-benefit programs. Only 11 percent of the labor force is organized into unions (which are very weak), although the percentage is much higher for industrial workers than for other workers in urban areas. In short, public statements to the contrary, national policy has generally favored concentration of income in the upper income decile. This is doubly harmful because it also limits domestic market expansion and generates social dissatisfaction.

The strategy and pattern of development in Mexico is showing increasing signs of obsolescence, as is clear from the accumulation of mounting problems associated with the balance of payments, the labor market, regional development, income distribution, and public sector financing. These fundamental problems are a reflection of the lack of decisive changes and adjustments in the country's development strategy. The government's approach to economic policy has essentially remained unchanged since the 1940s and consequently is incapable of meeting the needs of the economy. This strategy has been based on (1) the substitution of domestic goods for imports and excessive protection of domestic supply, as a means of promoting industrialization; (2) the implementation of infrastructural programs and programs to expand basic services (frequently subsidized) which have generally benefited the urban centers and the relatively more developed areas; (3) the provision of special incentives for production and investment; and (4) the establishment of forms and rates of taxation whose impact on income from property and capital is very slight.[8]

Conclusions

The major task of Mexico's future economic policy should be to provide much more productive employment for millions of the existing labor force and to absorb those reaching working age. Rural development must bear the brunt of the task. This will require a change in the pattern of growth, since there are signs that the common strategy of industrialization based on import replacement has already been carried too far and at the expense of the promotion of exports.

It would be wrong, however, to end this analysis on too critical a note. By most standards Mexican economic performance has been very impressive. Rapid economic growth has been accompanied by a high level of economic stability. Skillful economic policy has prevented bottlenecks from developing in the supply of one or two key resources, which might have held up economic progress; it has also managed to secure for Mexico most of the advantages that foreign capital can bring without compromising Mexico's strong national desire to control its own destiny.

The country's current problems have in fact been explicitly recognized by the Echeverria government, whose declared economic objectives include redistributing income, reducing unemployment and underemployment, bringing the marginal social groups into national economic life, promoting a new basis for foreign trade, and reducing technological dependence. In other words, emphasis has been placed on rectifying a number of basic inequalities, and a new national development strategy is beginning to take shape.

BRAZIL

Brazil has been added to the honor role of postwar economic miracles, along with Germany and Japan. But as Brazil still belongs in the category of semiindustrialized economies, it has further to go than those two highly industrialized countries. However, if its present accomplishments afford legitimate grounds for satisfaction, the very fact of its underdevelopment opens up new vistas for the future of this immense country. Perhaps Brazil is succeeding to the enviable position, long enjoyed by the United States, as the "country of unlimited possibilities."

The turnabout in Brazil in less than a decade (1968-73) from a land beset by threats of revolution, anarchy, and general civic and economic decline is indeed a miracle. To understand the transformation of the economy, it is necessary to (1) follow the evolution of the dynamic forces underlying the current surge in economic activity and (2) examine the manner in which the government has manipulated these forces to achieve its objectives.

Growth of the Economy

During 1973 the Brazilian economy expanded at a rate of 11.4 percent in real terms, thus marking the sixth consecutive year in which the rate of increase in output exceeded 9 percent. The average rate of growth of GDP in the six-year period from 1968 to 1973 was equivalent to slightly over 10 percent, showing a sharp acceleration with respect to the previous five-year period (1963-67) when the average annual rate was 3.4 percent. With population growing at about 2.9 percent a year, GDP per capita in the 1968-73 period rose by 6.9 percent, in contrast with a rise of less than 1.0 percent a year for the 1963-67 period.

The expansion of the economy since 1967 has been led by a continued rise in industrial output, which increased at an average rate of 12.5 percent a year, or over four times faster than in the 1963-67 period. Manufacturing output, particularly motor vehicles and chemicals, grew faster than total output. The expansion in the industrial sector in 1968 and 1969 was made possible through the utilization of previously idle installed capacity, but since 1969 productive capacity has expanded at a very fast pace to meet increased demand, especially from the export sector. Investments in infrastructure, electric energy, and the production of basic materials such as steel and cement have also risen considerably, in line with the government's intention to avoid supply bottlenecks.

Agricultural production advanced at a slower pace than did total output, increasing by 5.7 percent in the 1968-73 period. Coffee output fluctuated considerably from year to year, but its total production during those years was well below that of the previous five years and was sufficient to cover only about 70 percent of total demand (domestic and foreign) with a corresponding large reduction in official stocks. During the 1968-73 period Brazil diversified its primary exports, becoming a major world producer and exporter of soybeans and sugar and increasing significantly its supply of meat to world markets. By 1970 agriculture accounted for 14 percent of GDP, while industry, commerce, transport and communications, and other services accounted respectively for 23, 10, 4, and 49 percent.

One of the most alarming economic phenomena prior to the 1964 Brazilian coup had been a spiraling inflation, which by 1964 had reached an average annual rate of 87.8 percent. Clearly, remedial measures were needed. Thus policies were applied that brought about a steady decline in the ratio of the government budget deficit to GNP and a downward trend in the rate of money expansion that had come about because of the deficiencies in the government's tax system. Consequently, the rate of inflation after 1964 was gradually brought under control and it declined to an annual rate of some 20-25 percent. While this may seem high to some observers, many of the distortions previously accompanying the inflationary process have been lessened and neutralized by an indexing of all assets according to the price index.

Government Economic Policies

Several factors account for the favorable performance toward the end of the 1960s of the Brazilian economy with respect to growth, export expansion, and reduction of inflation. In large part, it is the use of effective economic policy that has succeeded in restoring confidence and providing the basis for continued economic expansion. Beginning in 1964 the public sector's finances underwent a major overhaul. Federal expenditures were put on a more sound economic basis by reducing subsidies to the railroads and other public entities. Major strides were also made in reforming the tax system. As a result of such reforms, real tax revenues have accelerated.[9]

In short, the resurgence of growth toward the end of the 1960s can be attributed to the stabilization policies of the mid-1960s which corrected the distortions that had arisen during the peak industrialization drive of the 1950s. By the late 1960s many price distortions were eliminated, inflation was brought under control, more realistic exchange rates were adopted, efforts were made to expand and diversify the country's export structure, financial institutions were modernized, tax incentives were developed to attract funds to lagging regions and backward sectors, and government investments in infrastructure were stepped up.

It is probably too early to determine if Brazil's boom is only a short-run phenomenon and if the stagnation of the early 1960s stemmed simply from the political turmoil which led to the stabilization policies instituted soon after the 1964 change in government. If this is the case, the prospects for long-run growth are likely to be excellent. On the other hand, if the stagnation was related to long-run phenomena —structural factors that to date have not been corrected—then there is the possibility that the current boom may soon come to a halt.

Distribution of Income

In general, although economic policy since 1964 has been effective in restoring growth and reducing inflation, this success has not been optimal or without cost. Very clearly, post-1964 Brazilian economic policy, like all economic policy, has had a differential impact on certain groups. In keeping with the political character of the new Brazilian regime, it is not surprising that the burden of stabilization has been borne largely by the lower classes. The increase in inequality of income distribution and the detrimental effect of policy on the real incomes of lower-income groups were caused in part by the stabilization policies which forced the real minimum wage to decline; between 1964 and 1970 it had fallen over 25 percent in purchasing power.

Despite subsequent rates of real income growth of over 9 percent, under the new regime there is cause for dissatisfaction: the upper 3.2 percent of the labor force commanded 33.1 percent of the income in 1970 compared to about 27 percent in 1960. Although the concentration of income is less in agriculture than in nonagricultureal sectors, thereby reversing their 1960 ordering, this accomplishment is not indicative of greater welfare in rural areas. Rather the sectoral differential in reported census incomes has widened, a phenomenon corroborated by the independent quarterly surveys of households conducted since 1968.[10]

It appears that in the absence of an effective and far-reaching alteration in government attitudes, there is likely to be little progress and, quite possibly, future deterioration in the distribution of income.

Conclusions

Judged by the restoration of high growth rates and the relative control of inflation, economic policy since 1964 must be termed a success. However, economic problems remain, and no basic changes in the structural foundations of the economy have been made. In sharp contrast with the radical changes in the political system, economic policy has only manipulated the existing system rather than drastically restructuring its institutions.

Without major reforms in the economic system, the feasibility of maintaining the high growth rates of the late 1960s and early 1970s may prove extremely difficult. To provide the basis for those continued growth rates and to maintain social peace, several steps must be undertaken: investment and reform in agriculture in less favored regions of Brazil, better educational opportunities, and a more equitable distribution of income. The policies followed by the post-1964 regimes have been only halfway measures. Doing away with distortions in the price mechanism, slowing down inflation rates, modernizing the capital market—these all work on the supply side. The basic problem of preventing the stagnation experienced in the early 1960s cannot be solved without parallel measures on the demand side, that is, increasing the productivity and incomes of the masses of low-income workers so that their demands for domestic products will become significant.

SOUTH KOREA

In comparison with most other developing countries, South Korea today seems to have wrought an economic miracle. It has become a showcase for development based on private enterprise achieved under the most difficult circumstances. One must remember that postwar development in South Korea started with an economy that was dislocated by the partition along the 38th parallel and then completely devastated by the Korean War from 1950 to 1953. Less than 20 years later, however, the economy had reached an extremely high rate of economic and industrial growth.

Throughout the 1950s, Syngman Rhee's government became increasingly autocratic. Meanwhile, largely as a result of the American presence in Korea,* a whole new generation was being exposed to Western democratic values and institutions through the greatly revamped and expanded Korean educational system. As a result of the contrast between the dictatorial structure of the Rhee regime and the democratic ideals of Korean youth, a clash was almost inevitable. In 1960 a national uprising led by the nation's college students overthrew the Rhee government.

The subsequent military coup of 1961 brought into power a nationalistic and pragmatic leadership that began mobilizing the nation's resources. After the military regime was transformed into a civilian government in 1963, the government moved increasingly toward the recognition that economic development and growth were the keys to its own political success, as well as to the establishment of a stable and viable Republic of Korea.

Growth of the Economy

Since the signing of the truce agreement in 1953, the GNP has increased consistently. During 1954-56 the average growth rate in real terms averaged 4.5 percent annually, made possible by reconstruction aid from the United States and the good harvests of 1954 and 1955. But the growth rate dropped to 1.2 percent in 1956 because of crop failures. At the same time, inflation increased sharply—the average GNP growth rate at current market prices was 47.9 percent.

---

*Throughout this study, "Korea" and "South Korea" are used interchangeably.

INCOME AND GROWTH PATTERNS

In 1957-59, financial stabilization programs were carried out and caused inflation to slow down substantially. During 1957-61 the average rate of price increase declined 7.2 percent per annum. The stabilization programs, however, by drastically reducing the rate of growth of the money supply, had adverse effects on aggregate demand. This was compounded by the decline in foreign aid after 1957. As a result, the real GNP growth rate, which was 8.8 percent in 1957, declined to 5.5 percent in 1958, 4.4 percent in 1959, and finally 2.3 percent in 1960.

The military revolution of 1961 not only brought about political and social changes but also marked the turning point in economic growth. Except for one year of crop failure in 1962, the real GNP growth rate has accelerated to become one of the most rapid in the world in per capita terms. Between 1960 and 1965, per capita GNP grew at a respectable 21.2 percent in real terms; between 1965 and 1970, however, it grew by a remarkable 95.2 percent. In terms of averages, the real annual per capita rate of growth in GNP between 1960 and 1965 was 3.6 percent, compared with 10.0 percent for the next five-year period. These growth rates have continued into the 1970s.

Along with these impressive growth rates, a radical change in the structure of production has taken place. The share of primary product in GDP fell from 47.3 percent in 1953 to 38.7 percent in 1965, and to 28.4 percent in 1970. At the same time, the contribution of the industrial sector rose sharply from 14.3 percent in 1953 to 28.2 percent in 1965, and to 35.0 percent in 1970. The relative decline of the agricultural sector obscures the fact that a substantial increase in agricultural output took place. From 1957 to 1969 agricultural production in real terms increased by over 75 percent. Within the industrial sector as a whole, the growth of manufacturing output has been the dominant feature, but the steady growth in the share in GDP of construction, power, and transport facilities has characterized the rapidly industrializing economy.

As a result of its rapid expansion, the economy had reduced unemployment. Official sample surveys indicate that unemployment has fallen from around 8.0 percent in 1964 to 4.5 percent in 1970. Also as a result of the rapid expansion of the economy, a considerable shift has taken place since 1964 in the composition of persons employed by the industrial sector. At that time 61.9 percent of the working population was engaged in the primary sector, 8.9 percent in mining and manufacturing, and 29.2 percent in the infrastructure and service sector. By 1970 these respective figures were 50.5, 14.3, and 35.2 percent. The shift in these ratios accords with the substantial shift that has occurred in the pattern of output. At the same time, the number of people employed increased from 8.2 million in 1964 to 9.6 million in 1970. In the primary sector the number of people employed declined absolutely from 5.1 million in 1964 to 4.8 million in 1970.

Government Economic Policies

Despite the stabilization programs of the 1950s, excessive monetary expansion in 1961-63 resulted in price increases of nearly 45 percent annually by 1963. Beginning late in 1963 the newly elected government initiated a firm antiinflationary financial program.[11] At the same time, the First Five-Year Development Plan (1962-66) was scaled down to match a realistic reappraisal of the country's available resources. Maximum priority was placed on the development of exports as a leading growth sector. The antiinflationary program was implemented after 1963 on a sustained and comprehensive basis and with a growing sophistication in financial techniques. The primary policy emphasis during the early years of stabilization was on curbing the pace of monetary expansion and on expanding the role of the pricing system in order to achieve a more efficient allocation of resources. Once a substantial measure of success was achieved on the antiinflationary front, the government was able to pay increased attention to its development program, particularly the Second Five-Year Plan (1967-71). In fact the original annual growth target of 7.0 percent in the government's First Five-Year Plan (1962-66) was exceeded slightly. An annual growth rate of 10 percent was targeted for the revised Second Five-Year Plan.

The government's strategy was straightforward. In order to shift the productive structure from what were essentially land-based food and raw material exports (areas in which Korea did not have a comparative advantage) to the exportation of labor intensive manufactures (products on which Korea did have a comparative advantage), the country first had to achieve a more realistic relative price of foreign exchange, that is, cheapen its products in international markets.

In 1964 the government devalued the exchange rate, which resulted in a 40 percent average annual rate of growth of exports, and permitted the liberalization of imports. This strategy not only imparted a substantial impetus to domestic investment, but also eliminated the foreign exchange constraint which had prevailed through much of the 1950s and early 1960s. Furthermore, an interest rate reform in 1965 allowed interest rates to be determined by free market forces.[12] This resulted in a doubling of interest rates on savings deposits. By increasing the volume of savings flowing through the banking system this reform freed the economy from its dependence on inefficient nonmarket rationing devices for its allocation of investment.

Finally, the distribution of the real burden for financing the government's development program was made considerably more equitable by greatly increasing the efficiency of tax collection and by a series of tax reforms. The result of these reforms was the sustained growth rate of over 10 percent per year in real terms.

INCOME AND GROWTH PATTERNS

Income Distribution

Korea has one of the more equitable distributions of income among the semiindustrialized countries.[13] During the 1960s the overall income distribution in Korea remained fairly stable. But a major problem still lies in the rural sector where agricultural income fell from 33.1 percent of national income in 1966 to only 25.5 percent in 1970. Total farm and nonfarm income of farm households grew at an average of 2.5 percent annually during this four-year period.

For the country as a whole, the bottom 60 percent of households earned 34.2 percent of total income and the top 10 percent of households earned 30 percent of total income in 1970. Within both the nonfarm household and farm household groups, the bottom 60 percent of households earned 33.4 percent and 37.8 percent of total income respectively, and the top 10 percent of households earned 30.5 percent and 25.3 percent of total income respectively. For the bottom 10 percent of households in the nonfarm and farm household groups, the share of total income earned was only 2.5 percent and 3.0 percent respectively.

Conclusions

In the past the spectacular growth achieved in Korea's economy depended on the accelerated growth of exports and the large inflow of foreign resources to overcome the financial and technological barriers to rapid development. Limits to that growth were set by the availability of complementary domestic resources, including in particular a basic infrastructure and an abundant supply of disciplined, mobile, easily trained, and cheap labor. In the present situation the physical limits of the labor supply have been nearly reached, and real wages have been increasing at least as rapidly as has productivity. And the increasing debt service has become a burden on the balance of payments. Finally, the limits of industrialization through domestic production of light consumer goods have been approached.

Still, the almost irresistible conclusion from the Korean development experience is that with proper economic policies and the maintenance of factor prices that reflect adequately the country's relative factor scarcities it is possible to achieve high rates of growth even though the country may not be blessed with an abundance of good farm land or natural resources. Furthermore, the country has not sacrificed social justice and concern for the quality of life in order to achieve such rapid growth. It has accomplished this by eliminating price controls (particularly interest rates and foreign exchange). These policies have dramatically increased Korean saving and resource productivity and apparently have resulted in giving most income groups relatively equal access to an increased share of output.

A RELATIVELY SIMILAR SEQUENCE OF DEVELOPMENT IN THE FOUR COUNTRIES

The four countries examined have all apparently gone through a somewhat similar sequence of development stages. The replacement of imports through the industrialization stage of growth has to a large extent been completed in each country; and in each country, despite high rates of growth in national income and manufacturing, this growth has, with the exception of Korea, left in its wake a relatively skewed distribution of income. To overcome this inequality, and sustain growth, it is probable that Iran, Mexico, and Brazil will be forced to adopt a new development strategy. A possible approach could consist in transferring the impetus for development from a wealthy minority, which has been responsible for an important proportion of the total demand in the economy, to the demand generated by the bulk of the population, by redistributing income. This new growth strategy would not merely solve the problem of social justice, but would also effect change in the structure of production. By increasing the purchasing power of the wage-earning class, a new type of demand would be created, accompanied by a change in the structure of supply and production.[14] In short, popular demand would provide the stimulus for continued growth. With the exception of Korea, previous development strategies that relied on imported technology were basically labor saving. The result was not only modernization in some activities in relatively few cities and regions, but also concentration in property ownership and income, to the exclusion of a large part of the population from the system, and a high level of unemployment. It is quite likely that, if continued, the strategies would prove to be self-terminating—a result either of a drying up of domestic demand or of political revolution.

The question at this stage therefore is both the devising of an appropriate set of measures to assure the new consumption-oriented model of development and the defining of the best set of policy measures to achieve the distribution of income necessary to assure its success.

INCOME AND GROWTH PATTERNS

STRATEGIES FOR FUTURE GROWTH

There is no question that particular importance in any development strategy should be attached to the improvement of the system of financial rewards and penalties, so that it may be better adapted to reflect an individual's economic success or failure. This holds true for entrepreneurs, government enterprises, and private and public employees. Improving the market system would eliminate the continued existence of nonviable products of subsidized government enterprises, the restrictive access to credit that discourages the economically successful businessmen, and inadequate wage differentiation on the basis of productivity.

The existing pattern of production, resulting from distorted market prices in Iran, Brazil, and Mexico that are caused by government intervention, has often been a serious counterincentive to personal improvement and economic growth of the national economy. The need for rapid economic development and the strategic role of individual initiative means that in these countries—perhaps even more than in advanced economies—access to resources (human and nonhuman capital) and incomes should be scaled in direct relation to the abilities of individuals. The resulting production structure and income distribution would in this sense be a fair one.

What we are proposing is not that the gap between the richest and the poorest groups in these countries be eliminated, but simply that it be sufficiently wide to provide adequate scope for enterprising people to look forward to tangible improvements in their earned income. Obviously, the incomes and wealth of a few at the top would have to be scaled down through such devices as high income taxes, wealth taxes, and estate duties; but by and large we are proposing that the majority of the people simply be provided with adequate incentives for greater effort to achieve capital accretion for themselves, and incidentally for the economy, through market-induced incentives for increased savings, investment, and productivity. In this sense we are proposing a nonradical alternative to the income distribution problem in developing countries.

Our approach centers around stimulating economic activity in sectors which, compared with other groups or sectors, display greater capabilities or are better organized for undertaking productive initiatives. The opportunities provided by such a differentiation should be suitably utilized, possibly by expanding relevant activities beyond the traditional sphere of operation found in mature economies. This is especially advocated with respect to the banking system, which has great responsibilities in the developing countries and is normally better organized than are other sectors of the economy. In such countries the banks have the important duty of effecting an optimal distribution of credit among the various sectors of the economy, according to their economic potentials.

Each of the countries examined achieved high rates of growth during the 1960s and in their own ways have been looked upon as success stories by neighboring countries. It is quite likely that all (with the possible exception of Korea) are reaching a critical stage in their development in which increasing attention will have to be given to income distribution if their rates of growth are to be maintained. Each country has had several special factors that have allowed growth to occur despite the lack of demand for industrial output. Iran, for example, has grown most rapidly because of the rapid increase in oil revenues; Mexico has benefited through lack of civil strife, a result of the land reforms carried out after the revolution in the early 1900s; and Brazil has benefited from an unusually large market resulting simply from the size of the country.

It is the thesis of this study that many of the favorable factors that have contributed to growth in Iran, Mexico, and Brazil in the past will not be viable in the future because of their inability to offset the depressing forces associated with increasing income disparities. A new strategy must be adopted that will, through improved income distribution, allow for increased purchasing power among the masses of the population. In this sense the strategies followed by these countries must be centered more around demand for output rather than on the supply of output.

In developing this new strategy for growth, it will first be necessary to identify the most important factors responsible for the existing distributions of income in the four sample countries. This will then lead to an identification of the most effective policies for restructuring these income distributions. Of particular concern in this regard is the important role the governments have played in affecting the pattern of income distribution. They have accomplished this through their policies toward credit and capital markets, taxation, education, agriculture, and industry. Of these, government policies toward credit and capital markets have had the greatest effect on income distribution.

NOTES

1. Cf. Mohammad Riza Shah Pahlevi, Mission for My Country (London: Hutchinson & Co., 1961).
2. The sections on Iran are based on Robert Looney, The Economic Development of Iran: A Recent Survey With Projections to 1981 (New York: Praeger Publishers, 1973).

3. These points are developed in more detail in N. L. Whetten, Rural Mexico (Chicago: University of Chicago Press, 1948), and Clark Reynolds, The Mexican Economy—Twentieth-Century Structure and Growth (New Haven: Yale University Press, 1970).

4. Roger D. Hansen, The Politics of Mexican Development (Baltimore: Johns Hopkins Press, 1971), chap. 2.

5. Growth data for Mexico, Brazil, and Korea are derived from Gross National Product—Growth Rates and Trend Data by Region and Country (Washington: Agency for International Development, various issues); Yearbook of National Account Statistics (New York: United Nations, various volumes); Balance of Payments Yearbook (Washington: International Monetary Fund, various volumes); and Trends in Developing Countries (Washington: World Bank, 1973). In a number of cases there are discrepancies in the figures given by each of these sources, yet these are not sufficiently large enough to alter the general pattern of growth for each country presented here.

6. Income Distribution in Latin America (New York: United Nations, 1971), pp. 61-69; Encuesta Sobre Ingresos y Gastos Familiares 1968 (Mexico City: Banco de Mexico, 1972); and Ifigenia M. de Navarrete, "La Distribucion del Ingreso en Mexico: Tendencias y Perspectivas," in El Perfil de Mexico, en 1980 (Mexico City: Instituto de Investigaciones Sociales de la Universidad Nacional Automa de Mexico, 1970), pp. 15-72.

7. Benjamin Higgins, Economic Development—Problems, Principles, and Policies, rev. ed. (New York: W.W. Norton & Company, 1968), pp. 635-653.

8. Cf. R. Carrillo Arronte, An Empirical Test on Interregional Planning (Rotterdam: Rotterdam University Press, 1970), chap. III.

9. Details are given in Alexandre Kafka, "The Brazilian Stabilization Program, 1964-67," Journal of Political Economy (August 1967), pp. 166-200.

10. Income Distribution in Latin America (New York: United Nations, 1971), pp. 69-78; Albert Fishlow, "Brazilian Distribution of Income," American Economic Review (May 1972), pp. 391-402; and C. Langoni, Distribuicao da Renda e Desenvolvimento Economico do Brasil (Rio de Janeiro, 1973), pp. 26, 64, 68, 70.

11. S. Kanesa-Thasan, "Stabilizing an Economy—A Study of the Republic of Korea," International Monetary Fund Staff Papers (March 1969), pp. 1-24.

12. John Gurley, Hugh Patrick, and E.S. Shaw, The Financial Structure of Korea (Seoul: United States Operations Mission to Korea, 1965), p. 81.

13. South Korea, Annual Report on the Family Income and Expenditure Survey (Seoul: Bureau of Statistics, Economic Planning Board, 1970); Report on the Results of Farm Household Economy

Survey of Agricultural Products (Seoul: Bureau of Statistics, Economic Planning Board, 1971).

14. An approach of this sort was first proposed for Colombia in Laughlin Currie, Accelerating Development—The Necessity and the Means (New York: McGraw-Hill, 1966).

CHAPTER

2

CREDIT, CAPITAL MARKET POLICIES, AND INCOME DISTRIBUTION

The level and expansion of per capita income has always been the central focus of growth and development studies. Unfortunately, development theory contains no single, consistent explanation regarding the interrelationships between investment, output, income distribution, and monetary and credit policies in developing countries. This chapter attempts to construct a viable framework for studying these interrelationships in the four selected countries, and is concerned primarily with the direct and indirect effects of monetary and credit policy on income distribution.

Since the 1960s economists have become increasingly aware of the deficiencies in their customary treatment of the distribution of income and wealth. Previously they had a somewhat conservative bias toward accepting the distributional pattern generated by the market system. But now this approach has been sharply eroded by the accumulating evidence of market imperfections, such as controlled interest rates in money and capital markets.

Market imperfections in the financial sector of an economy are particularly serious because this sector greatly affects the process of economic development and patterns of income distribution, by assisting in the breakaway from repetition of repressed economic performance to accelerated growth. If capital markets are repressed and distorted therefore, they can intercept and destroy impulses to development and social equity[1] in semiindustrialized countries.[2]

NATURE OF THE FINANCIAL STRUCTURE

In Mexico, as in the case of Iran, Brazil, and, to much less an extent, Korea, the financial structure is such that (1) individual economic units issue relatively few primary securities as a proportion of saving—thus indicating that firms place greater reliance on internally generated funds compared with firms in wealthy countries; (2) most of this limited flow of primary securities is acquired by financial institutions rather than being placed directly with the ultimate savers; and (3) the liabilities of the monetary system—the central bank plus deposit banks—account for a high percentage of all claims on intermediary financial institutions that are held by the public.

In short, the most noticeable characteristic of capital markets in these countries is that they are not highly developed as evidenced by the low ratio of financial issues and national wealth. In the early 1960s, for example, this relationship had a value of 1.70 in the United Kingdom, 1.40 in Japan, and 1.25 in the United States. It was only 0.40 in Mexico.

Still, the present financial structure[3] of Mexico is quite developed by low-income country standards. Keeping in mind the institutional peculiarities of each country, the Mexican market is used to illustrate the lack of financial development in our sample countries. That market is characterized by the following:

1. The important role of government financial institutions, particularly the development banks. These institutions (excluding the Bank of Mexico) now account for about one-third of the assets of all financial institutions in the country and occupy a crucial position in the long-term financing of the economy.
2. The dominating position of a small number of financial groups, each having a close relationship with one of the large commercial banks, but also controlling the most important private development savings and mortgage banks.
3. The great importance of liabilities of private and public financial institutions, particularly development banks. These liabilities usually are of medium- or long-term duration but are in effect redeemable on demand and bear high interest rates.
4. The minor importance of publicly offered and traded securities held outside financial institutions, with these fixed interest-bearing securities amounting to only a little over one-half of the total outstanding debt and less than one-fifth of all claims against financial institutions held by the public. Most of these securities are issued by the central government or by government agencies.

CREDIT AND INCOME DISTRIBUTION

The Mexican financial system is deficient in a number of areas: Government interference of all sorts, primarily through regulation of flows, is very strong; the information available to most market participants is very deficient and extremely unevenly distributed; the flexibility of financial institutions and financial instruments in adapting to the specific needs of supporters and users of funds is still unsatisfactory, with the possible exception of the needs of large business; the integration of the great mass of households into the financial system, particularly in rural areas, is still very limited; the facilities of the system remain overconcentrated in Mexico City; and these markets are sometimes dominated by monopolistic elements.

In general a developing economy requires both the formation of real and financial resources and the creation of transfer mechanisms that permit the allocation of savings to more efficient uses. In Mexico, particularly prior to the 1940s, the fiscal and financial mechanisms were inadequate to sustain the transfers of funds that were required for accelerated growth and the changing economic conditions in the country. Therefore the transfer of resources was carried out initially by means of the price mechanism rather than by the financial system, through a drastic redistribution of income that permitted the creation of savings and their conversion to investment, expediting the formation of capital and channeling it toward new uses on the basis of greater profits. It was a relatively crude transfer mechanism, which limited the market for certain goods produced domestically and created serious social frictions.

The rapid development after 1940 of capital markets made long-term credits and capital more easily available. But in Mexico today it is still very difficult for those who do not have substantial capital to start a business or expand a small one.[4] Lenders typically use credit-rationing criteria in addition to interest rates in the allocation of funds. For those fortunate enough to receive credit, the increased availability of funds as a result of financial intermediation is probably considerably more significant than is a simple reduction in costs. The availability of funds from financial institutions enables the entrepreneur to assume a greater debt position than he otherwise could and consequently to undertake larger investments. In addition, access to funds on reasonable terms probably has favorable expectational or psychological effects on entrepreneurs in Mexico. Closely related to financial intermediation is the fact that the monetization of both the agricultural sector and handicrafts has encouraged the shift to commercial production, and because of specialization, to increased work efforts, emphasis on high-yield products, and enhanced responsiveness to changes in relative prices of different products. Still, the country has a long way to go before the majority of the population will be able to participate on equal terms in the modern sectors of the economy.

While few economists question the positive direct effect of the development of a capital market on the rate of growth of output of a market economy, many have doubts about its consequences on income distribution. It is our purpose here to throw some light on the effect that monetary policies and development of capital markets in Mexico and the three other sample countries have had on personal income distribution. This analysis centers on the direction of the impact on (1) the cost and availability of credits as well as on (2) the existence of financial investment possibilities on personal income distribution.

USE OF MONETARY CONTROLS

A classical example of application of reserve requirements, so as to regulate not only the quantity but also the distribution of bank credit, has been offered by the Banco de Mexico (the other countries use these methods to one degree or another). In effect, private financial institutions in the country are given the option of either maintaining marginal reserve requirements of 100 percent or agreeing to distribute credits among potential borrowers along government-determined lines. Thus the government is not only able to force funds into production credits for directly productive activities rather than commercial trade, but is also able to regulate the flow of funds from private financial institutions to particular sectors of the economy. For example, by modifying marginal reserve requirements the Banco de Mexico could bring about a shift in private bank assets that would result in increased (decreased) holdings of government securities and more (less) credits to the agricultural sector as opposed to trade credits. Furthermore, the Banco de Mexico could change marginal reserve requirements for one type of financial institution and leave unchanged the reserve requirements for other financial institutions.

The bank has thus exerted pressure for the extension of loans to those activities, in volumes and under conditions that were not considered sufficiently attractive by commercial banks, but which were important from the standpoint of general economic development and stability.

Among the most important effects of the bank's policies after the 1940s were the following: (1) there was a reduction in the relative share of credit to the commercial sector and more direct contact between banks and industrial firms—and the decision concerning the use of funds was put in the hands of entrepreneurs who made decisions for the purchase of machinery and equipment; (2) banks were forced to use new techniques in lending, in order to make loans to those activities which, though profitable, had been neglected; (3) the

CREDIT AND INCOME DISTRIBUTION 27

commercial sector, given its high elasticity of supply, was not affected adversely, since its self-financing capacity was higher than that of other sectors; and (4) agricultural and industrial entrepreneurs were given access to credit that was tantamount to a reduction in their borrowing rates of interest.

The Mexican authorities appear to be satisfied with the results obtained under their system, which has been in use since the 1940s. They believe the system was instrumental in inducing commercial banks to take an interest in types of productive loans that they had not previously made because of inertia or force of habit. Furthermore, there seems to be a feeling that, since banks have become accustomed to making such loans and have found them to be remunerative, they may well continue such lending in the absence of the Banco de Mexico's reserve requirement policies. But in general, measures to influence the composition of bank portfolios have been difficult to enforce since it has not been easy to ascertain whether or not the loans were made for the purpose stated or whether the funds were used for the purpose that the bank intended.

PROBLEMS OF CONTROLLING CREDIT ALLOCATION

Difficulties stemming from the inability of governments to control tightly the asset portfolios of commercial banks have resulted in the perpetuation of existing production and income patterns, however uneconomic they may have been. This situation can be traced to the fact that the main source of funds of a commercial bank is deposits. Since the receipts and payments of funds in such a bank take place at times selected by the depositors, commercial banks prefer short-term credit to commercial trade. They also prefer large loans rather than small ones whose administrative cost and risk are substantial; and hence a number of gaps arise in the credit structure. This position is compounded in countries where there is no well-developed securities market that would enable the mobilization from outside the banking system of funds needed for long-term investment.

One of the most serious gaps in many developing countries is that connected with agricultural credit, both short- and long-term, for by its very nature agriculture is not an area to which commercial banks usually cater. The small farmers generally are forced to resort to middlemen and moneylenders who charge exorbitant interest rates, partly because of the large risk involved; and payment of these interest charges wipes out most of the farmers' gains from increased output and thus dampens the incentive for farming.

Two methods have generally been adopted to channel funds into the agricultural sector: the use of controls by the central bank and the creation of special agricultural credit banks.

AGRICULTURAL CREDIT IN MEXICO

In Mexico agricultural credit is supplied to the ejidatario (communal farmer) by the National Ejido Credit Bank. Interest rates are set at 10 percent.[5] The implication of the fixed rate is that price credit rationing is not allowed, that is, that the free market rate is considerably above 10 percent. In addition, the bank has several institutional peculiarities that should be noted. First, a large portion of its risk is absorbed through its collaboration with the National Crop and Livestock Insurance Program. The ejidatarios are required, when they borrow from the bank, to take out insurance that covers the farmers' out-of-pocket costs (including outstanding credit) in the event of a natural disaster.[6] The bank has first claim on any indemnities paid, and this serves to eliminate its risk derived from these sources. This practice does not, however, eliminate risk arising from unfavorable events that are short of natural disasters, such as unfavorable prices, borrower dishonesty, or incompetent management. Still, for many crops the bank is protected against unfavorable prices by the government's program of guaranteed prices. With respect to dishonesty and management, the bank tries to diminish risk by screening loan applicants, by providing technical assistance and regular checks on the borrower, and by acting as sales agent for the ejidatario at the time of harvest. All these factors tend to reduce the bank's risk in lending, although they do not eliminate it entirely.

Second, it is widely accepted in Mexico that the bank performs a social welfare role for the ejidatarios by lending them funds at a rate of interest considerably lower than that charged by alternative sources. Thus the bank is subsidizing the ejidatarios.

These measures, while apparently well meaning, are not in the nation's best interest, if in fact concern for disparities in rural income is the main reason for this form of credit. For one thing, at 10 percent there is a shortage of funds, and all ejidatarios who want credit cannot obtain it. Second, funds are available only for sanctioned purposes—and sanctioned activities are determined by the bank in accordance with national agricultural policy. Third, the loans are made by the bank to an ejido (communal land) credit society, which in turn lends the funds to the individual ejidatario. Under this arrangement, the ejidatario may be restricted in his borrowing since he is forced to conform to the farm plans of his credit society, which may not be consistent with his own. Fourth, the upper limit of the size of the loan to the ejidatario is well defined and may be insufficient for his purposes. Article 55 of the Agricultural Credit Law specifies a legal limit on short-term loans of 70 percent of the estimated value of a product at harvest time.[7] This limit was established to prevent abuse of the credit system by any one farmer and to cover what were arbitrarily considered to be the necessary capital requirements. In practice, however, the bank has established a lesser maximum loan limit called a quota that is equivalent to approximately 70 percent of the bank's established out-of-pocket production costs for activities undertaken with the loan. According to the bank's officials, this quota was set because they think the farmer should supply the remaining 30 percent of the costs out of his own resources.

In addition, the bank rations credit in a nonprice manner through two means: (1) sanctioning and (2) quota and legal limits. Other things being equal, the sanctioning process, as determined by agricultural policy, severely limits the income potential of the ejidatario. Among the sanctioned crops, the quota and legal limits are insufficient to cover expected operating capital requirements unless the ejidatario has substantial savings. The shortage of owned capital among some ejidatarios may be a reason why the Ejido Bank has a continuing record of many loans not being repaid in full. Thus under the quota or legal limit systems, the bank should make larger loans to ejidatarios who have little or no savings—for example, those receiving credit for the first time or those whose savings have been wiped out by a disaster.

The bank could spread its funds over a larger number of ejidatarios in the country and thus improve total income and income distribution in the ejido sector by increasing its lending rates. In fact, given the demand for loans, income distribution and total income could be improved considerably by even more stringent credit rationing. Instead, the bank's policy of charging a fixed 10 percent rate of interest (lower than the market rate) regardless of loan size only uses society's resources inefficiently (that is, the most productive farmers or areas are constrained by lack of credit), while at the same time granting an income subsidy to the ejidatario. In order to eliminate this subsidy, the bank should raise the rate of interest to a level that would coincide with the rate of return on that credit. Higher interest rates would not only cause the farmer to operate more efficiently, given the new rate of interest; it would also cause him to operate at a position that would optimally allocate resources from society's point of view.

An increase in the interest rate would, however, reduce the income of those ejidatarios now receiving credit by eliminating their subsidy. The consequences of this could have important implications for both the ejidatario and the bank, since the reduction in farmer income would reduce the ejidatario's potential to increase his standard of living, to undertake capital formation, and to have funds available for use as operating capital in future crop cycles. On the other hand, the policy would put the bank on a sounder financial basis by raising its income on loans. The latter would appear to be particularly attractive in view of the fact that the bank has a continual record of financial losses and consequently is actually subsidized by the Mexican government. The larger income to the bank would tend to eliminate the need for subsidization (thus reducing the cost to society) and remove the bank's dual image as a welfare and banking institution and make it solely a financial institution. In addition, a reduction of the size of the loan per ejidatario would also enable the bank to spread its funds over a larger number of farmers, thus enhancing income distribution in the ejido sector. Should subsidization of the ejido sector still be determined appropriate, the subsidy could be given directly to the farmer via a direct payment plan rather than being given under the disguise of credit.

AGRICULTURAL CREDIT IN BRAZIL

To date, the problems of extending credit to small farmers in Brazil have been viewed largely from the demand side, that is, the farmer. The government has assumed that small farmers are of a conservative nature—that they are unwilling to change or assume debit risks, they lack knowledge on how to use credit, they fear dealing with formal credit agencies, and they lack profitable investment alternatives on their farms. Many of the special government credit programs have been focused on some aspects of these problems, and almost all have included a low interest rate policy. Much less attention has been given to problems on the supply side of credit. Yet it is quite likely that major credit distribution problems in this area may exist; if this is the case, some adjustments in current policies might substantially increase the flow of credit to small farmers through regular banking channels.

Interest rates on bank credit in Brazil have been closely regulated since at least 1933. Enactment of a usury law in that year prohibited rates above 12 percent per year. In 1938 a special division within the Bank of Brazil was organized for the purpose of providing official credit at subsidized rates to Brazilian agriculture. Since 1950 nominal interest charged on agricultural credit has been less than the annual rate of inflation and this has resulted in a negative real charge for the use of agricultural credit.[8] The 12 percent interest ceiling on agricultural loans was enforced until 1967, although a number of devices were used to circumvent the ceiling. In a few cases, additional interest was collected sub rosa. In other cases, banks used measures that required the borrower to sign for a loan for more than he received. The balance of the loan was left on deposit with the bank and the borrower was required to pay interest on the unused money. More commonly, service charges were loaded on top of the interest rate to raise total credit costs.

In 1965 the Banking Reform Law reaffirmed the 12 percent rate but added the additional proviso that interest charges on agricultural credit could not exceed 75 percent of the rate for normal commercial lending. In 1967 the Central Bank Resolution authorized a maximum 6 percent administration and inspection fee in addition to the 12 percent for agricultural loans greater than 50 times the farmer's minimum salary. Small borrowers were given loans on a less costly basis. The administration and inspection fees were limited to 2 percent or less on loans valued below 50 percent of minimum salaries. Borrowers of small amounts generally paid 13-to-14 percent while larger borrowers paid 17-to-18 percent per annum. With inflation in excess of 20 percent per year in the late 1960s, these rates resulted in significant negative real rates of interest.[9]

Interest rates in Brazil have a very restricted role to play in allocating credit under those circumstances. In fact, interest charges are irrelevant to some borrowers, particularly smaller ones, since they cannot get bank credit at any price. Increased credit is absorbed mainly by those who apply first or have special connections in the banking system. At negative interest rates, farmers have been asked to use loans for projects whose marginal rates of return are near zero. Under these excess demand conditions and to the extent they are legally allowed, banks have concentrated their funds in large loans to minimize operational risks by lending mainly to those operators with high equity to credit ratios, that is, larger farmers.

An interesting associated point is that low interest rates on credit for small farmers have often been justified in the past because policy makers believed these farmers would not significantly increase their borrowing unless interest rates were lowered by large amounts. Little empirical evidence has been generated to substantiate this point. It is likely that the proposition is suspect, on the basis of the Brazilian experience. As such, the low interest rate policy may not be needed to induce small farmers to use credit where it can be profitably applied. Instead, the inexpensive credit policy may only seriously thwart the incentives of the lender to make loans to those farmers who are the intended beneficiaries of this policy.

Incentives for the banks to make more loans to smaller farmers could be provided through any one of a number of policy alternatives.

As a minimum, credit charges on all sizes of agricultural loans could be equalized in Brazil: banks should not be penalized for making small loans. Higher real (corrected for inflation) interest charges across the board for agricultural credit would in fact improve the credit allocation to small farmers. Increased credit charges to large borrowers would force them to reduce their borrowing substantially and expand the funds available for small loans. Banks could also be encouraged to make small loans by a differential discount rate policy through the central bank; that is, a larger discount spread might be allowed on small loans than on large loans.

The overall supply of credit does not seem to be the major agricultural credit problem in Brazil; rather, it is the lack of appropriate policies that provide banks with economic incentives to lend to small farmers that appears to be the main constraint. As was the case in Mexico, Brazil's policy of cheap agricultural credit, while well intended, has been no bargain to small farmers.

AGRICULTURAL CREDIT IN IRAN

During the 1960s, Iranian agriculture underwent a major social and economic upheaval arising from land reform. This abrupt change in traditional patterns of production and marketing created a number of important problems. For one thing, village farmers (who now owned the land) lost services which their former landlords had traditionally provided, such as credit. More significantly, they became encumbered with an additional expense—that of paying for their land over a 15-year period (a major condition stipulated in the land reform laws). This means that their credit needs expanded considerably in volume and type; but institutional credit has not kept pace with this development. The total credit now available is inadequate and much of that which comes from traditional sources (money lenders) carries an exorbitant interest rate. Outside of agribusiness and farm corporations, for which special provision has been made, the credit that has been granted has been mostly short-term. Long- and medium-term credit has not been available to any appreciable degree.[10]

Institutional credit represents only a quarter to a third of the credit obtained by farmers, the bulk still coming from private sources (traders, moneylenders, relatives). The farming sector contributes about a quarter to the gross domestic product, yet farm loans to the sector represent about a tenth of all institutional credit to the private sectors. Commercial banks in Iran have traditionally kept away from financing agriculture, except for limited amounts advanced to big agriculturalists or to exporters.

The land purchase and resale scheme developed at the time of Iranian land reform (1962) obliged the government to pay 6 percent on land compensation funds. The government, however, sold the land to the peasants interest-free. This policy neglected an excellent opportunity to have strongly improved the financing of support programs for the land recipient. A 6 percent interest charge to the peasants on their land purchases could have been readily borne, since the rate of return on these funds was much higher and as a result the peasants were accustomed to paying much more than this on nearly all credit received. This interest income could have been collected by the newly established land reform cooperatives and allotted to farmers to augment their credit funds from other sources. This would have given the cooperatives capital reserves of about three times the amount they now have, and at no added cost to the government.

The official interest rate charged by the Agricultural Cooperative Bank of Iran is 6 percent. There has not been any change in this rate since the mid-1960s.[11] The main rationale for this policy has been to bid away borrowers from high-interest, noninstitutional sources. It is very unlikely, however, that such an interest rate can cover the various costs of lending, so that some of the costs must be borne by the government.

Farms undertaking investment in wells, other capital improvements, and intensive cultivation with the use of fertilizer can afford to pay higher rates of interest than the 6 percent charged by the Agricultural Bank.[12] To ensure both the economic use of scarce capital resources and the ability of credit institutions to employ staff of the required ability and number, it is necessary to increase the rates charged on agricultural loans. This would not only assure a greater supply of those loans (since it would attract additional savings into the banks), but also efficient use of the loans (since only viable, productive projects capable of generating income for repayment would be undertaken.)

AGRICULTURAL CREDIT IN SOUTH KOREA

In 1970 the average interest paid for all Korean agricultural credit was 59 percent per annum, with most credit from private sources carrying interest rates in excess of 10 percent per month. Credit from the National Agricultural Cooperative Foundation (NACF) averaged about 13 percent per annum. And as agricultural credit needs increase, the public sector through NACF will be called upon to provide the largest share of the increase.

Thus while NACF is a private federation of cooperatives with funds of its own to lend, it also is charged with the responsibility of carrying out government policy with government funds or with a government subsidy. The NACF is therefore often caught in the middle in discharging its duties as both a private and public agency. The result is that it attempts to operate as a businesslike credit agency, while at the same time making poor-risk loans on the recommendation of local government officials. Since the government has limited funds and has subsidized credit at relatively low interest rates, it has created a system in which potential favors and payoffs are necessary to qualify for loans. Because of the large gap between demand and supply on loans at the controlled low rate of interest, government-subsidized funds account for a small proportion of total rural credit (44 percent in 1970). The rest comes from private sources. NACF deposit funds from both rural and urban sources also fall far short of meeting the rural credit demand. And procedures for extending government credit often lead to poor results. For example, in country cooperatives, local village leaders decide who receives loans. This approach often leads to splitting the loan funds equally among a large number of people so that none receive enough funds to make major capital investments in productive capital.[13]

Rural credit has a twofold purpose. For the best use of funds, the government intends that credit be used to increase food production (and consequently national income). Yet much rural credit is used for consumption purposes, simply because the rates of return on investment in modern inputs in agriculture are so high that farmers can consume a large proportion of their loan and still pay it off.

Korea has been active in reforming interest rates, but its loan rate structure is still characterized by a marked dispersion of interest rates. For example, eight varieties of financial intermediaries that utilize savings from private domestic, government, and foreign sources divide the capital market into segments. Each offers credit at different rates; for example, negative real loan rates are reserved for some of the segments, while loan rates that approximate the scarcity price of savings prevail in others. All of the rates are fixed by the government at the decreed levels. Since the market system is not allowed to function the excess demand for these funds at each rate must be eliminated by arbitrary rationing procedures.[14]

Because government loan rates are lower than are free market rates, a large subsidy element exists. In 1969 for example, loan rate subsidies amounted to 8 percent of all loans outstanding at Korean banking institutions, and to 17 percent for certain preferential government loans.

Since the Korean economy has relatively abundant labor, yet has relatively limited amounts of capital (resulting in a high rate of return to capital), it is hard to see how these rates of interest artificially pegged at such low levels are necessary in order to stimulate investment. For example, from 1962 to 1967, returns on investment amounted to 17-to-19 percent. There is therefore no shortage of investment opportunities in the country; but there is a shortage of savings to finance these investments.

PROBLEMS OF INDUSTRIAL CREDIT

The methods of rationing credit and restricting its access to only a limited number of potential borrowers in the agricultural sector is also a common phenomenon in the industrial sector. For example in Iran large establishments rely on commercial banks for their needed additional working capital. This capital is initially obtained for one year or slightly longer and the contract is renewed with the same bank or with another bank for a number of years. But the small industrial establishments and craftsmen requiring long-term loans or capital usually cannot obtain these funds. These private sector credit transactions are carried out in three loosely related markets. The largest source is that of the commercial banks, which supply some two-thirds of total credit extended; these are usually short-term (up to one year) loans at an annual interest of 13-to-14 percent. The remaining credit is split roughly equally between nonbank private lenders and government banks.

The government has established a number of specialized banks to fill the credit needs of small borrowers for productive activities (since commercial banks do not invest in these areas); and these banks extend credit at interest rates ranging from 6 percent (to agriculture) to 9 percent (to industry). The government also initiated a special credit scheme for exports, through commercial banks, at 4 percent, and for a portion of agriculture's and industry's working capital requirements, through specialized banks, at 10 percent. It is also noteworthy that the government is a monopolist in the medium- and long-term funds market. Probably the only source for funds borrowed for more than one year is the government. Still, government funds are directed toward the short-term market, and this is especially true in agriculture.

At the other end of the market, there is the nonbank private credit. Not much is known of the size or credit terms in this market, but it is estimated that they are about the same as those of the government banks. Funds available are for the short, sometimes the very short, term. In some cases no interest rate is charged (when money is provided by relatives and friends) in view of the religious tradition against usury. But in most cases the implied interest rate is very high, ranging anywhere from 20 to 100 percent.

At the government end of the credit market, an excess demand for funds exists, as one would expect because of its low interest rates. Specialized banks reject a considerable amount of total applications for funds every year, the annual rejection rate typically ranging around one-third of total applications. As a result, the Agricultural Cooperative Bank of Iran had to institute a penalty rate of 12 percent due when the loan is not used for the original stated purpose. There are views, undocumented, that credit-worthy borrowers, not in need of funds themselves, borrow at the low interest rate only to relend the money at a higher rate. The fact that the interest rate is spread so wide suggests a highly imperfect market wherein the government policy is to reduce, sometimes considerably, the price of capital.

The real problem is that no attempt has been made by the government to assess the impact of its credit policy on economic activity and on the relative use of labor and capital. In view of the special structure of the credit market, it seems reasonable that at rates between 6 percent and 12 percent in the rate of interest, the demand for funds does not change with small alterations. This is particularly so since annual rates of return are estimated to be around 20 percent for the economy as a whole, and some 30 percent for industry. Government help seems to be required not so much in reducing the price of capital, but in making it available to those (primarily small farmers and manufacturers) who for various reasons do not have access to bank credit.

Two problems may be specifically mentioned in this context. The Agricultural Cooperative Bank has some 160 branches in Iran, compared to several thousand for commercial banks—hence the phenomenon that, as one moves away from the cities, the reliance on nonbank credit increases. In addition, this bank has not adapted itself to the seasonal demand for credit typical of agriculture.

Second, small-scale industries in the cities find it difficult to obtain bank credit because of lack of sufficient collateral. Funds for more than one year are available only at the government banks and they deal only with big customers.

Availability of credit to agriculture and small-scale industry is an important factor in determining the rate of job creation. Therefore measures are needed to minimize the distortions in the price of capital and to increase the accessibility to bank credit, at normal prices, to those who cannot obtain it at present.

To summarize, the traditional or informal credit markets are quite inadequate for reducing dispersion in real rates of interest for

CREDIT AND INCOME DISTRIBUTION

both the majority of small-scale urban entrepreneurs and the rural population. Because of limited government funds, these groups usually have access to only two sources of credit—a moneylender or a village store. This fragmentation permits the exercise of monopoly power, which inevitably leads to highly differentiated rates of interest.

Not all of this is the fault of the commercial banks. It is usually the fault of various regulations, such as usury ceilings on the interest rates charged on bank loans. These ceilings have emasculated the ability and willingness of commercial banks to serve small-scale borrowers of all classes. A maximum interest rate of 10 percent does not begin to cover the administrative costs and potential default risks inherent in small-scale loans; hence the great mass of small farm households is driven to the moneylenders. In addition to restricting the overall volume of bank lending, the interest ceiling ensures that the trickle of available finance flows to completely safe borrowers whose reputation is known or whose collateral is relatively without risk. Or worse, the great excess demand for loans allows allocations to be contingent on political or establishment connections. Importers holding exclusive licenses, or the largest landowners, or various government agencies are likely to be the beneficiaries. Since these individuals frequently have large visible incomes and asset holdings, loans made to them at low regulated rates of interest tend to exaggerate the already skewed distribution of income.

SUMMARY OF CREDIT AND FINANCIAL POLICIES

In Mexico, Brazil, Iran, and to a certain extent, Korea, governments have attempted to meet the financial needs of small-scale industry, agriculture, and retail trade—areas in which commercial bank financing is ordinarily available. Public lending to these sectors has generally concentrated on direct and indirect subsidies to borrowers through special credit facilities provided by development institutions. This public activity has not, however, succeeded in satisfying more than a small part of each sector's credit needs. Moreover, contrary to each government's intention, these policies on the whole have benefited mainly the more affluent of the population.

Paradoxically, therefore, cheap credit may not benefit the little man at all. Quite the contrary, it may effectively prevent him from competing for long-term finance from the organized banking system, and as a result he is confined to obtaining month-to-month credit from the village storekeeper.

Employment effects of this strategy have been minimal: lack of credit in traditional sectors impels labor migration to the city, and capital intensive growth in urban areas (stimulated by low interest rates) absorbs only a portion of the rural migrants. The labor force not absorbed builds its slums. Current distribution effects result in an urban elite, an urban proletariat of underemployed, and a rural class on a flat or falling trajectory of income and wealth. The filter-down or spillover or linkage effects from industrialization stimulated by artificially low interest rates are not impressive in our sample countries.

NOTES

1. For a general description of this process see Edward Shaw, Financial Deepening in Economic Development (New York: Oxford University Press, 1973), and Ronald I. McKinnon, Money and Capital in Economic Development (Washington, D.C.: The Brookings Institution, 1973).

2. An excellent description of the characteristics of semi-industrialized countries is given in Carlos F. Diaz Alejandro, Exchange Rate Devaluation in a Semi-Industrialized Country—The Experience of Argentina, 1955-1961 (Cambridge: MIT Press, 1965).

3. Raymond Goldsmith, The Financial Development of Mexico (Paris: Development Center of the Organization for Economic Cooperation and Development, 1966), chap. 2.

4. Robert L. Bennett, The Financial Sector and Economic Development—The Mexican Case (Baltimore: Johns Hopkins Press, 1965), chap. 2.

5. Folke Dovring, "Land Reform in Mexico," in Land Reform in Brazil, Cuba, Guatemala and Mexico (Washington, D.C.: Agency for International Development, Spring Review of Land Reform, 1970), p. 5.

6. Cynthia Hewitt de Alcantara, "The Green Revolution as History: The Mexican Experience," Development and Change, no. 2, (1973-74), p. 35.

7. Jerry Ladman, "A Model of Credit Applied to the Allocation of Resources in a Case Study of a Sample of Mexican Farms," Economic Development and Cultural Change, January 1974, p. 229.

8. Richard L. Meyer, Dale W. Adams, Norman Rask, and Paulo F. Cidade de Araujo, "Rural Capital Markets and Small Farmers in Brazil, 1960-1972," (Washington, D.C.: Agency for International Development, Small Farmer Credit in South America, 1973), p. 11.

9. Donald Syvrud, Foundations of Brazilian Economic Growth (Stanford, Calif.: Hoover Institution Press, 1973), chap. 9.

10. Abdolhossain Zahedani, <u>Evaluation of Agricultural Development Strategy, 1962-1972</u> (Ph.D. diss., University of California, Davis, 1974), chap. 2.

11. Thomas Stickley and Ebrahim Hosseini, "Small Farmer Credit in Iran—The Supervised Agricultural Credit Program of the Agricultural Cooperative Bank of Iran" (Washington, D.C.: Agency for International Development, Spring Review of Small Farmer Credit, vol. 9, 1973), chap. 1.

12. International Labor Office, <u>Employment and Income Policies for Iran</u> (Geneva, 1973), p. 89.

13. George Rossmiller et al., <u>Korean Agricultural Sector Analysis and Recommended Development Strategies, 1971-1985</u> (East Lansing, Mich.: Department of Agricultural Economics, Michigan State University, 1972), p. 28.

14. Shaw, op. cit., p. 159.

CHAPTER

3

THE EFFECT OF GOVERNMENT TAX POLICIES ON INCOME DISTRIBUTION

Public finance is a subarea of economics that embraces two variables: (1) the level of taxation and the tax structure and (2) the level and distribution of government expenditures. Unlike some areas of economics, public finance involves issues that are highly controversial and that must be resolved not on the basis of precise scientific analysis, but on the basis of political, social, and economic value judgments.

In the following discussion of the impact of tax policies on income distribution, we will spell out the criteria by which we are judging the appropriateness of government revenue systems. Nevertheless, the reader should be aware that great controversy in this area exists even among public finance experts.

IRAN

Until the late 1960s, one of the major constraints on Iran's economic growth was the low level of domestic savings which in turn made necessary high levels of borrowing in order to maintain high levels of investment.[1] In recent years the need to prevent the gap between government expenditures and taxes from becoming too excessive has given rise to some upward revisions and readjustments in the tax system.

Despite the fairly rapid increases in tax revenues since 1968, it is petroleum revenues that have permitted the public sector to break away, at least temporarily, from the trap of low savings and investment. In doing so, petroleum revenues have relieved immediate pressure on the nonpetroleum tax system in order to provide sufficient revenues to achieve a balance between government expenditures and receipts. However, in spite of several tax reforms, the misallocation of revenues and the distributive inequalities resulting from deficiencies in the structure and performance of the tax system remain and, unless the government takes corrective measures in this area, these problems are likely to be magnified by the unbalanced growth generated by the petroleum revenues.[2]

Tax Policies

A major step in tax reform was undertaken in a 1967 law designed to eliminate the dependence of the country on oil revenues. That law divides direct taxes into two parts: income taxes and other direct taxes. Moreover, the direct taxes can be divided into four major categories:[3]

1. <u>Taxes on Agricultural Land</u>. The income of those engaged in agricultural activities, irrespective of their legal status with regard to landownership, is subject to the provisions of the 1967 law. Certain exemptions are allowed: on an annual income of less than 60,000 rials (76.25 equal one U.S. dollar), no tax is levied on individuals who are either owner-farmers or who owned their land during the land reform of 1962; and exemptions are given to those who retained their land according to the provisions of the 1967 land-reform act and who farm those lands. Exemptions are also allowed for losses greater than 25 percent caused by natural calamities; income from newly developed irrigated land for a period of ten years; income on agricultural products deemed indispensable to national development; income acquired from above-average yields (up to 50 percent); income from cattle farming for a period of ten years; and income from agricultural activities located in border areas.

Most of these provisions are designed to achieve certain national goals—self-sufficiency in agricultural production, particularly cattle, and stable political borders. It should be noted that prior to the 1967 law, small landowners were subject to a tax on their agricultural incomes. However, the 1967 law benefited this group by allowing an exemption for a period of ten years.

2. <u>Taxes on Occupations</u>. All persons who earn wages or salaries, who receive income from estates or from agricultural activities, or interest on investments on bank deposits, or who have occupational earnings, are subject to a tax on occupations, whether they maintain commercial offices or not. Exemptions are given to those who do not maintain commercial offices, that is, those who

receive regular annual earnings of less than one-half million rials; and those who receive irregular annual earnings, —for example, 80 percent of income from services is taxable, and 65 percent of income earned by artists and writers is taxable.

3. <u>Taxes on Wages and Salaries</u>. Persons who work for an employer and are paid in money or in kind are subject to taxes on earnings greater than 60,000 rials per annum. There are certain exemptions: pensions, travel expenses, the entertainment expenses of provisional and local governors, annual holiday bonuses of up to 30,000 rials; houses and vehicles belonging to organizations; and insurance contributions made by employers.

4. <u>Taxes on Legal Persons (Companies)</u>. The total income of companies and other profit-making activities of other legal persons is taxed as follows: income from state-owned commercial ventures— (amortization + costs) - (taxable income not included in other categories + total sales) = taxable income; income levied on private companies—(amortization + costs) - (taxable income not included in other categories + total sales) = income subject to a general company tax rate of 10 percent. The remaining profits are counted as profit for distribution to shareholders and company reserves; the undistributed profits are taxed in the following way—15 percent tax on profit distributed to those holding registered shares and to partners; 25 percent tax on profits accruing to bearer shares; and 25 percent tax on undistributed profits. The purpose of the structure of taxes in this category is to encourage the transformation of bearer shares into registered shares.

Numerous exemptions are allowed: 25 percent of the taxable income of mining companies and mineral processing plants founded before 1967 and 20-to-100 percent of the taxable income of those founded after the new legislation; southern fisheries for five years; companies providing for the needs of ships in the Persian Gulf for ten years; the capital reserve of companies; building companies that construct low-cost housing; exporters of selected goods; companies engaged in educational and health activities for ten years; and agricultural joint stock companies for ten years.

In 1973 there were additional changes in income taxes.[4] These included (1) the exemption of all agricultural and animal husbandry activities from income taxes for a period of ten years; (2) a change in the tax brackets for income in excess of six million rials and in the marginal tax rate for some tax brackets; (3) an increase in the corporation tax on taxable income in excess of twenty million rials that effectively raised the maximum tax rate from 25 percent to 55 percent and made the tax progressive; (4) the exemption from tax for the next five years of income earned from the construction and sale or rental of medium- and low-cost residential property and automobile parking facilities; (5) a 10-15 year tax holiday for new factories located more than 120 kilometers outside Teheran or for existing factories that locate outside this radius; and (6) an increase in tax rates for government employees' salaries (they still remain somewhat lower than the rates for nongovernment employees).

While progress is being made in reforming the national tax structure, municipalities are still suffering from antiquated tax structures. One of the most common endemic problems remaining for municipalities in Iran is insufficient funds to support both current and development activities. Because there is little correlation between municipal revenue and city size, some cities find it impossible to provide even a minimum of public services. The resulting need for loans from central government organizations has produced an ever increasing debt burden, approaching 30 percent of total municipal revenues in some cases. Three major kinds of revenues can be identified: levies and taxes administered and collected locally; taxes and duties collected by central agencies and reapportioned to municipalities; and grants and loans from central government agencies.

City taxes are imposed by each municipality, acting under authority given by the national laws and operating under the general supervision of the Ministry of Interior. In general, these are indirect taxes, usually sales and excise taxes and user charges, with the important exception of a property tax, newly initiated under the Town Reconstruction and Development Act of 1968. This tax, which replaced the land tax, is imposed on the value of land and buildings at a rate of 2 1/2 rials per 1,000 rials. A minimum value per building unit, below which a property is exempt, is determined by the city council, and property valuation is undertaken by the city. This property tax, which has great potential as a revenue generator, is as yet unproductive, because the rate is low and the exemption level usually excludes all but the most expensive properties.[5]

No generalization can be made about the strength of other local revenues, for their returns and incidence vary from city to city. Among the more common revenue forms taxed and collected locally are fees for registering cars and bicycles and for issuing licenses for trade and construction; taxes on entertainment, primarily a cinema tax; revenue from the sale of water, from the bus system, and other user charges; money resulting from the liquidation of assets, such as the sale of municipally owned land.

As can be seen, there is a plethora of local taxes which, in most cases, do not produce much revenue and are only marginal increments to city income. Moreover, there is little consistency or standardization from city to city.

The second category of local tax revenue, as noted above, comprises taxes and duties collected by central agencies and reapportioned to municipalities. A multitude of revenue sources fall under this category:

1. All granulated and solid sugar sold in Iran is taxed by the Ministry of Economy and part of the tax is given to municipalities.
2. A tax of 0.59 rials is imposed on the sale of every liter of gasoline and given to municipalities.
3. The Customs Organization of the Ministry of Economy collects a levy on all imported dutiable items for the benefit of the port cities.
4. A tax is collected on passports issued to travelers, with the revenue turned over to the city in which the passport was issued.
5. Taxes collected by the Ministry of Finance at a rate of 3 percent of the taxable income of certain taxpayers are given to the municipalities.
6. A portion of the proceeds from a tax on alcohol reverts to the municipalities.

In general, these taxes are collected within each city and thus the revenues generated reflect the level of economic activity in each city. The most important of these taxes, in terms of the revenue they provide, are sugar and gasoline levies. The municipalities have no control over the rates imposed on these taxes, nor have they any say in the distribution of the revenues to particular cities.

Regarding the third source of tax revenues for municipalities—loans from central government agencies—substantial funds come from the central government on an annual basis via the Ministry of Interior and on an ad hoc basis via the Plan Organization, the Ministry of Finance, and government banks. The municipality is a silent partner to these types of central aid, with little or no say in the amount or frequency of grants received.

Iran therefore has a system of taxing income which, because of the variation in tax rates and bases among the numerous taxes, results in tax liability being determined as much by the type of income received as by the level of income. As a result, the Iranian system of taxing income places differential burdens on different income receivers. Placed in order of the lightest to the heaviest burden, the sequence is roughly (1) civil servants, (2) private employees, (3) self-employed individual investors and private entrepreneurs, (4) investors in Iranian corporations, and (5) owners of foreign corporations. For some tax purposes, these differential burdens may be weighted with respect to equity objectives and the desire to encourage development by inducing higher levels of savings and investment.

Effect of Tax Policies on Income Distribution

It is clear that the exemptions stated in the law are primarily designed not for income distribution considerations but to attract capital to the industrial and mining sectors; to encourage the repopulation and development of border areas; to prevent the centralization of investment in Teheran; to protect new industries; to encourage exports; to encourage investment in industry; and to encourage both the construction of low-cost housing for low-income groups and educational and health activities.

Perhaps some of the government's motivation was to reduce the disparities in the income distribution by using more steeply progressive tax rates. However, this motivation was not backed by the necessary skill to collect the taxes. Therefore much of the reform in tax laws in the country has only led to corruption of the tax-collecting authorities and to widespread evasion. Tax evasion and corruption have undoubtedly widened the income disparities rather than narrowed them, since the resultant nonpaid incomes have distorted the investment pattern in favor of luxury consumption goods; this in turn has created a self-generating growth spiral in that sector and a consequent reduction of resources devoted to the nonluxury consumption goods sector. This has caused shortages in many of these products, many of which cannot be imported.

Despite its recent progressive tax reforms and modifications, the government is still primarily dependent on regressive indirect taxes for the bulk of its revenues. In 1969, 55 percent of Iran's federal revenues, apart from oil, came from indirect taxes, mainly customs duties. An additional 22 percent came from government monopolies and other agencies, from the sale of government services, and from miscellaneous sources. Less than 23 percent of nonoil revenues came from direct taxes, most of which were levied on individuals. Only 5 percent of the nonoil revenue total came from taxes on the profits of private and public corporations. The reliance on customs revenue and oil revenues—taxes which cannot be expanded easily when the government wishes to undertake higher levels of investment—was, in addition to accelerated spending, one of the major causes of the government deficits in the late 1960s. The preliminary Fifth Five-Year Plan (1973-77) projected that only 10 percent of the total, and 20 percent of nonoil revenues, would come from direct taxes; thus the tax system will continue to play a relatively minor redistributive role.[6]

Conclusions

A general tax reform concentrating on income and wealth taxes is supported by considerations both of economic growth and equity. Iran is dependent on oil revenues, import, and other indirect taxes for the overwhelming proportion of its revenues. These are only slightly supplemented by a group of miscellaneous taxes, fees, and licenses on internal production and exchange. All of these sources of revenue stultify trade and production in varying degrees by restricting and distorting efficient patterns of consumption and factor allocation. The burden of these levies is shifted largely to low-income groups, with the result that the distribution of wealth is made more unequal by the tax system.

Because of the extreme concentration of wealth among an elite group of high-income recipients in Iran, and the unimportance (due to oil revenues) of the nonoil revenue system in generating government funds, it is essential that the government adopt a net wealth tax. This is so because the tax is not only firmly rooted in equity but it also has desirable economic effects. Briefly, a net wealth tax could be introduced as a tax to be imposed annually on the net value of all assets less liabilities of individual taxpayers. As such, the tax would differ from gift and inheritance taxes; these also tax net wealth but only when transferred. The tax would also differ from the property tax, which is only on real property and on a gross rather than net basis. Thus an annual tax on net wealth would be desirable on equity grounds in the sense that the base would include all of a taxpayer's wealth, would provide a deduction for outstanding liabilities and, for equity purposes, would provide exemptions and a progressive rate structure.

In a country where the income tax is an imperfect instrument, both in structure and in application, where oil provides sufficient government revenues to carry out normal government operations, and where the distribution of income is markedly unequal, the arguments for a net wealth tax are much more compelling than in most developing countries. The issue is not simply that income is an incomplete measure of taxable capacity and that wealth taxation for this reason is needed to supplement income taxation; rather, it is the inequitable distribution of wealth that gives rise to the inequitable distribution of income, and if any improvement is to be achieved in the structure of distribution of income, it is necessary to get to the source of the problem, that is, wealth. The net wealth tax is the only feasible and practical measure for taxing wealthy individuals who largely escape their income tax liabilities through structural faults in the income tax law, by exemptions, evasion, and administrative inadequacies.

To summarize, the Iranian economy is characterized by glaring inequalities of income and wealth and by extremes of opulence and poverty—a situation which is the result of centuries of landlordism and undue privileges, in which heredity, custom, and environment have all played their part. And it is evident that disparities in income and wealth are increasing. Furthermore, the tax system has not adequately taxed the gains from capital appreciation and unearned increments. In these circumstances an optimal strategy is undoubtedly the imposition of an annual tax falling directly on wealth, a tax which would also automatically assess a substantial part of capital gains over a period of years.

A net wealth tax would also facilitate the enforcement of the income tax by requiring that balance sheet information be a part of a wealth tax return. This is because in Iran most evasion of the income tax is facilitated by concealing income derived from wealth. Therefore the more data that the income tax authorities have on the wealth of taxpayers in the form of balance sheet information, the easier it is for them to determine the income that should be reported for income tax purposes.

Finally, a net wealth tax would be conducive of an efficient use of resources, because the burden of tax would not vary with respect to profitability. Thus it would encourage the activation of under-utilized wealth in order to meet the tax payments. This is especially important in instances in which urban land is held off the market for speculative purposes, or when large tracts of agricultural land are underutilized. There is ample evidence of both problems in Iran.

Recommendations

If the tax policy of Iran is to meet the requirements of sound fiscal policies or the needs of the Iranian people, the following steps should be undertaken:

1. The personal income tax should be widened by lowering exemptions and raising the tax rates in all brackets. Also, a net wealth tax should be introduced. This would probably entail a reinforcement of the staff in charge of assessing and collecting net wealth and income taxes and supervising the application of the relevant legislation.

2. At present the redistribution of income through indirect taxation is not favorable to low-income groups. To rectify this, taxes on necessities such as sugar and tea should be abolished. New or higher taxes should be levied on luxury or semiluxury goods.

3. The country should raise more revenue from sources other than the oil industry, because of possible shortfalls in oil production. In the absence of a well-established taxation system ready to take over, a falling off of oil revenues for any reason would substantially reduce the government's ability to finance a development program.

4. The agricultural sector through the net wealth tax should contribute more to the national revenue. This is especially important because of the benefit which that sector has been deriving from public expenditures, particularly high-cost dams and irrigation projects.

5. Real estate taxes should be administered in such a way as to bring in more revenue. This is important not only as an end in itself but also as a means of preventing land speculation (particularly in Teheran) and of forcing capital funds into productive uses. The net wealth tax is ideally suited to this.

With respect to land taxation, a system of progressive taxation should be put into effect on the basis of the potential output from land, that is, the output that the land would yield if it were managed with average efficiency. A net wealth tax based on potential output would have a certain built-in incentive: the inefficient farmer whose production is less than the average for the region and for the type of land concerned would be penalized, whereas the efficient farmer would be correspondingly encouraged. The actual tax liability could be changed from year to year by estimating the average value of output per acre for the country or region as a whole and multiplying this by the coefficient that relates the fertility of any particular acre to the national average. In specific form the land tax should be levied taking into account the following:

    a. The potential income from each holding under average conditions of production should form the tax base of land revenue. The potential output of each holding should be estimated on the basis of soil classification according to to productive capacity. The average potential output per acre for each region should be updated occasionally to allow for changes in the drainage situation, sedimentation, erosion, and land improvement programs. Once these steps are adopted, annual revision of the assessment on each holding could be made on the basis of changes in the agricultural price level in each region. In years of extreme distress due to drought or flood or other calamities, complete remission of land revenue should be granted to those regions affected.

EFFECT OF TAX POLICIES

    b. The assessment should be applied to the entire holding of household. This would avoid the artificial partitioning of land among members of the same household to escape higher marginal rates of taxation.
    c. Nonfarm incomes should be added to the farm income of each household and the total income taxed at the appropriate rate.
    d. Under the new system, tenant farmers also should be subject to the land tax. In assessing the tenant farmers, the government should allow them a tax credit in recognition of their rental obligations. The landlords, however, should be taxed according to the full potential income from the land, making due allowance for the share of the produce that goes to the tenants.
    e. The appropriate rates of tax should be applied to the potential income from the entire landholding of the household in their locations. In other words, holdings are to be treated on a consolidated basis.
    f. A basic minimum exemption should be allowed in all cases irrespective of the size of the household or status of the agriculturists (tenants or owner-cultivators). This exemption limit should be fixed at a certain level of income and not at a certain size of landholding.
    g. Land revenue taxes should be made progressive with increases in income. The rates should be comparable to those for nonagricultural incomes that are required under the personal income tax.
    h. As a measure to promote economic development, certain approved categories of savings and investment should be given credit in calculating the taxable income of the farm household. For example, savings in the form of government bonds could be exempted. Similarly, investment in the form of tractors, irrigation equipment, or other farm equipment could be exempted.

  6. The numerous concessions and tax incentives granted corporations must be reexamined.

  7. In order to achieve a better regional distribution of income, there must be changes in tax policy and tax administration. The principal need in Iran is decentralization of tax authorities, especially on land and other property, among regional and local planning agencies. People in these areas would be more willing to pay taxes if the money is used to improve their own communities.

MEXICO

In general, central government finances in Mexico have been managed prudently and with a flexible adjustment to changing economic circumstances. Still, the long-standing weakness of the revenue system has not been removed, and this is one area wherein the government will have to take more direct action in the near future. The major weakness results in a failure of revenues to grow automatically at the same pace as GDP—let alone more rapidly—thus making recurring tax increases necessary for the government simply to maintain its share of national resources.[7]

Since the mid-1950s, the rapid advance of the economy's growth in income has been financed in large part by foreign credits, unequally distributed throughout the country. The resulting concentration in certain areas has caused an unequal and unjust distribution of income. To correct this situation, it has been necessary for the federal government to start obtaining more resources from domestic saving rather than from external credits. This has required a number of revisions of the tax structure.

Tax Policies

In some of the developing countries the governments have mitigated the inequalities in income distribution that have followed the early stages of industrialization by imposing tax and expenditure policies. In Mexico, however, the fiscal system has not been oriented toward redistributing the gains from rapid growth. In fact, until the early 1970s, equity considerations have played a small role in the government's overall development strategy.

To overcome the low revenue yield of the tax system and to improve the system's impact in income distribution, a number of reforms have been undertaken. Of these, the reform of 1971 was probably the most important. The main idea of the reform was not to tax either wage earners or business more than other groups. Until 1971, wages were the most highly affected area, while the combination of wages and capital was only lightly taxed and returns to capital were exempt from taxation. Under the new system, the income tax was made more progressive and the concept of total income, that is, earnings from both a person's work and his capital, was introduced so as to tax real earning capacity.

In comparison with the tax treatment applied to wages from labor, however, income derived from capital still continues to receive more preferential tax treatment. The marginal tax rate on income from labor is now 42 percent, while the tax on income from fixed income assets and from distributed dividends is only 20 percent.[8]

It is clear that due to high profit rates, it would be possible for income from capital to be taxed much more heavily if the government wished, and this is the main reason that the government could channel more resources to itself. At present the income tax on individuals adds very little to total revenue and in context simply indicates a move in the right direction rather than an important measure in itself.

Effect of Tax Policies on Income Distribution

The fiscal weakness of the public sector (as evidenced by chronic government deficits) is both a cause and an effect of the income distribution prevailing in Mexico. One of the functions of the tax system and of the public sector should be to help correct the unequal distribution of income, not only for moral reasons but for sound economic reasons connected with development. If the tax system does not perform this function and the services provided by the government through current expenditures do not adequately compensate for the reduced income of the majority of the population, the vicious cycle will continue in which the concentration of national income and industrial and urban wealth distorts the fiscal system in a way that intensifies the inequality. Inequality in turn obstructs economic development by adversely affecting the balance of payments—a situation not only promoting unproductive and luxury forms of consumption and investment but lowering the purchasing power of the rural, and most of the urban, population.

Fiscal policy in Mexico is directed largely toward promoting rapid economic growth, primarily through the development of the infrastructure of the economy, and toward encouraging both private sector savings and investments, particularly in modern industry. These policies have had a marked impact on the distribution of national income.

For example, throughout the late 1930s and 1940s, the Mexican government relied on inflationary financing of public sector expenditures. Revenues remained low, investment programs grew in size, and central bank lending covered a major portion of the growing deficits. This fiscal policy mix contributed substantially to the annual price increases of between 6 and 22 percent during the period.[9] Government officials therefore made a quite conscious choice to finance public sector programs through inflation rather than through direct taxation. In retrospect, it is clear that Mexico could have achieved even higher rates of growth during the period if taxes had matched expenditures and prices had been held stable. Those responsible for government policy at that time, however, apparently felt that growth with price stability was impossible; they feared that increases in taxation would simply undermine all the other investment incentives. Thus taxes on higher income groups and capital gains were not raised and price increases continued to average 10 percent a year through 1955. The best statistical evidence available suggests that during the 1940-50 period, inflationary taxation to stimulate industrialization caused real wages to fall in both agricultural and nonagricultural activities while the real incomes of the entrepreneurs rose rapidly.[10]

Conclusions

The most glaring weakness in the Mexican revenue system, and one that has prevented income equalization, is the failure to tax income from capital on the same bases as that derived from labor. Particularly deficient in this respect are measures to tax transfers of wealth effectively through the inheritance tax, which is a sieve of loopholes, and the relatively lax taxation of capital gains under the income tax. A failure to tax all capital gains under the income tax destroys the neutrality of the income tax and directly benefits upper income groups.

Recommendations

Further tax reform in Mexico would have incalculable favorable consequences. It would reduce much of the luxury consumption and even investment carried on by higher income groups. It would increase the overall rate of savings and transform part of these savings into public savings. Budgetary expenditures financed from increased tax revenues would improve income distribution, promote a larger domestic market, combat the rigidities of supply that inhibit monetary policy, and ensure sufficient funds for the official banks that play a special role in economic development. Fiscal policy, through adequate tax measures, would also induce business savings and thus raise the capacity to finance industrial expansion. The tax system could be severe and still stimulate development and enterprise.

EFFECT OF TAX POLICIES   53

    More precisely, a tax exclusively on income does not reflect the economic capacity of the individual; this also depends on his wealth. A tax on the profits of a firm would therefore be a more effective way of taxing the income of its owners. Similarly, a tax exemption for undistributed profits should not be given. Under the existing system, there is a bias in favor of the owners of capital; to overcome this the tax on income from wages and salaries should be fixed annually and that on income generated by capital should be modified in order to tax all capital gains. As in Iran, a tax on a broad concept of wealth as well as on income should be introduced.

BRAZIL

    After the revolution of 1964, Brazil achieved in less than a decade tax reforms unparalleled in the nation's history. These reforms totally restructured state finances, offered substantial revenue-sharing programs for local governments, greatly improved the collection of federal income taxes, and initiated an imaginative system of tax incentives. Such changes all had profound effects on the allocation of resources, distribution of income, stabilization of the economy, and rate of economic growth—the major concerns of the government.

Tax Policies

    The structure of federal income taxes before 1964 was rudimentary, with generous exemptions, lax administration, and no widespread withholding of taxes. As a result, both the federal and state governments were obliged to make more intensive use of regressive taxes on consumption, which tended to distort private production and consumption patterns.[11] The first step taken to improve the national revenue system was the creation of the Reform Commission of the Ministry of Finance. This commission, which began its operations in 1963, was given the task of examining the structure of Brazilian public revenues and making proposals on needed changes.
    As a result of the commission's studies, a general reform of the national fiscal system was outlined in constitutional Amendment 18 of December 1965, and detailed in Law 5172 of October 1966. Both pieces of legislation became effective on January 1, 1967, and they embraced the following reforms:[12]

1. The state turnover tax [imposto sobre cirulacao de mercadorias (ICM)] was transformed into a value added tax, with uniform rates on all taxable items. It was originally intended that the states and municipios would both collect the ICM, but this provision was later abandoned in favor of a system of revenue sharing. Under this latter system, the states would administer the tax and transfer 20 percent of the proceeds to their respective municipios according to origin criteria.

2. The exclusive power to collect taxes on property transfer inter vivos was returned to the states (this tax had been shifted from state to municipal jurisdiction).

3. The exclusive power to tax exports was transferred from the states to the federal government, with the revenues earmarked for the formation of monetary reserves. This change in the national tax system altered not only the administrative jurisdiction of the tax but also its conception. The new export tax was henceforth to be utilized not as a source of income but as a regulatory instrument of foreign trade.

4. Certain noneconomic municipal taxes were abolished. Included among these were the taxes on industries and professions, amusements, and licenses, and the stamp tax. A new local tax on services was enacted to cover some of the areas of incidence lost through the abolition of the tax on industries and professions and the amusements tax.

5. The previous method of sharing federal income and excise taxes with the municipios was replaced by an arrangement which also included the states. To this end, 14 percent of the collections from each of these taxes was to be deposited in "participation funds." The total amount thus to be distributed was divided equally between a state participation fund and a municipal participation fund. Shares from these funds were to be transferred automatically by the Bank of Brazil at monthly intervals. Finally, a method of distributing individual shares based on land area, population, and need was substituted for the old equal-shares formula.

Effect of Tax Policies on Income Distribution

The tax changes accomplished certain positive effects: federal indirect taxation in Brazil now tends to be varied on the basis of "essentiality" (higher prices for luxuries); for the first time the government has begun effective tax registration (if not always payment) of the rich; and the government has shifted investment funds to some degree from the richer to poorer states and municipios.

These positive steps, however, have been more than offset by the legal structure and rates of income taxation (taxes on dividends, interest, upper incomes, urban property, and companies are low by international standards, and those on capital gains are virtually nonexistent) and by the use of massive incentives for investment (tax holidays) for the entrepreneurial class. Many of these tax incentives are for the lowest income area in Brazil, the northeast, but the area's property owners usually reside in the south.[13] The incidence of taxes presented in Table 3.1 shows only proportionality in the tax structure; it has had a minor redistributive role.

The markedly skewed distribution of income in Brazil may be accounted for by the number of economic myths that have been perpetuated by business interests and a number of influential post-revolutionary conservative economists (notably Roberto de Oliveria Campos and Antonio Delfim Neto). For example, these observers stress the potential discouraging effect exerted on private investment by increased taxes on income or profits.[14] However, since private investment rates have been particularly strong since the income tax increases of 1964, their position is scarcely credible. There is no evidence, as they maintain, that the increase in savings associated with income increases of the rich in Brazil is higher than that associated with the poor.

Conclusions

Two serious problems that should be addressed by the government are those of increasing the productivity and incomes of the agrarian sector and widening the markets for industrial goods. In both fields tax policies have been unsatisfactory. In the first case a rigorous collection of the progressive land tax within a fully implemented agrarian reform should improve the allocation of resources, increase output, and bring about a more even distribution of income and wealth. In the second case the government must carefully evaluate the costs and benefits connected with increased taxation. Desirable as the rapid improvement of public finances might have been since 1964, the negative impact on the purchasing power of consumers has hampered the expansion of various consumer durable industries.

TABLE 3.1

Brazil: Estimated Effective Tax Rates, by Income Class
(thousands of old cruzeiros)

Year	Less than 99	100-149	150-249	250-349	350-499	500-799	800-1,199	1,200-2,499	Over 2,500
1961-62									
National	5.2	7.8	10.6	10.5	14.3	17.0	18.7	15.3	14.8
Rural	3.6	4.4	4.6	4.1	4.1	4.6	5.3	6.4	6.5
Urban	16.2	19.8	21.6	22.5	23.3	24.1	23.3	19.9	18.0
1962-63									
Rural	3.6	4.4	4.6	4.2	4.1	4.7	5.4	6.4	6.3
Urban	16.0	19.5	21.3	23.1	23.4	23.2	24.2	19.7	18.3

Note: One new cruzerio is equivalent to one thousand old cruzerios.

Source: Data for 1961-62 are compiled from Henry Aaron, "Estimates of the Distributional Impact of Brazilian Taxes and Expenditures," mimeographed (Council for International Progress in Management, Inc., July-August 1968); and Gian Sahota, "The Distribution of Tax Burden in Brazil," mimeographed (Sao Paulo, June 1968).

SOUTH KOREA

Korean thinking on taxation and savings has stressed two themes. One is that since income levels are low and private savings can be increased only gradually, most savings and investment in the near future must be done by the government. The other is that taxation of income must be moderate in order to encourage private savings and investment and to reduce the inequality of poorly administered income tax laws, while substantial commodity, excise, and other indirect taxes are needed to curb consumption (increase private savings) and provide revenue. Lower income tax rates have been popular with middle- and lower-income taxpayers for the reason that they were hit hardest by the tax system in force under Japanese occupation. Income taxes before World War II were very inequitable, since those who were honest or could not avoid the tax (that is, employees of larger private businesses and corporations whose taxes were withheld) were hit the hardest. The less honest or less exposed usually paid little or nothing. This stress on increasing private savings, and on indirect taxes was a basic feature of the important tax reform in 1954, and has been conspicuous in subsequent major reforms, particularly the reform of 1960.

Tax Policies

Measures to stimulate savings and investment in the 1960 tax reform included the abolition of the taxation of capital gains, provision of a 50 percent tax exemption for corporate profits retained for reinvestment, lower personal and business income tax rates, and exemption from taxation of 30 percent of income earned from exports and of 20 percent of income from other foreign exchange activities, such as sales to U.N. military forces in Korea and income from tourism. At the same time, taxes on consumption were increased by imposing higher liquor, restaurant, and admissions taxes, by doubling taxes on gasoline and other petroleum products, and by imposing new or increased commodity (excise) taxes on imported and domestically produced luxury consumer goods, such as electric fans, radios, and photographic equipment.

A major tax reform at the end of 1967 reduced income taxes on lower-income groups and small business, and raised them on higher-income groups and larger business. Further increases in exemptions on wage and salary income were introduced. A capital gains tax was also reestablished, but limited to real estate. However, higher alcohol taxes (which were shifted to an ad valorem base), a new doubling of the number of items subject to commodity taxes, higher petroleum product taxes, and the introduction of a telephone tax were enacted.[15]

In general the Korean tax structure can be characterized by a moderate degree of progression in income taxation; supplementation of income taxation by a system of commodity taxes which imposes heavier taxes on luxury items; and the same tax rate for people receiving equal amounts of income from different sources.

Effect of Tax Policies on Income Distribution

Because the Korean income tax system is only mildly progressive, the major tax-related modification of the pattern of income distribution comes from excise taxes on commodities. In Korea Commodity taxes cover about 80 categories of imported and locally manufactured and processed commodities. The base of the tax is the commercial price of the commodity at the time of either removal from the factory or delivery from the bonded area.

Rates range from 2 percent, on paper, to 70 percent, on gambling and sporting events, semiprocessed wool, and imported yarn. Rates on yarns and fibers range between 10 percent and 70 percent; rates on electrical equipment range between 5 percent and 50 percent; and on passenger cars, 10 percent.

If Korean families are grouped into low-income, middle-income, high-income classes on a basis of their percentage of income spent on food, low income can be arbitrarily defined as that in which more than 70 percent of expenditures is for food; middle income can be said to include food expenses between 50 and 70 percent; and high income, food expenditures of about 50 percent.

On this basis, since the types of commodities typically consumed by high-income groups have relatively high tax rates, the net effect of the Korean commodity tax on income distribution is progressive.[16]

Recommendations for Tax Reform

Despite strong efforts at tax reform, several deficiencies remain. These could be overcome by better coordination of information on taxpayers' reports obtained from various sources; eventual abolition of exemptions and deductions offered to export industries; raising of income tax schedules, since the private sector is now capable of generating sufficient domestic savings; heavier taxation on urban lands and buildings to discourage speculation in real estate; and heavier taxation of petroleum, alcohol, cigarettes, and other nonessentials.

In conclusion, government tax policies have increased national savings without causing the income distribution to change significantly. In this sense tax policies have been relatively successful. But more difficult tasks remain for the future, particularly in achieving sustained financial stability and effective tax collections.

THE IMPACT OF TAXES ON INCOME DISTRIBUTION FOR THE FOUR COUNTRIES

Acceptable as our sample countries' growth rates are, they are (perhaps with the exception of Korea) still not sufficiently adequate to utilize the countries' available resources fully and efficiently. Therefore an attempt must be made to obtain even higher economic growth rates. To this end, the governments should be provided with all the resources that they can use effectively in productive investment. At the same time, private savings and investment increases should be encouraged and conspicuous consumption and speculative activities curtailed.

The appropriate goal of tax policy for these countries is to obtain higher levels of investment, both public and private, but to do so in such a way that the net effect is a more equitable redistribution of income and wealth.

The main factors responsible for the failure of each country's taxation system to attain its objective of a more equitable distribution are the following:

1. Absence of a clear and comprehensive notion of what constitutes income for tax purposes.
2. Failure to recognize that the ownership of disposable assets confers a benefit on the owner over and above the income that the property yields; and the failure to supplement taxes on income with taxes on net wealth.
3. The often imprecise definition of expenses as permissible deductions to be set against receipts in the calculation of trading profits, together with overgenerous recognition of the notion of, and overgenerous provision for, the relief of losses.
4. Failure to secure the true aggregation of a man's (or a family's) total property or income for tax purposes due (in

part) to defective provisions concerning the compulsory aggregation of family income, and to provisions concerning the transfer of income or property into trusts and settlements (quite apart from any illegal concealment of income).
5. Failure to secure the full reporting of income or property due to the absence of any automatic reporting system for property income and property transactions; the failure to make the return required of the taxpayer comprehensive enough to ensure that it is self-checking in character; and the methods afforded in common law for the concealment of income and property through the registration of property in bogus names, or through anonymous holdings (like bearer bonds), or the system of blank transfers in the case of shares.

Our major conclusion is that some form of tax on wealth is the most effective way of using the tax system to improve the distribution of income. Taxes, however, cannot make the poor richer, which is, after all, the main concern of distributional policy. Even the complete removal of all taxes on the poorest members of each country would not make them much better off, simply because of the low absolute amounts involved. Furthermore, many of the poorest people, particularly those in rural areas, are at best marginally within the economic life of the country, and are thus little affected by taxes. While the regressive portions of the tax system ought to be reduced as much as possible, it is clear that if a country's main concern is with poverty as such, any fiscal corrective must be exercised primarily through the expenditure side of the budget.

Public expenditures of course cover many items. We have confined our discussion mainly to expenditures for the development of financial institutions and well-organized capital markets and expenditures on education.

This emphasis is based on the assumption that the rise in the investment in human capital relative to that invested in nonhuman capital increases earnings relative to that derived from nonhuman forms of capital, and that more equal distribution of investment in nonhuman capital equalizes earnings. The hypothesis examined is that increases in the investment in human capital can be the basic factor reducing the inequality in the personal distribution of income. One of the implications of this formulation is that changes in income transfers, in progressive taxation, and in the distribution of privately owned wealth have been overrated as factors in altering the personal distribution of income.

In order to take advantage of the educational system and be able to purchase additional amounts of education, developed capital markets must exist so that students can borrow now in order to achieve higher income streams in the future. If limited to self-financing, many adults would have to forego additional investment in their human capital.

NOTES

1. Robert Looney, The Economic Development of Iran: A Recent Survey with Projections to 1981 (New York: Praeger Publishers, 1973), p. 104.
2. Jahangir Amuzegar and M. Ali Fekrat, Iran: Economic Development Under Dualistic Conditions (Chicago: University of Chicago Press, 1971), p. 57.
3. A more detailed description of the Iranian tax system is given in Terence J. Grove, The Iranian Tax System (Teheran: Industrial and Mining Development Bank of Iran, 1970).
4. These changes are described in Annual Report and Balance Sheet, Bank Markazi Iran, various issues, and the Bank Markazi Iran Bulletin, various issues.
5. Battelle Memorial Institute, Battelle Regional Development Project—Unified Report on Regional Development Plan Framework (Teheran: Iranian Plan Organization, 1972), pp. 193-198.
6. The Fifth Five Year Plan (Teheran: Echo of Iran, Iran Trade and Industry Publications, 1973).
7. An excellent description of the Mexican fiscal system is given in James W. Wilkie, The Mexican Revolution: Federal Expenditure and Social Change since 1910 (Berkeley: University of California Press, 1970).
8. Review of the Economic Situation of Mexico (Mexico City: Banco Nacional de Mexico, S.A., various issues).
9. Clark Reynolds, The Mexican Economy—Twentieth-Century Structure and Growth (New Haven: Yale University Press, 1970), pp. 84-88.
10. Ariel Buira, "Development and Price Stability in Mexico," Weltwirtschaftliches Archiv (1968), pp. 60-62.
11. An excellent description of the Brazilian tax system is given in Carl S. Shoup, The Tax System of Brazil (Rio de Janeiro: Fundacao Getulio Vargas, 1965).
12. Cf. Ministerio do Planejamento e Coordenacao Economica, Plano Decenal de Desenvolvimento Economico e Social, Tomo 2, Aspectos Macroeconomicos, vol. 1 (Rio de Janeiro: Politica Tributaria, 1967).
13. An excellent description of the various tax incentives given for investment in northeastern Brazil is given in David Goodman,

"Industrial Development in the Brazilian Northeast: An Interim Assessment of the Tax Credit Scheme of Article 34/18," in Riordan Roett, ed., Brazil in the Sixties (Nashville: Vanderbilt University Press, 1972).

14. See Roberto de Oliveria Campos, Reflections on Latin American Development (Austin: University of Texas Press, 1967).

15. The details of these reforms are contained in An Outline of Korean Taxation, 1967 and An Introduction to Korean Taxation, 1968 (Seoul: Republic of Korea, Office of National Tax Administration).

16. P.D. Ojha and George Lent, "Sales Taxes in Countries of the Far East," International Monetary Fund Staff Papers (November 1969), pp. 576-579.

CHAPTER

4

THE EFFECT OF EDUCATION ON INCOME DISTRIBUTION

An underdeveloped country is literally an underdeveloped society, not merely an underdeveloped economy. Thus to develop that economy it is essential that the gap be reduced between the ignorant and enlightened, between the economically free and the economically deprived, between those whose education gives them freedom of choice in the deployment of their skills and those who cannot choose because they have no skills to offer.

Whether or not an expansion of the education system is a sensible policy toward achieving a better distribution of income depends on the rate of return to education at different levels. That human capital per se is not a perfect substitute for physical capital in generating income streams over time is evidenced by the specter of unemployed university graduates in countries such as India.

The problem is not necessarily to determine whether education is desirable or not, but to ascertain the right kind of education and how to ensure that broadening educational programs will benefit the lower-income groups. The problem of ensuring access to education for lower-income groups is equally important. There is growing evidence that in many countries educational expansion, especially when it involves higher education, tends to be directed disproportionately toward higher-income groups in urban areas. Even where educational facilities are directed at the poor, the poor may not be able to benefit from them. These are formidable problems, but ones that must be dealt with if education is to be an instrument promoting both equality and growth.

IRAN

Two main features of Iranian education are, first, its rapid extension to greater numbers of people since the mid-1960s and, second, a marked disparity in educational opportunity between the rural and urban sectors of the economy in favor of the latter. Since the end of World War II, enrollments at every educational level have been increasing at a faster rate than has the growth of population.

Iran's population increased from 25.8 million in 1966 (the year of the second census in the country) to 30.7 million in 1972 and is projected to increase to 36.2 million by 1977 (the last year of the Fifth Five-Year Plan). Because of this rapid growth, a marked skewness has developed in favor of younger age groups. In the census of 1966, around 46 percent of the population was in the 15-year-old-or-less age group; by 1977 this percentage will still be around 45 percent, and the increasing number of youths has necessitated huge investments in education and training.[1]

A remarkable fact about Iranian education is that these relatively large numbers of new students have been educated very inexpensively. During the Third and Fourth Plans the total expenditures allocated to the educational sector as a percentage of gross national product (GNP) stayed constant at a rate of slightly over 3 percent. Moreover, the percentage of expenditures for education in the total government budget has gradually decreased.[2] The result has been that the growth in the education budget has been less than the growth in the number of students.

The preliminary budget requested by the Department of Education of the Plan Organization for the Fifth Plan indicates that for gradual improvement of the educational standard in the country the expenditure share of the educational sector should be raised by at least 70 percent[3] (corresponding to 5 percent of GNP). This figure is still considerably less than that spent on education in most European countries. Two alternative conjectures come to mind—either Iran has been especially efficient in allocating its resources to education or the cost per student has been low because the quality of education has also been very low.

Educational Structure

Iran has had compulsory education since the late 1940s, since it is believed that education is necessary to the economic and political development of the nation. The result has been somewhat successful.

EFFECT OF EDUCATION

The proportion of literate to total population increased from 15.4 percent in 1956 to nearly 30 percent in 1966.

In 1971, 74 percent of Iranian children entered primary school, and more than half of the pupils who completed primary education entered secondary education. According to the 1966 census, however, only 1.1 percent of the labor force had completed more than one year of higher education (universities). In 1971-72 the total school enrollment was as follows:[4]

Kind and level of education	Numbers enrolled
Primary general	3,500,000
Secondary general	1,060,000
Higher (in Iran and abroad)	105,000
Technical	35,000
Teacher training	14,000
All vocational training	170,000
Total	4,884,000

Concealed in these aggregate figures is a significant difference in the educational distributions for the rural and urban sectors of the economy. For urban areas, 64 percent of the children in the 6-12 age group were enrolled in primary schools, while in rural areas only 30 percent of this age group were enrolled;[5] furthermore, the dropout rate in the rural areas is quite high.

The relatively low participation rates in rural schools to a large extent reflect not only the demand by parents for their children's time in productive activities on the farm, but a dissatisfaction with the curriculum, which is classical in nature rather than applied and is of recognized low quality. Vis-a-vis urban schools, rural schools have fewer books and materials and are operated by less qualified, more poorly paid teachers.

Effect of Education on Income Distribution

In Iran, where all of the educational levels have experienced significant growth it is not obvious how the educational system has affected the income distribution. However, several deductions can be made.

An imbalance between middle- and upper-skill levels clearly exists and is increasing in Iran. At present (1975) more than 97 percent of pupils in secondary schools are following courses of a nonvocational academic nature, and at this stage of education, dropout rates are even higher than in elementary schools. In 1970 only 36 percent of entrants in the first year of secondary education completed the program.

The resulting lack of skilled workers is confirmed by interviews with employers, who report difficulty in finding people with appropriate vocational skills but no difficulty in finding university graduates. Indeed, employers most often resort to hiring university graduates to undertake office and technical jobs that could be performed by individuals with lesser educational attainments.[6]

Secondary graduates lacking these skills then find themselves unable to compete for jobs and have little alternative but to drop out or continue to the university level. As a result, university enrollment has expanded very rapidly. In 1968, 106,000 took the university entrance examinations and 16,000 were admitted; in 1970 the applicants numbered 63,000, of whom just over 12,000 were admitted to full-time undergraduate classes.[7]

Economic theory would suggest that such an imbalance would result in lowering the wage of college graduates relative to those with secondary school training. This would make investment in a university degree less profitable, thereby discouraging some individuals from undergoing a college education. Thus any imbalance in the educational structure would tend to be corrected over time. Yet in Iran the fraction of individuals receiving a college education is rising; the equilibrating mechanism suggested by theory does not appear to be operative. The important question is why. The answer would appear to lie largely in the low availability of secondary education but also in the set of incentives confronting students. These incentives are the result of institutional arrangements surrounding higher education and job selection.

In Iran the direct cost of a university education borne by the student is quite low, since higher education is highly subsidized. The result is that private rates of return to higher education are considerably higher than are social rates of return (see Table 4.1). In fact the government's share of direct costs is several times as great as the private share. This ratio, however, varies from subject area to subject area. The result is a greater difference between private and social returns* in agriculture and engineering, which

---

*However this is not the case for investments in education (or human capital). Not only is free trade in this type of investment impossible, thus preventing the market mechanism from equalizing rates of return on different types of education, but government policies cause each individual's return to be removed from the value of the

TABLE 4.1

Iran; Private Rate of Return for Five Fields of Education, 1968
(percentages)

Fields of Study	0 percent Growth in Real Per Capita Income			3 percent Growth in Real Per Capita Income			5 percent Growth in Real Per Capita Income			Private Share of Direct Costs of Education
	No Ability Adjustment	60 percent Earnings Differential	40 percent Earnings Differential	No Ability Adjustment	60 percent Earnings Differential	40 percent Earnings Differential	No Ability Adjustment	60 percent Earnings Differential	40 percent Earnings Differential	
Literature and humanities	20.0	14.0	10.3	23.7	17.5	13.7	26.1	19.8	15.9	—
Science	23.6	16.6	12.4	27.4	20.2	15.8	30.0	22.6	18.1	—
Business and public administration and economics	23.9	16.9	12.6	27.8	20.5	16.1	30.3	22.9	18.3	—
Agriculture	27.4	19.5	14.6	31.4	23.2	18.1	34.0	25.6	20.5	—
Engineering	30.7	21.9	16.5	34.8	25.7	20.1	37.5	28.2	22.5	—
Differences between Social and Private Rates of Return under Different Circumstances										
Literature and humanities	4.7	3.5	2.8	4.6	3.4	2.8	4.5	3.4	2.7	
Science	9.4	6.9	5.6	9.3	6.9	5.5	9.3	6.9	5.5	
Business and public administration and economics	5.4	4.0	3.2	5.4	3.9	3.2	5.2	3.9	3.0	15.15
Agriculture	13.6	10.2	8.1	13.7	10.2	8.1	13.7	10.1	8.1	5.99
Engineering	12.5	9.3	7.3	12.5	9.3	7.3	12.4	9.2	7.3	8.79

Note: Earnings differentials are due to education.

Source: Mohammad Rahmani, "The Application of a Systems Analysis Approach to Educational Planning in Iran," Tahqiqat Equtesadi (Winter 1971), p. 24.

have a lower private share of the direct costs, and a lesser difference in literature and the humanities and public administration, which have a higher private share of the direct costs.

Thus if Iranian students decided upon the number of years of education strictly on the basis of economic criteria, rational behavior would be to continue through university. This conclusion is strengthened when it is recognized that the capital market in the country is extremely imperfect and that the nominal returns available to most individuals on financial assets do not exceed 8 or 9 percent. Hence from a private viewpoint, rational behavior would suggest not only that continuing one's education is a sound investment, but also that the rate of return is far higher than on available alternatives.

If this model of Iranian students' behavior is correct, the question is why anyone finishing secondary school fails to attend a university. The answer would appear to lie in rationing: there are entrance examinations which must be passed and a minimal rate of progress required for continuing student status.

In Iran, where public policies determine the supply of educational opportunities to different income groups, it has been possible for the government to discriminate in the returns to investment in education to a degree that would not be feasible in markets for physical capital. Free markets and active trading in physical capital (equity shares) always tends to equalize the rate of return on this form of investment. Also the Iranian government, dominated by elites, has been able to exclude generations of low income, politically impotent groups from access to as much education as they would like. Since the government investment for universities has not expanded very rapidly until quite recently, rates of return have remained high for students completing this level of training. Coupled with the fact, therefore, that the private rate of return on a year of primary education in Iran is less than a year of university education, it is likely that the growth of educational capacity has done little to improve income distribution and in fact may have made it worse.

During the Fifth Five-Year Plan (1973-77), the government's intention has been to moderate as much as possible the expansion of

---

individual's contribution to society. For example, agronomists are principally employed by the Iranian government at low, civil service salaries. Thus private returns to potential agronomists are small. Yet, because agriculture is the major nonoil economic activity in Iran and much of it is still practiced as it was a hundred or more years ago, a well-utilized agronomist should produce enormous returns for the society. That is, social returns are far greater than private ones.

university and secondary education, so as to accelerate the amount of funds devoted to primary education. The wisdom of this strategy is somewhat questionable given the lack of reliable manpower statistics. The statistics identify the bottlenecks that are likely to occur after 1977 and thus indicate the direction that future investments should take, but fail to answer the question of how much investment should be undertaken if rates of return are to be equalized at every educational level at a yield equal to the return on physical capital.

Increasing the relative supply of primary school graduates in Iran will have the initial effect of widening the wage differential between low and high educational levels and offsetting any improvement in income distribution attributable to a larger number of primary school graduates. To what extent this is an important offsetting factor depends on the case of substitution among skill levels. If it is relatively easy to substitute one skill level for another, then a widening wage differential will be counteracted (until good vocational schools become established) on the side of labor demand, as employers substitute lower for more highly skilled (university) workers. Some studies[8] have measured extremely high substitution rates, so it may be possible to expand the supply of primary school graduates and encounter only slowly diminishing returns to investment in this type of education. Increasing the relative supply of primary school graduates would therefore improve the overall distribution of income.

Policy Recommendations

Tuition in Iran is generally free, or scholarships are provided to cover tuition and other expenses; nevertheless, many talented children from low-income homes do not avail themselves of educational opportunities, largely for economic reasons (they cannot afford the lost income involved in attending school). Thus the best government program would seem to be a modest scholarship program for the poor from the most backward areas and student loans for everyone; these would be financed by a special "graduate tax" on future income. If there were no income, no repayment would be required.

The higher educational system in Iran has the potential to bring about income equality, and this could be achieved by raising tuition fees to cover the full costs of higher education. The result would reduce the private rate of return on higher education, bringing it more in line with the social rate. This policy should simultaneously be accompanied by the more vigorous use of scholarship programs for talented poor students or, better still, by loans for everybody to be repaid out of a graduate tax on future incomes if the amount of the loan were sufficiently generous to cover all fees and all maintenance expenses. The magnitude of the loan and corresponding graduate tax could be varied from time to time to produce whatever scale of higher education is thought desirable. It is certain that such a scheme would give a much greater stimulus to income quality than prevails under the present system.

It is likely that this policy would encourage poorer students to seek higher education. It could be defended on the grounds of the benefit principle of taxation—that is, that graduates earn more than those who do not, and further that there is no reason why the average taxpayer who earns less should be asked to subsidize higher education for the fortunate few.

MEXICO

In Mexico education is now considered by most citizens as the only means of permanently improving one's income and status and it is the main reason that they are demanding increased access to formal training. Politically, this was reflected in then President Avila Camacho's all-out campaign of 1944 to eliminate illiteracy in the country. In 1959, when the program appeared to be faltering, the goal was reaffirmed, and measures were undertaken to attain excellence in the educational system. Particularly since 1970 the government has earmarked substantial budgetary resources for education.

Educational Structure

By 1960 the country was in the midst of an Eleven-Year Plan, designed to provide at least an elementary school education for every Mexican child by 1970. This was indeed to be an expensive crash program, made necessary by the rapid growth in school-age population. For example, the rate of literacy among those children six years of age and older rose from 42 percent in 1940 to 62 percent in 1960. Because of the rapid rise in population, however, the total number of illiterates rose to 10.5 million, a gain of 1.2 million.

In 1960 many children were still without instruction of any kind, and the majority did not attend school beyond the first year. In addition, most of the schools were without sufficient operating funds.

In the 1965 budget, education received the largest allotment of any segment of the economy: over $365 million, or $40 million more than the previous year and over 23 percent of total spending.[9] A major reason for this change in emphasis was to reduce skilled labor bottlenecks that are increasingly responsible for the underutilization of plant and equipment.

Still, the federal and state governments appear to have been less dedicated to the advancement of postprimary education than they purported to be, despite claims to the contrary. In 1958, after the country had experienced its marked economic development, only 332,000 students were enrolled at the advanced levels. Somewhat more than half of them were in preprofessional or prevocational schools—that is, at the secondary, preparatory, and prevocational levels. Prevocational and vocational students made up nearly 6 percent of the total. The post primary group as a whole represented about 6 percent of those aged fourteen to twenty-nine who were eligible for advanced work. Five years later, surveys indicated the disturbing fact that of every thousand children who entered primary school in any given year, only seventeen completed the sixth grade; and of course there were further casualties, as those transferring from the primary to the postprimary levels dropped out.[10] The dropouts occurred essentially for economic reasons; that is, students had to drop out because, given the low levels of their family income, the earnings lost while they attended school significantly lowered the rate of return on education.

Effect of Education on Income Distribution

The rate of return on education in Mexico is quite high, and is the largest single determinant of income differentials. In terms of unstandardized rates (rates not adjusted for by factors other than schooling) the private returns ranged from 21 percent for three years of schooling to over 36 percent for fifteen years of schooling (see Table 4.2). The corresponding social rates of return ranged from 17 percent to over 29 percent. A point that is of extreme importance is that adjusting for factors other than education reduced the returns for the lower educational levels by about 15 percent, whereas returns for the higher levels were reduced by only 2-to-3 percent. In other words, the lower the level of education, the lower that part of earnings which is strictly due to education.

This result may seem unusual, as one would expect to find an inverse relationship to be true; that is, the higher the level of education, the lower part of the earnings differential strictly due to education. However, two other factors are in play here—ability and socioeconomic background. Whereas ability enhances the flow of students to higher educational levels, their socioeconomic background hinders the flow of students from the lower grades.

TABLE 4.2

Mexico: Estimated Rates of Return per Years of Education

Years of Education	Internal Rate of Return		Years of Education	Rate of Return	
	Marginal	Total		Private	Social
0-1	—	—	—	—	—
2	17.8	—	—	—	—
3	17.8	—	—	—	—
4	17.8	17.8	2-4	5.2	4.6
5	37.3	—	5-6	32.1	26.8
6	37.3	24.3	7-8	24.0	17.1
7-9	20.0	—	9-11	16.8	13.2
10-11	15.1	22.5	12-13	22.4	16.7
12-14	14.4	—	14-16	34.6	27.9
15 and over	29.9	21.4	—	—	—
Physical capital	20.0	—	—	—	—

Sources: Internal rates of return are drawn from Marcelo Selowsky, Education and Economic Growth: Some International Comparisons, Economic Development Report, no. 83, Project for Quantitative Research in Economic Development, Center for International Affairs, Harvard University, 1967, Table II; rates of return are from Donald B. Keasing, "The Process of Educational Growth," mimeographed document based on data from Martin Carnoy, "Rates of Return to Schooling in Latin America," Journal of Human Resources 2 (Spring 1968).

The private rate of return on the costs of completing the first five grades of school in Mexico is higher than is the rate of return on subsequent schooling up to 8 years. Then the rate of return increases for further schooling over 12 years. The explanation for this is that the costs of elementary schooling are low mainly because at this level there are no earnings foregone, whereas earnings foregone are large for schooling beyond the eighth grade. Since rates of return on the primary system are relatively high, it will not only be necessary to increase the capacity of that segment of the system, but it will also be desirable to introduce an intensive expenditure policy to encourage school attendance. Among the suggested programs are the provision of school breakfasts and lunches, free transportation, and footwear, in accordance with the number of days of school attendance. These policies are vital since only a small percentage of the children continue their studies after the second year of primary education in rural areas. What is more, fewer than 33 percent of the children enrolled at the beginning of primary education complete the final year, which indicates that there are many areas in which expenditure could be increased and thus yield a high rate of economic return and considerable improvement in the distribution of income, especially if high priority is given at the same time to improving the curricula.

Policy Recommendations

Referring again to Table 4.2, it should be stressed that the marginal rate of return on education in grades five and six is 37 percent; for grades seven to nine it is 24 percent; and for over 15 years of education it is 29 percent. Since the rate of return on education for all primary education (24 percent) is higher than that for physical capital (20 percent), if a larger part of government funds were allocated for education, the effect would be a higher rate of growth in the medium and long term. The same is true for the return on all secondary education. The wastage, implied by the high dropout rate before these levels are reached, is obvious. The low-income effect for poorer children has resulted in part from government policy which has concentrated on the first grades of elementary education. Mexico's future education policies will have to be directed not only toward improvement in the quality of the education, but also toward encouraging the largest possible number of students to complete the education cycles.

This policy would be consistent with the aim of improving the utilization of the labor force. Apparent or concealed unemployment is common in the rural sector and is of greater incidence among the less skilled workers, measured by years of schooling. In this connection, a high return may be expected from programs for the training or retraining of adults.

Continued mass education, adult training programs, and improvements in the quality of education will bring about broader social participation in the benefits of economic growth. A broadening of the total capital stock in Mexico to include a greater share of human resources at all levels will facilitate the redistribution of income by widening the distribution of labor skills. This is in fact an investment policy that would meet the objectives of economic growth and social progress in a positive manner.

BRAZIL

The need for improvement in educational levels has been well recognized in Brazil, which started the decade of the 1960s with a level of human resource development well below the international standard for countries with similar levels of economic development. Progress since then has been impressive, at least in terms of official statistics, which indicate the number of students enrolled at each educational level. Public education is to a large extent free, thereby widening opportunities for children from poorer homes. Nevertheless, rapid population growth has made the already formidable task of improving the educational attainment of the country's citizens even harder—a situation that promises to continue for the foreseeable future.

Educational Structure

The Brazilian population of children aged seven to fourteen in primary and lower secondary schools is at present growing at approximately 3 percent a year. This rate of growth is not likely to drop significantly until toward the end of the 1970s, and only then if a decline in the birth rate can be achieved. The population aged fifteen through nineteen is growing even faster, and it will still be growing at nearly 3 percent in the mid-1980s. This implies that either a higher proportion of national income must be devoted to education or the country will take longer to achieve its educational targets.

An examination of enrollment between 1953 and 1967 indicates that only 40 percent of the entering first-grade class were promoted to the second grade; 29 percent went to the third grade; and 18 percent to the fourth grade. The consequences of this structure are clear: no more than 10 percent of any entering body of primary students ever reaches the secondary level. Only 5 percent of those who enter school ever complete the first four-year cycle, and only 3 percent finish the second four-year cycle.[11] Briefly, the educational system creates a nation of dropouts. This has given rise to two related problems: a surplus of unskilled manpower and a shortage of trained qualified workers.

The surplus of unskilled manpower, which has reached staggering proportions in the urban areas, is due to a number of causes:

1. Rural inhabitants have migrated to urban centers in search of better living and employment conditions.

2. A high proportion of young persons are in the labor force.
3. Unplanned industrial developments have attracted handicraftsmen and home-industry workers at a greater rate than they can be absorbed.
4. Urban development is outstripping industrial development.
5. A higher level of education is required for employment in tertiary occupations—that is, commerce, banking, insurance, public administration—so that it is difficult to incorporate unemployed industrial manpower into the tertiary sector.
6. There is a lower demand for labor, which has resulted from increased productivity in certain sectors.

Effect of Education on Income Distribution

The educational system in Brazil, which regulates access from the traditional (rural) to the modern (urban) sector, has perpetuated income disparities. Those individuals who have received some of the benefits of formal school have had the opportunity of acquiring the skills necessary for an industrial job, and thus have a greater chance of entering the modern sector than those who have not had schooling. These latter are more likely to remain in the traditional sector, with its low incomes and little chance for improvement. In general the rate of return on education is not only high, but it also increases rapidly with additional training. In 1962, for example, the private rates of return based on the assumption of zero direct costs of schooling were as follows: 11 percent for primary education 22 percent for the first four-year cycle of secondary, 20 percent for the second three-year cycle of secondary, and 38 percent for higher education. The corresponding social rates were 10 percent, 17 percent, 17 percent, and 14.5 percent.[12]

The high rates of return on higher education reflect the very rapid industrial growth in Brazil, especially in the Sao Paulo area but also throughout the industrial triangle of Sao Paulo-Rio de Janeiro-Belo Horizonte. This growth has required quantities of professional managerial talent far beyond the available supply. Still, even though the education system is expanding fairly rapidly to meet these needs, it will be a long time, given its low stage of development, before it will be able to play a significant role in improving income equality.

In addition, education at all levels is most available to the economically advantaged because of (1) the importance of private (that is, nonfree) secondary education and (2) the increasing importance of income foregone by students in the postprimary years.

On the other hand, the tax structure appears substantially regressive in nature, bearing more heavily on the poor than on the nonpoor. Frankly stated, the poor are taxed to subsidize the education of the nonpoor. On balance, therefore, the current method of financing public education would seem to increase rather than reduce the unequal distribution of income in the country.

The economic consequences of government policies with respect to schooling in Brazil have been embodied in the population's earning power and the income distribution. The government's philosophy that the objective of the country should be to maximize income growth, while leaving the distributional issues to resolve themselves through the political process, has served as a rather transparent rationale for ignoring distributional issues altogether. The idea that these two fundamental issues—efficiency and equity—can be segregated is simply fallacious. The need for an integrated efficiency-and-equity approach is particularly great in the analysis of education whose intrinsic functions include both the generation of income and its distribution.

Policy Recommendations

The federal government in Brazil is aware that the system of financing higher education is both economically inefficient and socially unjust, and it intends to eliminate both free university and free upper secondary education.[13] But this would not be a good policy for the latter since there is no sign of an excessive output of graduates at this level, and upper secondary education could be publicly supported through a grant or loan scheme for students from poorer families.

A loan scheme might be easier to implement than a complicated scholarship formula, though there is clearly an appropriate place for both in the present system. Several alternatives are available: deferred payment through a fixed income obligation, and deferred payment through a progressive income tax system.

However, the income tax scheme for repayment of educational loans may raise important questions concerning its use to help finance higher education because of the inherent regressive features of the Brazilian tax system. In practice, only those who appear on a public or private sector payroll pay their fair share of income taxes in Brazil (in part because their taxes are withheld at the source). Those who earn income outside the organizational framework of a public or private sector payroll (all independent professionals, self-employed businessmen, wealthy farmers, tradesmen, and merchants) can escape a large part of their income-tax obligations. Even more importantly, higher income groups enjoy an added advantage, in that capital gains are not taxed in Brazil. Thus any proposal designed to have graduates repay part of the costs of their higher education through a fixed percentage of the gross income, as reported in their future income returns, would very likely penalize the less affluent graduates (those subject to payroll deductions) and favor the more affluent (those upper-income groups not subject to payroll deductions and able to enjoy untaxed capital gains). It would be unfortunate indeed if the original objective of introducing equity into the financing of higher education in Brazil, using a deferred payment linked to the income tax, would in the end result in another inequity, with those most able to pay the cost of their education escaping much of their repayment through the route of a defectively and imperfectly administered tax system.

SOUTH KOREA

Korea's educational system is very developed for a country at its level of income. Yet there is still an increasing shortage of technicians and a growing imbalance between the supply of and demand for particular skills. The problems of education and the need for improving the quality of technical manpower were explicitly recognized in the Second Five-Year Plan (1967-71). As stated in the plan, the problems are excessive classroom size and inadequately trained teachers; the still pervasive influence of the Confucian ethic on educational values; and excessively rigid government control. Although the first problem can probably be solved in the near future, the other two difficulties are more resistant to change.

Educational Structure

The literacy rate in Korea is high, evidence of the fact that education for one's children is placed high on the priority list of necessities. The educational system is administered by the Ministry of Education and includes elementary schools, middle and high schools, public and private colleges, and universities. Quality varies considerably, and parents in a position to choose will go to great lengths to see that their children attend superior schools. Unfortunately, a relatively high percentage of the better quality schools are located in Seoul and relatively few in the poorer rural areas.

Education through the ninth grade has increased rapidly, and secondary and higher education has grown even more dramatically.

In the 20 years after liberation (1945), the number of college students rose about 18 times and the number of middle and high school students 14 times.[14]

The expansion of higher education created for the first time in Korea a chance for large numbers of its people to receive more than a ninth-grade education. Some of the best secondary schools and colleges were public, with relatively modest tuition and other fees; private schools also increased rapidly. Entrance to all schools above the elementary level was by competitive examination until 1968, when the examinations for admission to middle school (grades 7 through 9) were abolished. This opening up of educational opportunities led to a decline in individual reliance on the family and gave the individual a greater opportunity for nonfamily experience; it further leveled the traditional class structure by opening a wide channel of upward mobility and abolished to some extent the intellectual isolation of the rural area.

In 1971 there were 100 public and 15 private agricultural high schools in Korea, with 39,788 students. Of the graduates from these schools, about 6 percent in 1971 went on to higher education and approximately 33 percent went into salaried employment.[15] No statistics are available, but rough estimates indicate about 30 percent of the agricultural high school graduates returned to farming.

Effect of Education on Income Distribution

Calculations of the rates of return on education in South Korea are sketchy (see Table 4.3). The rates from primary school education cannot be estimated, since the primary school attendance is compulsory and universal. Hence with no workers lacking a primary education, it is not possible to compare differences in graduate versus nongraduate income.

A curious fact apropos education in Korea is that the higher the level of school, the lower the rate of return. The relatively low rate of return on university education has resulted in income distribution and patterns of earnings similar to those found in the Western European and North American countries.

For example, as in the more advanced countries, the estimated rates of return from all levels of schooling are much lower in Korea than is the rate of return on investment in physical capital. This averages about 20 percent in real terms.[16] It seems therefore that in Korea there has been some misallocation of resources between educational and physical capital (that is, plant and machinery). There should have been more investment in physical capital than in education,

TABLE 4.3

Korea: Rates of Return on Education

Type of Education	Rate of Return (percent)
Middle school	12
High school	9
College and university	5

Source: Kim Kwang Suk, "Rates of Return on Education in Korea," mimeographed (Seoul, 1968), p. 10.

because the economic return from physical capital is much higher than that from education. Within the education sector itself, it appears (since its rate of return is lowest) that relatively too much has been invested in higher education.

This is not necessarily a criticism of the Korean strategy of development. At least two positive benefits of the high level of educational attainment have stood out in Korea's growth experience. One has been that the economy has been able to expand at a rapid rate because the large pool of college and vocationally trained talent has been generally able to meet the demands of rapid modern industrial expansion. And the benefits of the high rate of literacy have included the ability to introduce quickly new practices into agriculture with the help of printed material, the rapid learning rate of new factory labor, the ability of government leaders to speak to the general public, and public awareness of events and changes taking place in the country. It is significant that several of the most rapidly developing countries—including South Korea—have educational levels above the average for countries with comparable levels of per capita income. Not only is there some tendency for a certain national level of educational attainment to be associated with a given level of productivity, but educating the work force above that level pulls up productivity and tends to equalize the distribution of income.

Conclusions

The evidence (though incomplete and rather sketchy) lends weight to the conslusion that the high rates of economic growth, together with an equitable distribution of income attained in Korea by the 1960s, was attributable to effective mobilization and use of the country's resources. The most plentiful of these resources was manpower, and educational policies were designed to make the most effective use of manpower in all sectors of the economy.

CONCLUSIONS ABOUT EDUCATIONAL PLANNING IN THE FOUR COUNTRIES

Educational planning directed toward improving income distribution must include questions about the appropriate educational scale in the four countries or the sort of educational system or the financing of that system.

Empirical evidence indicates:

1. In the countries examined, returns from investment in human capital is well above the returns in physical capital. This suggests that these countries should give greater emphasis to investing in human rather than in physical capital.
2. Per capita income differences can be better explained by differences in the endowments of human rather than physical capital.
3. Investment in education can contribute substantially to the rate of growth of output in these countries.

Government policy indicates:

1. In general, tax laws in the countries studied discriminate against human capital. Human capital, like other forms of capital, depreciates, becomes obsolete, and entails maintenance. Tax laws are all but blind to these matters.
2. Capital market imperfections bias investment toward physical rather than human capital. Much could be done to reduce these imperfections by reforms in tax and banking laws and by changes in banking practices. Long-term private and public loans to students are warranted.
3. There is ample opportunity for improving not only the educational but the health and nutritional levels of individuals in these countries. There is also ample opportunity in these areas for indigenous government aid donors to reexamine their approaches and attitudes, in terms of assessing effective inputs to create a more dynamic system of education for change. This is an appropriate time for renewed emphasis in this area, as foreign aid levels decline and as self-reliance is more widely sought as a matter of national and personal pride.

NOTES

1. F. Amin-Zadeh, "Population Growth and Manpower Problems in Iran," in Symposium on Manpower Planning and Statistics (Teheran: Central Treaty Organization, 1969).

2. Educational Statistics in Iran (Teheran: Ministry of Education, 1963-71).

3. The Fifth Five Year Plan (Teheran: Echo of Iran, Iran Trade and Industry Publications, 1973), chap. 20.

4. Employment and Income Policies for Iran (Geneva: International Labor Office, 1973), p. 64.

5. Ibid., p. 65.

6. The situation in traditional industry, somewhat different, is indicated in William H. Bartsch, "The Industrial Labor Force of Iran: Problems of Recruitment, Training and Productivity," Middle East Journal (Winter 1971).

7. George Baldwin, "The Iranian Brain Drain," in Ehsan Yar-Shater, ed., Iran Faces the Seventies (New York: Praeger Publishers, 1971), p. 272.

8. Bartsch, op. cit.

9. Mexico (Mexico City: Banco Nacional de Comercio Exterior, 1968), p. 375

10. Cf. V.L. Urquidi y A. Lajous Vargas, Educacion Superior, Ciencia y Tecnologia en el Desarrollo Economico de Mexico (Mexico City, 1967).

11. Americo Barbosa de Oliveria and Jose Zacarias Sa Carvalho, A Formacao de Pessoal de Nivel Superioe e o Desenvolvimento Economico (Rio de Janeiro: Campanha Nacional de Aperfeicoamento de Pessoal de Nivel Superior, 1970).

12. Cf. M. Carnoy, "Rates of Return to Schooling in Latin America," Journal of Human Resources (Summer 1967) and S.A. Hewlett, "Rate of Return Analysis: Its Role in Determining the Significance of Education in the Development of Brazil," mimeographed (1970).

13. For a description of the government's educational reforms see William A. Harrell, Educational Reform in Brazil (Washington: Office of Education, U.S. Department of Health, Education and Welfare, 1968).

14. Statistical Yearbook of Education (Seoul: Korean Ministry of Education, various years).

15. Ibid.

16. Kim Kwang Suk, "Rates of Return on Education in Korea," mimeographed (Seoul: 1968), p. 11.

CHAPTER

5

THE EFFECT OF GOVERNMENT AGRICULTURAL POLICIES ON INCOME DISTRIBUTION

Government policies have had an uneven impact on the income distribution in the various sectors of the economy in the developing countries. For example, in electric power, transportation, and commercial trade, they have had relatively little impact, but in agriculture and industry the impact has been significant.

The basic fact that the poor are disproportionately located in the rural areas and are engaged in agriculture or allied rural occupations is well established. The percentage breakdown varies in different countries, but in all cases the poorest group corresponds to the lowest 40-to-50 percent of the population. About two-thirds of this group earn their livelihood from agriculture, and can be assumed to be small farmers and farm workers. The remaining third are artisans and small traders, but these, too, live in rural areas; it is possible therefore that as many as 70 percent of the poverty group lives in the rural areas.[1]

To deal with their rural problems (particularly in agruculture), the governments have followed a number of different policies: (1) emphasis on relatively rapid agricultural output through the concentrated application of high-yield inputs on a small number of large-sized commercial farms (Mexico and Iran); (2) a rapid increase in agricultural output through competition, and the utilization of free market forces, without a major redistribution of land or wealth; and (3) a redistribution of wealth and political power together with attempts to utilize the rural labor force more effectively (Korea).[2]

MEXICO

Agriculture poses some of the most difficult problems to Mexico's development, and since it is essential to the development of the country, it is important that the problems be solved. In the first place, the sector employs close to one-half of the labor force and contains the greatest income disparities in the country; second, for the last several years, some essential items of the country's food supply have been growing less rapidly than has the population. The first of these factors has led to widespread underemployment and poverty; the second has led to increases in food prices which lower even further the real incomes of lower-income consumers in urban areas.

The historical experience of Mexico is of great interest because many developing countries are following a development strategy similar to that introduced originally in Mexico.

Government Policies toward Agriculture

Mexico's policy is generally directed toward land reform; however, the government has tended to follow a changing set of policies on agriculture and consequently an inconsistency often exists between what the government proclaims and what it actually does. Nevertheless, it has attempted to reconcile what it considers to be a conflict between greater equality and faster growth, by changing various agrarian institutions to give security to the peasants while adopting expedient measures to increase production on large modern commercial farms. To this end, and to alleviate the distress in the traditional agricultural sector, it has been carrying out the land reform that began after the revolution of 1910, brought about largely because of unequal ownership of land. Since that time it has generally upheld the principle of limits on individual landholdings and redistribution of large estates in favor of landless peasants. A consequence of this has been the creation of many ejidos—which can best be described as communal farms in which the members own land and often farm it collectively.[3] Ejidos are mainly small, but where they include good cropland, they can produce as effectively as other types of farms. They account for 43 percent of the country's total cropland.

While creating the ejidos, the government's agricultural policies have been oriented toward favorable conditions for the expansion of large-scale modern agricultural production by investing a great proportion of the budget in the development of power, transport, fuel, irrigation research, and credit institutions to serve the sector. Tax privileges, overvalued exchange rates, and minimum price supports have also been used extensively to subsidize the larger commercial farmers.

In order to increase wheat output, the government instituted a research program supported by the Rockefeller Foundation. Research carried on at the International Maize and Wheat Improvement Center (CIMMYC), located in Puebla, has resulted in increasing the average yield per hectare of wheat from 800 kg. in 1950 to nearly 2,800 kg. in 1970. The increase in yields, often referred to as the Green Revolution, results from the application of improved grain varieties, heavy fertilizer and pesticide usage, and most important, controlled irrigation. Without fertilizer or controlled irrigation, the new varieties usually yield no more and sometimes less than traditional strains.[4]

Commercial agriculture, supported by public investment in irrigation, yields incomes comparable to those of the industrial sector. But unfortunately, subsistence agriculture continues largely untouched by the country's rapid development. It receives disproportionately little help from public expenditures for irrigation and is concentrated in regions which, although usually highly populated, receive little expenditure for education or other public services.

Together with its conflict of policies on land tenure, the government's policy of regulating agricultural prices has also been complicated by a number of publicly espoused government goals. It has, at the same time, attempted to achieve self-sufficiency in agricultural production, to encourage the cultivation of export crops to earn badly needed foreign exchange, to maintain relatively low food prices for the low income urban dwellers, and to raise the living standards of the rural masses. It is understandable that measures taken to cope with such diverse and frequently inconsistent objectives—particularly when the priority of goals has been subject to change because of shifting world conditions and changing governments—have been characterized as lacking orientation and as contradictory or self-defeating.[5] Although regulated agricultural prices have made farming less profitable, there are no direct subsidies on either acreage or production.

Effect of Government Policies on Income Distribution

It has taken skillful manipulation on the part of successive Mexican presidents to convince peasants and workers that the government had remained faithful to the ideals of the revolution, that it was striving toward the establishment of a welfare state for the benefit of the underprivileged. However, this was largely an illusion, for government policies have definitely favored the privileged classes.

Government agricultural policies which were undertaken to assist the people have in fact adversely affected them by increasing the numbers of unemployed farm labor. The subsidy given to modern agriculture has saved labor—not used it—despite a rise in population which is one of the highest in the world. The average number of people employed on large farms declined from 6.1 per farm in 1950 to 5.0 per farm ten years later; at the same time, it rose only slightly on small holdings and on ejido land. Landless laborers, as well as a younger generation of ejido and small farm youth, have found it more difficult every year to get a job. In 1960 farm workers were employed for an average of only 100 days a year, compared with 190 days a decade before, and their yearly income had diminished from 850 pesos to 700 pesos. By 1980, if current trends continue, the 3.2-to-3.6 million farm workers that were in the countryside in 1960 will have doubled.[6] In terms of employment—the basic problem of development facing the country—the productive absorption of a rapidly growing population has thus been frustrated by government policies rather than being resolved (as could have easily been the case) during the course of the Green Revolution.

It is still too early to evaluate the preliminary results of the 1970 Mexican Census of Agriculture; as a consequence, data from the 1960 census must be used. In that year, the degree of concentration in Mexican agricultural output among a handful of agricultural producers was quite apparent. Over 40 percent of the agricultural marketings came from about 11,000 farms or 0.3 percent of the nation's producing units. By including a wider group of intermediate-sized or private farmers and the better situated ejidatarios (members of ejidos), three-quarters of the agricultural marketings usually came from about 15 percent of the farming units.[7]

Given the set of policies in addition to credit which favor (or at least do not encourage) the small landowners, these concentration ratios are likely to have significantly increased, and with them disparities of rural incomes, since the mid-1960s.

The process is as follows: price supports above the world level at times have induced large surpluses. If demand could have grown rapidly enough to purchase this output, or if the government could purchase all that was supplied above the absorption by regular commercial channels, the prices of foodgrains could be maintained. This, however, has been beyond the capability of the government—prices of a number of crops declined sharply in the mid-1960s.[8] The consequences are that the great bulk of the small farmers, not able to gain access to the new technology, have seen their net incomes decline because of the falling prices offered for their small marketable surpluses. On the other hand, large farmers have found that in order to spread the fixed costs of machinery, their operating acreage had to be further expanded. An additional consequence of the government's pricing policies therefore is the illegal expansion in acreage that is now taking place through the renting of ejido lands to private groups. The economic explanation of this process is simple: the investments made on fixed assets (such as tractors) by the larger farms have resulted in their short-run costs of production becoming lower than their long-run costs since depreciation on machinery is only a small proportion of their expenses. Due to their financial resources, their fixed costs can be foregone in the short run. Falling prices will therefore not affect their short-run supply of output. Prices of products such as wheat can therefore fall to the levels that will cover only variable costs and not fixed costs. The impact of such a situation has disastrous effects on small farmers whose total costs are largely variable. Many have been bankrupted and forced to rent on increasingly unfavorable terms to the larger, expanding landowners.

Given the tendency for agricultural prices of staple foods to fall, the real loss of income would be greatest for small farmers who could not cover their costs of production. The real gain of income would be greatest for urban workers who consume a high proportion of staple foods in their daily diet. One would predict therefore a transfer of income from small villages (where mechanization has not been introduced) to large towns.

This line of reasoning is substantiated by the fact that monthly family income by size of community indicates that there is a clear trend toward a rise in monthly income by city size. Average monthly income in communities with fewer than 2,500 inhabitants in 1968 was less than half that in communities with a population of from 10,000 to 150,000 and less than one-fourth of the average monthly income in the Federal District. In terms of relative distribution, 46 percent of families residing in communities with fewer than 2,500 inhabitants received 23 percent of income, while at the other extreme 14 percent of those residing in the Federal District received nearly 30 percent of total family incomes. In fact, since 1965 when food prices began to fall, the average level of real income for the 10 percent of the families in the lowest income brackets has been deteriorating. The next 20 percent of families have apparently increased their real income moderately while families in the median stratum have received an appreciable increase in real income.[9]

Admittedly, causes of this decline in relative incomes by city size are complex and not exclusively related to changes in food prices. It is clear, however, that during the 1960s the agricultural sector expanded much more slowly than did the national GDP. While the national GDP rose to an average annual rate of 7 percent at 1960 prices, the GDP of agriculture increased only 3.6 percent per year. Various indices show that this expansion by farming and other agricultural activities has been concentrated in the group of the largest-scale farmers. Yet most Mexican farmers are small landowners and ejidatarios, and it is on this level that production has remained at a standstill.

Also, price supports financed from the general treasury have simply transferred money from the poorer sectors of the economy to the larger farmers. In 1965, for example, when the artificially high wheat price of 940 pesos a ton, which had been in effect since 1954 at the insistence of pressure groups of large landowners, was finally lowered to 800 pesos, one federal agency estimated that this change alone saved the country some 250 million pesos a year.[10] In short, the impact of government support of the Green Revolution inputs in Mexico has been to improve the upper end of the spectrum of income receivers more than the lower end; this has simply added to the incomes of the already rich.

Conclusions

Government pricing policy has therefore not favored small-scale agriculture. Both credit and price policies have increased the incomes of the larger farmers, and there has been no reason for the government to maintain the domestic price of any particular commodity above that prevailing in the world at large or in subsidized farm machinery. On the contrary, a sensible objective of government policy would have been to ensure that lower costs, due to increased output made possible by the Green Revolution technology, were passed on to the lower-income groups (particularly in urban areas) in the form of lower food prices.

The Mexican authorities have long neglected the two interrelated problems that are emerging as a direct outcome of their policies with respect to the rural sector—unemployment and a highly inequitable income distribution. Indeed, as the new technology of the Green Revolution continues to be adopted in the agricultural sector with the utilization of heavy machinery at an increasing rate, as is probable during the 1970s, more joblessness and increased income flows to the already privileged are likely. Even if the spread of new technology were not so pervasive, the employment problem would probably become more serious as the 1970s ended; a work force born in the population explosion that is currently taking place will be reaching a labor market that may well not be able to absorb it.

Ironically, the Green Revolution's biological and chemical innovations can be applied equally well to small farms as well as to large ones in terms of yields per acre. They can therefore be incorporated into the existing institutional framework of Mexican agriculture without drastic increases in capital formation (tractors, combines). Small-scale peasant farms can adopt these biological and chemical innovations with relatively minor adjustments in contrast to technical innovations involving tractors and combines.[11] The potential benefits of the Green Revolution are therefore not necessarily limited to a few large farmers, and, if used wisely, cannot only raise the income of farmers but can promote growth elsewhere in the economy. Indeed, the new wheat varieties could stimulate the rural regeneration that is so essential to the country's income distribution problem.

Government-instigated price distortions have stifled this development by cheapening the price of capital through overvalued exchange rates and low interest rates. Since yields per acre of lands with and without tractors and combines are about the same, the result has simply been unnecessary mechanization.

Recommendations

The Mexican authorities should discontinue designing policies exclusively directed toward large-scale commercial farmers. A more realistic, and probably the best, approach requires an overall reform of pricing, credit, and supporting educational institutions. Higher real interest rates in the credit markets (both public and private) would somewhat reduce the incentive and ability of large farmers to acquire a disproportionate share of public resources and expand acreage at the expense of smaller farmers.

Often the best price policy is to have no policy at all; that is, let the market reflect the supply and demand conditions with respect to particular locations in the country, so that storage and transportation costs are also determined in competitive markets. Yet because of the large rural-urban per capita income differential, price policy in Mexico must still be used by the government, but now take on a good measure of an income policy for the benefit of the majority of the rural population. Since food occupies about 40 percent of the urban cost of living, the government through its buying and selling of wheat should let its price rise relatively faster than others (that is, manufacturing) and yet hold the increase of the total cost of living index at an acceptable annual rate. This policy would of course improve also the incentives on the part of small farmers to expand production while at the same time maintaining their viability. This would be a temporary measure for the period when increased interest rates would prevent the further overmechanization on large-sized commercial farms.

At the same time, there should be a strengthening of agricultural research and extension centers with the object of developing seed varieties adaptable to the specific climatic conditions of each region. Most importantly, the relatively large number of subsistence farmers in relatively arid regions require special attention.

Although it is unreasonable to expect immediate results, expanded research, extension services, and technical assistance should be important instruments for increasing the productivity of small farmers and the ejido type of communal farms. Such a policy, combined with increased investments in rural education and public works, is necessary for the rural rejuvenation so vital for the country's continued prosperity, and at the same time would increase equity.

BRAZIL

Brazil's diversity is nowhere more widespread than in its agriculture, which is characterized by wide differences in productivity between regions and even within each of the geographical divisions of the country. Average figures for the country as a whole consequently mean little, though it is worth noting that average agricultural productivity and incomes are less than half the national average and probably less than 20 percent of industrial productivity.

Public policy is beginning to reflect real concern over the great income disparities not only between urban and rural populations but within the rural sector. The highly unequal distribution of the accessible land and that of access to financial resources and modern technology has caused the concentration of the great bulk of farm income and employment to be in the hands of a limited number of producers. In the past the rural employment problem has been alleviated in part by the ability of the rapidly growing urban economy to absorb rural dwellers and agricultural workers at a relatively high rate. But this increase in urban job expansion is now threatening to slow down.

Government Policies Toward Agriculture

Brazilian agricultural policies have relied on market incentives to achieve the expansion and modernization of agriculture necessary for the country's continued development. The policies have concentrated in five main areas.[12] First, investment in marketing facilities has been designed in good part to improve price incentives to farmers and thus expand production. This was the major agricultural policy throughout the 1950s. Second, subsidization of inputs, primarily fertilizers and farm machinery, in the 1950s took the form of exchange rate subsidies and tax exemptions, while in the 1960s subsidized credit was the principal means of lowering farmers' production costs. Third, a massive increase in credit was granted to agriculture for cultivation expenses—particularly between 1960 and 1965; fourth, the implementation of a minimum price program for basic commodities (excluding coffee, sugar, and cocoa), was begun in 1963 under the Goulart government, chiefly in response to a continuous rise in agricultural prices, but after 1964 was eliminated. Fifth, special incentives for investment in agriculture have become more prevalent since 1964.

The common characteristic of these policies is their reliance on free market forces as the most efficient allocation mechanism. Each aspect of policy is oriented toward increased production and productivity through higher profitability and reduced risk in farming. The government has hoped these policies will not only increase production, but will do so significantly enough to hold down increases in food prices to urban consumers.

In discussing Brazilian agricultural policy, it is much easier to outline what has not been done in terms of improving the income and employment opportunities for the great majority of the rural population than to examine what has been accomplished. For example, the government has shown little interest in improving rural education, and does not have an explicit policy in this area. As a result, rural educational levels are clearly deficient. Not only is the normal educational level of people working in agriculture extremely low (in 1960 less than 10 percent of persons active in agriculture had completed the primary course of four years), but worse still, there has been no real tendency for significant improvement.[13] Agricultural trade schools, which might be expected to have some importance in a country where 50 percent of the active population is engaged in agriculture, have contributed little to improve farming methods. This is in light of the fact that the payoff to education and training in Brazil seems to be very high.

Furthermore, the government has given little attention to agricultural extension services, to research, or to improving the land tenure system. Instead, it has granted large incentives to investment in agriculture. For example, it has cut the income tax liability in half for corporations investing in agriculture or other approved enterprises in northeastern and northern Brazil; it has granted a two-year tax holiday and reductions in taxes for an additional two years to corporations formed to engage in agriculture; it has offered special incentives for investment in fertilizer production and distribution facilities; it has removed duties on imports of agricultural inputs; and it has exempted many agricultural inputs and exports from the 15-to-18 percent value-added tax.

In its analysis of agriculture, the government has argued that agrarian reform was relevant only for situations in which an excess of labor existed, relative to current methods of production. It concluded that an excess of labor in the rural sector was not a common situation in Brazil. Therefore, instead of a major land reform program to stimulate production, the land reform law of 1964 (which has only been slightly modified since then), instead of redistributing landholdings, stressed changes in land taxation as a stimulus to effective land use. No tax was to be charged for farms under 20 hectares, while the tax rate for other farms was to rise with their size and with nonuse of potentially productive acreage. The maximum rate was 2.7 percent of land value.[14]

Effect of Government Policies on Income Distribution

While no official figures are available on unemployment in agriculture, the effectively employed labor force in 1965 was approximately 16.2 million. Given this figure, an indirect measure can be used to compute the degree of underemployment. For example, according to population projections from the 1960 census base, the total rural population between the ages of 10 and 59 was probably about 25.1 million in 1965.[15] For efficient production in agriculture, only about 0.67 percent of the rural population need be engaged in this sector. In 1965 this would have amounted to 16.8 million. The difference (25.1 million-16.8 million) is indicative therefore of the magnitude of the underutilization of rural labor.

In 1964 there were at least 10 million farm workers, or about 4.7 million farm families who lived under inadequate income and working conditions. The bulk of the needy rural masses is concentrated in the major agricultural states along or near the Atlantic Ocean. In 1950, seven states (Ceara, Paraiba, Pernambuco, Bahia, Minas Gerais, Sao Paulo, and Rio Grande do Sul) had a total of nearly five million or 67 percent of all needy farm workers in Brazil. For 1964 this would be equivalent to an estimated 6.5 million workers in these seven states alone, except that the proportion of workers in Sao Paulo is probably larger now than it was in 1950 due to migration to that state. However, there is not a state in the country, with the exception of Rio Grande do Sul and Cartia Catarina, where the number of underprivileged farm workers does not exceed and sometimes considerably exceed one-half of all farm workers.

The heavy concentration of Brazilian industry in the center-south region and the neglect of the agricultural sector have resulted in alarming regional inequalities in income distribution. This is particularly true with regard to the northeast region. Taking the northeast region as a whole, the per capita income in 1966 was only 26 percent of the average for the state of Sao Paulo. The corresponding figures for 1947 and 1957 were 24 percent and 20 percent respectively. Even within the center-south region, there are large differentials. In Minas Gerais, for example, the 1966 per capita income was only 42 percent of that in Sao Paulo. The three extreme southern states, all overwhelmingly devoted to agriculture, lost ground relative to Sao Paulo over the period, falling from 61 percent in 1947 to 54 percent in 1957, and 51 percent in 1966.[16]

The average size of all farms under 100 hectares declined (mainly through the process of inheritance) between 1950 and 1965. This is particularly serious for the small landholders whose land base is too small for more than subsistence living. In a country with enormous land resources (Brazil has 850 million hectares altogether) this has been a tragic development. It implies that small landholders on the average become poorer. In fact the average size of farms over 500 hectares increased from 15,115 hectares to 16,700 hectares between 1950 and 1965. In Brazil, therefore, access to land for the rural poor has meant access only to the smaller farms.[17] Given the government's policies in the 1960s, there is reason to believe that this trend in land concentration is continuing.

In 1965 approximately 4.6 million rural entrepreneurs were landless. While these estimates are crude, they give a fairly accurate approximation of the human dimension of the agrarian problem; and they cast strong doubt upon the efficiency of Brazil's attempt at agrarian reform, which uses taxation as its fundamental instrument rather than land redistribution to modify the agrarian structure.

Conclusions

Particularly since 1964, policies toward the agricultural sector have emphasized the market mechanism rather than land reform and rural education as the means toward increased production; consequently, they have induced the agricultural system to expand within its existing institutional setting. The crucial question of whether long-run agricultural growth would be greater if the expansion continued on the existing inequitable base or if instead the base should be first corrected has never been given serious consideration.

Yet there is good reason to believe that price distortions in the rural sector have caused much of the observed employment and income distributional problem. In Brazil large and small farms face an entirely different set of relative factor prices. This has limited employment creation and resulted in underutilization of land on the larger estates. The process is as follows: the wages paid by large farms are often higher than those paid by smaller farmers (because many small farmers do not abide by minimum wage regulations) and the interest rates paid by large farmers is, in most cases, lower than those of small farmers since their loans are less risky and easier to process. Finally, the rent on land paid by large farmers is lower than that of small producers (since they usually already own the land). This pattern of relative factor prices makes capital and land relatively cheap for the large farmer, and labor relatively expensive.

As a result, the large landowners tend to produce more capital-intensive crops, for example, irrigated cotton, and to use land rather wastefully, for example, by grazing cattle on natural pastures. On the other hand, the small farmers—facing extremely high prices of land and capital relative to the low implicit price of their own labor—tend to produce more labor-intensive crops, for example, food-grains, and to have high yields per unit of land.

In other words, the operation of the price system influences both the composition of output and the techniques of production employed on the two types of farms: land is overutilized on the small farms and consequently creates problems of erosion (particularly in the northeast) while land is underutilized on the large farms. As a result, total output is smaller than it would be if both groups faced equal factor prices.

Recommendations

The single most powerful policy instrument in Brazil for the combined objectives of rural equity productivity and output growth is land reform. Large estates in Brazil underutilize their available land resources, forcing labor into very small properties and into an underemployed landless labor force. In addition to factor price distortions, poor utilization of land on large farms results from the holding of land as a portfolio asset rather than for production.

The misallocation of resources within agriculture could be eliminated by creating a more equal size distribution of farms and allowing farmers equal access to inputs. Output could then rise by eliminating underutilized labor and land. Brazilian farm survey data indicate that the creation of family farms would incur no loss in potential efficiency of existing farms and that the redistribution of land into family farms of equal size would yield production gains of 25 percent.[18]

IRAN

The structure of farming, particularly the land tenure system, has undergone a profound change in Iran. In 1962 a far-reaching program of land reform was initiated with the aim of giving access to land ownership to the overwhelming majority of peasant sharecroppers, who until that time had farmed the land in villages owned by a small number of landlords. The program was carried out in three stages and is now virtually completed.[19] It has made some two million sharecroppers into owner-residents. At present (1975) half of the farm households own economically viable farmholdings and farm over 80 percent of the land. Yet the Green Revolution has not significantly reached the country, although it has had a substantial impact in West Pakistan on Iran's eastern border. It is therefore pertinent to ask and attempt to explain why the Green Revolution has not reached Iran in any appreciable degree. To answer this question, it is necessary to review the constraints on the agricultural sector's growth, with special focus on the rural technology promoted by the government.

Government Policies Toward Agriculture

The major government policy toward agriculture in Iran has been land reform. The Land Reform Law of January 9, 1962, limited the amount of land that any individual could hold to that farmed by not more than one village (irrespective of size) and provided for distributing the remaining holdings to peasants cultivating the land.

At the same time, the government undertook a series of less publicized measures between 1962 and 1972 which profoundly affected the development of agriculture. A law for the establishment of the farm corporations, with the stated aim of combining "un-economic" or "sub-economic" holdings and increasing output by mechanization, passed the assembly and the senate in December 1967 and January 1968. The important aspect of that law was that it removed the responsibility and private decision making from new landowning peasant farmers and placed them in the hands of officials. Whereas farm corporations were deemed best suited in dry-farming districts with marginal lands that could use farm machinery best, they were also established in districts in which good land and adequate water were available.

Another measure of importance was the Law for the Establishment of Companies for Utilization of Lands Downstream from Dams (the Downstream Land Use Law) enacted in 1968. This law authorized the establishment and promotion of agro-industrial (agri-business companies. Article One of the law states:

> For the purpose of the maximum utilization of the water resources, the land irrigable from the dams and the hydraulic power installation of the lands downstream of the dams, the Ministry of Water and Power is authorized, with due regard to the development programme of the agriculture-animal husbandry and the overall development of the country, to establish agro-industry companies with government capital, with private-local capital, foreign capital, or by joint companies being subscribed for by the government and private investors, either local or foreign.[20]

Beginning in 1961, the Iranian government set out to construct a series of multipurpose dams around the country; seventeen had been constructed as of 1972, making an estimated one million hectares of land irrigable. The area below these dams often is of the highest quality farmland in the country in terms of fertility, availability of water and electricity, and accessibility to transportation, and is contracted by the government to an individual or a corporation for a set period of time. The minimum size for such a contract is 5,000 hectares.[21]

Pricing policy is also important in Iran. In what is otherwise a free market, there are three types of government price interventions in the agricultural sector. First, the prices of oilseeds, tobacco, tea, and sugar are fixed by interministerial pricing boards, with the objective of increasing production of these crops. Second, the price of wheat is stabilized by the government which is prepared to buy and sell at preannounced prices. Third, the price of milk and meat is controlled in order to keep urban consumer prices low.

The remaining government policies toward agriculture include the provision of agricultural credit through special government subsidized banks, development of marketing channels, agricultural produce improvement, and rural regeneration.

As part of the regeneration of agriculture, a drive has been conducted to mechanize agriculture in suitable areas. Some 23,000 tractors were in use in 1972 and 3,000 units a year are currently

(1975) being imported from Rumania. Combine harvesters are increasingly being used in harvesting and it is estimated that more than 3,000 units were in use in 1969.[22] New agro-industries established in Khuzestan have led to rapid mechanization of 78,000 hectares in the south, while between 700,000 and 1.4 million hectares will be mechanized during the Fifth Plan period. This radical transformation of an increasing portion of the agricultural sector through government subsidies raises a series of questions relating to the institutional framework now being created and to the distributional impact of the spreading of new techniques, notably that based on large-scale, mechanized, capital intensive, commercial farms.

It is recognized by the Ministry of Land Reform that implementation of such a strategy will have strong labor-displacing effects. This is nevertheless regarded as desirable by the ministry (and the government as a whole) since it is the most rapid way of increasing individual labor productivity. However, the implicit assumption that this approach will also result in higher yields than could be gained through use of labor-intensive techniques on the small holdings may be highly questionable, as suggested by data from the 1960 agricultural census which indicates higher yields on smaller than on larger farms.

Effect of Government Policies on Income Distribution

A major factor affecting rural incomes has been the structural changes in Iranian agriculture that took place during 1962-72. As shown in Table 5.1, there were only 320 farms over 300 hectares in the country as of May 1972. Farms over 300 hectares accounted for less than 2 percent of the value added in agriculture and cultivated 1.75 percent of farms and orchards. Farms in this category are presumably operated by a manager, as distinguished from those in the next size category where the operator is the farmer. There are 645,000 farms in the farmer-operated category with sizes ranging from 10 to 300 hectares and producing 50 percent of the value added in agriculture and cultivating nearly 55 percent of the land. Subsistence farms comprise by far the largest number of farms, with some 2.2 million families, each farming between 0.5 and 10 hectares. There are one million farms of less than 3 hectares in the country supporting an estimated (5 in each family) 5 million people or about 16 percent of the total population.

The structural changes resulting from land reform and other measures taken have brought about institutions that are very new to Iranian agriculture. As a result, nearly a complete range of institutional structures exists in Iran: (1) private commercial farms;

(2) farm corporations; (3) farm cooperatives; (4) agro-industrial farms (agri-business); (5) agro-rural development projects; and (6) subsistence agriculture. Categories 2, 3, 4, and 5 are recent institutions and, insofar as their technology is concerned, the agro-industrial and some agro-rural projects are completely mechanized "modern" capital-intensive farms. Farm corporations and most of the private commercial farms are commercially operated semimechanical units. Farm cooperatives use basically traditional but semimechanical techniques; subsistence agriculture, on the other hand, practices completely traditional, fully animal-powered methods.

Despite these rapid changes in the structure of the agricultural sector, the urban-rural income differentials in 1969 were about 1 to 6, an increase from the level of 1 to 5 during the previous decade.[23] Thus a major problem of income distribution and employment relates to the conditions in Iranian agriculture. Roughly speaking, the rural labor force comprises about 50 percent of the total labor force, and it is likely that the total labor force will continue to grow at over 3 percent per annum, as in the 1960s. If this occurs, even if the nonrural labor force should grow at the very rapid rate of 4.5 percent per annum, the absolute number of the rural labor force is likely to continue to grow, at least through the 1980s. During the Fifth Five-Year Plan (1973-77), the increase is projected to be about 300,000. If, as in the 1960s, large numbers of the rural labor force cannot, or will not, remain employed in the villages, migration to the cities will accelerate and the problem of underemployment will then become transformed into one of open unemployment.

Quantitative measures of the shift of income, in favor of Iranian farmers, resulting from land reform are not available. It is generally agreed that those who received distributed lands in the early years of the reform benefited more than did those who obtained 30-year leases or other forms of tenure toward the latter 1960s. This is because 30-year leases were based on the average rents of the three years before leasing; the leases therefore usually did not give the peasant a measurable reduction in rents, but only protected him from future increases. On the other hand, a small number of the farmers joined their landlords in unit farm groups and these made definite gains in security and in income.

As to the reduction of inequality in income distribution, two facts are of interest. On the one hand, land reform has undoubtedly transferred a substantial share of agricultural income from the rich to the poor. On the other hand, there seems to have been some increase in the already wide gap existing between rural and urban incomes. Thus in 1959-65, per capita GNP in real terms rose by 11 percent in rural areas, compared to 17 percent in urban areas. And whereas in 1959 rural areas with about 67 percent of total population accounted

TABLE 5.1

Iran: Size Classification of Agricultural Units, End of 4th Plan (1972-73)

Size Category	Operator	Population		Land Areas Cultivated, Idle, and Pasture (hectares)		
		Families	Total	Unit Size Range	Total Land	Land Unit
Large	Agro-industry	20	—	5,000	210,000	10,500
	Large units	50	250	501–5,000	120,000	2,400
	Semilarge units	250	1,250	301–500	120,000	480
	Total	320	1,500		450,000	
Medium	Large farmer	1,000	5,000	201–300	270,000	270
	Medium farmer	4,000	20,000	101–200	630,000	157
	Small farmer	40,000	200,000	51–100	2,550,000	63
	Very small farmer	600,000	3,000,000	10–50	9,250,000	15
	Total	645,000	3,225,000		12,700,000	
Small	Tenant farmer (subsistence)	1,200,000	6,000,000	3–10	4,950,000	4.1
	Part-time tenant farmer (subsistence)	1,000,000	5,000,000	0.5–3	2,100,000	2.1
	Total	2,200,000	11,000,000		7,050,000	
Landless	Migrant herdsmen	100,000	500,000			
	Peasants	700,000	3,500,000			
Total		3,645,000	18,226,500		20,200,000	

98

Size Category	Operator	Annual Cultivation and Orchards (hectares)			Cultivation Per Unit	Value added of Production and Percentage in Billions of 1351 Rls. Market Value of Goods	
		Irrigated	Dry Farming	Total			
Large	Agro-industry	30,000	25,000	55,000	2,750		
	Large units	10,000	25,000	35,000	700		
	Semilarge units	20,000	40,000	60,000	240		
	Total	60,000	90,000	150,000		5	2%
Medium	Large farmer	55,000	58,000	113,000	113		
	Medium farmer	110,000	110,000	225,000	55		
	Small farmer	310,000	335,000	645,000	16		
	Very small farmer	1,525,000	2,180,000	3,705,000	6		
	Total	2,000,000	2,678,000	4,678,000		117	50%
Small	Tenant farmer (subsistence)	927,000	1,740,000	2,667,000	2.2		
	Part-time tenant farmer (subsistence)	450,000	620,000	1,070,000	1		
	Total	1,377,000	2,360,000	3,737,000		97	41%
Landless	Migrant herdsmen Peasants						
Total		3,437,000	5,122,000	8,565,000	2.3	235	100%

Source: <u>Coordinated National Food and Nutritional Policy and Plans</u>, Division of Health and Social Welfare Plan Organization, Teheran, May 1972, Appendix 3, p. 111.

for 37 percent of GNP, by 1965 they had 63 percent of population but only 32 percent of GNP. Similarly in that period, private consumption in constant prices rose by 5 percent in urban areas (6 percent in Teheran) but only 3 percent in rural areas.[24]

There is no doubt that despite land reform, the agrarian structure of Iran still reflects a relatively high concentration of land ownership, wealth, and income. Indications are that the distribution of agricultural income is more concentrated in the modern agricultural enclaves than in the relatively primitive agricultural areas.

For those farmers who have been fortunate enough to join farm corporations, their mean incomes have increased significantly. A comparison of the mean average income between 1968 and 1969 shows that farmers' incomes nearly doubled—from 29,464 Iranian rials to 53,671 Iranian rials. Further, on a man-equivalent basis, mean average incomes increased significantly—from 42,971 Iranian rials to 54,766 Iranian rials.

The income of farmers before they joined farm corporations was not symmetrically distributed about the mean (the distribution was skewed); that is, the majority had low incomes (around 20,000-to-40,000 rials) and only a few had incomes in the higher income ranges (above 40,000 rials).

In 1969 the distribution of farmers' incomes had changed, owing mainly to a significant difference among the distributed profits of the farm cooperatives. Therefore, in spite of the increase in the level of farmers' incomes, an uneven distribution of incomes still existed in much of the agricultural sector.[25]

Conclusions

The formulation and execution of agricultural development in Iran is being handled in the same manner as is industrial development. Foreign know-how and techniques are being adopted in the expectation that quick results will follow and that growth rates measured in output alone will soon match the achievements in the industrial sectors. The Ministry of Agriculture's officials and their counterparts in the Plan Organization speak of certain very modern farms (often foreign owned and operated) which have, for example, had yields of sugar beets nearly as high as farms in the United States. Because of their preoccupation with modern farms they are seldom aware that many fifty-hectare farms in the same area are operated by native Iranians and have even higher yields, and at the same time use local inputs.

These officials are first to propose more aids, tax exemptions, and subsidies to factors used by the modern company while the local farmer is almost totally neglected. The significance of this is that the government's strategy in encouraging foreign and domestic agribusiness is that the entire agricultural research in the country's few experimental stations be focused on problems of developing improved inputs for use in these types of farms. The most basic extension requirements of the small farmer are unattended by the numerous agencies, ministries, and banks that are supposed to perform such services.

Recommendations

Achievement of the objectives of an equitable distribution of income in the agricultural sector, together with growth, indicates that a far more general and indirect role should be played by the government. The following general rules are suggested for agricultural policy making:

1. The government should promote competition in production by allowing all farmers the chance to use land and water resources on an equal basis.
2. Water resources developed should be provided to all users at uniform costs.
3. The introduction of improved factors associated with the Green Revolution should be made available on a uniform basis to all farmers and should begin with the inputs commonly used by all.
4. Credits for the purchase of improved inputs of seeds, fertilizer, and chemicals should be provided uniformly to all farmers.
5. A national farm price policy should immediately be implemented. Marketing problems are perhaps one of the most important areas in which the government can undertake a major role.
6. The government has selected projects in a piecemeal and inconsistent manner. Many of these projects, such as dams and elaborate irrigation systems, affect only a fraction of the farms in the country. It is doubtful whether most of these projects can pass the most liberal interpretation of cost-benefit analysis. For example, the experiments with agro-rural projects like the one in Ghazvin have proved to be very costly for the number of people they affect. In addition, the

existing farm corporations in 1972 had some 52,000 hectares under cultivation. This amounted to no more than one-half percent of the cultivated lands and involved only 130,000 farmers.

The numerous rural projects undertaken by the government should explicitly take into consideration the impact of the project on income distribution.

Since the government's budget is so large, due to the country's increase in oil revenues, government project selection can directly alter the existing distribution of income in a fairly short period of time. In order to use project selection to full advantage in increasing the incomes of low-income groups, it would be necessary to establish some operational procedure for ranking projects in terms not on the size of the total net social return (or total net benefits) but on that part of total returns that accrues to beneficiaries below a certain income level. For example, in the case of an irrigation project, profitability of the project should not be based on the increase of income of all beneficiaries, but only on that of the beneficiaries below a certain income level. Since a close correlation exists between the size of holdings and farm income in Iran, the distribution between rich and poor farmers should not be too difficult to establish. The government could simply choose the poverty line in the region or area in terms of per capita income. The project, in its operating phase, would be expected to result in a permanent rise in the annual income of permanent employees.[26]

The resource cost R of providing these individuals N with higher incomes in the long run would be the social capital cost (including construction costs) of the project, when it enters its operating stage K at prices reflecting social costs; the social return to investment (which reflects only the efficiency and growth factors) in the economy r; the annual depreciation charge d, that is, depreciation and obsolescence; and the annual materials cost c at the operational stage of the project.

Then $R = rK + d + c$
and the desirability of the project is

$$r = \frac{N}{R} = \frac{N}{rK + d + c}.$$

It is also important to take into account the effects of the temporary income generated to workers during the construction phase of the project. Using the social rate of discount L_n, poor construction workers given temporary employment (income increases) could be considered equivalent to an annual number of sL_n poor workers given perpetual employment in the longer run. In addition, if the construction workers have H dependents, then the number of poor construction workers N$_c$ to be taken into account is

$$N_c = sL_n \cdot H.$$

Then $r = \dfrac{N + N_c}{rK + d + c}.$

The value judgments (assumptions) implicit in this project formula are, first, that the individuals whose annual incomes are raised from below the poverty line are given a weight of unity, while all other individuals' income increases are given a zero weight. Also, the index would be higher if a large number of individuals with per capita household incomes below the poverty line were employed half-time on a given project, rather than a smaller number full-time. This means that the more widely dispersed the income accruals are to income recipients below the poverty line, the higher the index.

It is also recommended that the allocation of government funds be based on alleviating regional income disparities. The model developed in Appendix A indicates that in Iran this would not result in reduced national income growth. Instead, a policy of gradually minimizing regional income differences would result in an acceleration of GNP.

SOUTH KOREA

At independence and partition in 1945, South Korea was primarily an agricultural country, with three-quarters of its working population engaged in farming. More than two-thirds of the farm families were full-time tenants, and most of the others were part-time tenants. The tenant-landlord relationship was harsh, with rents varying from 50 to 90 percent of the crop. There was extreme rural poverty.

Korea has one of the highest population densities and population-to-arable-land ratios of any country in the world, with 800 persons per square mile and less than one-fifth of an acre of cultivated land per person. This latter figure reflects, in addition to high population density, the very mountainous nature of the Korean peninsula. Except for relatively steep hillsides, most arable land is already under cultivation. Despite these handicaps, progress in agriculture has been substantial.

Government Policies Toward Agriculture

The South Korean government needed immediate land reform after the country was liberated, for two reasons: (1) the substantial acreage formerly belonging to the Japanese had to be redistributed to the Korean farmers and (2) the basic agrarian policy of "land to the tiller," which was endorsed and enacted by the constitution of the newly established Korean government, had to be enforced by redistributing land ownership to the actual tillers.

Land reform proceeded in two stages. Under American auspices in 1947 land once held by Japan was redistributed, reducing the full-time tenants from 70 percent to 33 percent of rural farmers within one year. A 33 percent ceiling on rates paid to the landowners was also established. A second land reform, in 1950, redistributed Korean landlord holdings, with nominal compensation, and virtually eliminated tenancy. It also established a structure of very small owner-operated farms; that is, reforms have limited virtually all farms to a maximum of 7.5 acres of arable land. The law even forbids farmers to pledge their land as security mortgages, in order to prevent reemergence of tenant-landlord relationships. Some illegal tenancy relationships, however, still exist—14 percent of cropland was rented in 1967 which is against the law, but these exceptions have not affected the basic structure of agriculture.[27]

The average farm comprises two-and-one-fourth acres, of which one-and-one-fourth acres is paddy land; 35 percent of all farms consist of one-and-one-fourth acres, and only 7 percent are more than 5 acres. The land is often scattered in small plots, although much consolidation of holdings is now taking place as a result of paddy rearrangement programs.[28]

Additional agricultural policies include agricultural price support programs, government marketing programs, and control of fertilizer supply. The government acquires rice during the harvest sale season (November through January) that usually amounts to about one-third of marketing during that period, and to 15-to-18 percent during the entire year. It also acquires about the same percentage of marketed barley and other grains harvested in early summer. The primary reasons for the government acquisition of grain are to provide for the government's own consumption needs (the army, prisoners, and welfare recipients), and to reduce the seasonal swing in prices by supporting them at harvest time and reducing them at peak market levels.[29]

The government has, as part of its agricultural policy, required the National Agricultural Cooperative Federation (NACF), the sole domestic buyer, to purchase fertilizers at a price adequate to provide a positive net return on the capital of government-owned fertilizer plants and a high profit to private fertilizer plants.[30] Often the government requires the NACF to cut the prices on fertilizer in order to provide relief for farmers as a result of droughts and to stimulate increased production.

Part of Korea's success in agriculture is that farmers, in contrast to those in Mexico, Brazil, and Iran, have not had to face the problem of unequal access to the market and factors of production. To increase accessibility to credit, the government has helped establish numerous rural cooperatives, which have allowed millions of small farmers to compete in modern agriculture on an equal basis. The result has been relatively high rates on agricultural productivity (see Table 5.2).

The Korean land reform and formation of rural cooperatives have allowed a strategy of agricultural development based on a succession of small improvements which the small farmer can adjust to, one by one, with each requiring only a modest increase in investment. This has turned out to be a faster way of achieving high levels of productivity than have the modern crash reaction programs often associated with the Green Revolution.

In general, there appears to be a uniformity in the technology adopted by Korean farmers which has increased productivity and includes (1) increased use of fertilizer, (2) improvement in farming techniques, (3) increased use of insecticides and of small-scale farm machinery, and (4) improvement in irrigation.

TABLE 5.2

Yields per Acre for Foodgrains, 1948-50 and 1968-70
(pounds per acre)

Country	1948-50	1968-70	Increase
Korea	1,640	2,850	1,210
Mexico	700	1,265	565
Brazil	1,170	1,225	55
Iran	900	950	50

Source: Derived from tables in the FAO Production Yearbook, Rome, 1970; and World Crop Statistics, FAO, Rome, 1966.

Effects of Government Policies on Income Distribution

Land reform, together with multipurpose farmer cooperatives, has made a significant impact on rural employment and incomes. The country has managed to involve all of its farmers in productive activities and has achieved the highest degree of agricultural progress in this century, with the exception of Japan, Israel, and Taiwan—countries which incidentally have a uniform size of landholding and effective cooperatives.

Korean industrial production grew more rapidly than did agriculture in the 1960-66 period, but agricultural population grew at only about 1.7 percent per year because of migration to the cities. This migration, induced by higher wages offered by industry, helped to relieve the population pressure on the land and thus increase rural income. As a result, daily wages paid agricultural workers are only a little lower than those of manufacturing production workers, and farm labor is in short supply at peak demand seasons. In absolute terms, the nonagricultural per capita GNP figure in 1966 was twice that of agriculture, but this undoubtedly overstates the personal income difference because of the usual problems of estimating agricultural income, differences in depreciation allowances and taxes, and farm populations earning nonfarm as well as farm income.

The principal effect of government rice procurement appears to have been to support the price of rice and hence farm income levels at harvest time, thus probably helping to improve the income distribution. Nonfarmers have also gained from government rice procurement, since this has increased the proportion of the crop sold in urban areas.

In comparison with practices in many countries, both developed and developing, subsidies to low-income farmers in Korean agriculture have been comparatively small. The poorest one-third of farm families, who are primarily subsistence farmers with no more than one-and-one-quarter acres of productive land, usually purchase no more than two or three bags of fertilizer a year and sell about the same amount of grain. Thus their benefits from subsidy prices are only a pittance, with most of the benefits going to middle- and upper-income farmers.

Yet a common feature of the farm economy in Korea is that the present tenure structure appears to allow considerable flexibility for families to participate in economic activity on an equal basis. The long-run prospects for the sector are therefore indeed bright.

Conclusions

Historically, a common pattern of farming—that is, that in which large and small farms face different factor prices for inputs—has not been stable, since large-scale farms, because they have been favored by the government, have driven out the small farms. In Korea the government has prevented this by limiting the maximum farm size in accordance with the balance of the supply of land and farm labor. Thus Korea has not only redistributed the land, but has imposed a limit on farm size. Originally, this was considered to be simply a matter of equity. In practice, however, these size limits have become part of a policy designed to maintain through equal access to factor inputs a structure of small farm, labor-intensive agriculture. This has allowed growth to occur simultaneously with increasing equity in income.

The current land, labor, and capital production pattern is generally one of high land productivity, low labor productivity, and high capital productivity. The present tenure system of Korea therefore seems to have contributed to the rational use of limited land, abundant labor, and relative shortages of capital.

The cooperatives have been used to solve precisely those problems of access for the small farmer that still remain unsolved in Brazil, Korea, and Iran—access to production inputs, the financial system, the market, and technical knowledge. Personal incomes and the introduction of new technology have risen accordingly as the cooperatives have grown.

One of the principal lessons to be derived from the Korean experience is the superiority of a policy whereby the government tries to create an environment conducive to the voluntary adaptation of modern farming methods on the part of the majority of the population, rather than the wholesale government-subsidized substitution of modern for traditional agriculture.

Recommendations

The only major deficiency in the government's agricultural policies is its subsidization of prices for fertilizer and grains. The cost of that subsidy is a poor use of capital which has a higher rate of return in other areas. In 1968, for example, the NACF sold about 45 billion won of fertilizer—which given a 10 percent subsidy cost about 4.5 billion won. This represents about 2 percent of total domestic saving, and nearly four times the total 1968 government expenditures on research and agricultural programs combined.[31]

If the government's objective is to improve the agricultural production and income distribution in the rural sector, there are more profitable ways to spend the same amount of money.

CONCLUSIONS FOR THE FOUR COUNTRIES

The new agricultural technology has failed to contribute to the improvement of the income distribution in Iran, Mexico, and Brazil, and because of the way it was introduced, the relative incomes of the poorer groups have declined. Clearly the problem can be solved only by introducing effective policies. In the long run, of course, industrialization will have to absorb an ever increasing proportion of the labor force in order to accelerate the transfer of labor from agriculture to industry. To do this, an increased rate of industrial growth will be required. Given the fact that the current rate of unemployment in Iran, Mexico, and Brazil is already significant, and the population growth is rapid, full employment through the transfer of labor into industrial occupations will not be obtained in the near future. Therefore, in addition to steps to accelerate the rate of industrialization, other intermediate policies are required.

These policies must be aimed at raising productivity in agriculture and simultaneously improving the distribution of income. To accomplish such a dual purpose, agricultural strategy will have to be oriented toward (1) obtaining an increase in the labor intensity of production and (2) stimulating the use of local resources.

Countries with great disparities in income in the agricultural sector should recognize that the only economies with rapid increases in yields for the agricultural sector as a whole since the mid-1950s are those in which nearly all farmers have access to a modern agricultural system as in Korea.[32] For example, in that country emphasis has been placed on the adoption by farmers of small-scale innovations.[33] Because of free markets, all farmers face essentially the same set of factor prices. As a result, the first farmers that adopt the new seeds and fertilizers still have the same factor proportions as those who have not introduced these inputs. Initially, differences in farm incomes resulting from this gradual adoption of new inputs was large. However, this was reflected mainly in differences in output per unit of input, rather than in major differences in the proportion of inputs used on the innovating farms.

In addition, the Korean agricultural strategy, emphasizing market forces as the major force allocating factors of production, has resulted in a level of capital and foreign exchange usage that is compatible with the semiindustrialized countries' factor endowments—abundant labor and a relative lack of capital. Market forces have conserved the use of these resources by forcing firms to use them in areas where they are most efficient. By not wasting these resources, most farmers in Korea have been able to expand their use of fertilizer and other yield increasing inputs. Thus the diffusion of innovations and their associated inputs have been broadly based in the country. The result has been a relatively equitable distribution of rural income.

Korea has therefore demonstrated that it is possible to design programs that increase agricultural output and simultaneously yield a more equitable distribution of income. In contrast Brazil, Mexico, and Iran have adopted a number of crash programs intended to increase agricultural output as rapidly as possible. These policies have often been ill conceived, and have only resulted in a deterioration in agricultural income distribution, without marked increases in output. From this it may be concluded, first, that government financial support of inputs, such as mechanization, is unjustified until and if empirical evidence substantiates the argument that these labor saving inputs can increase output rather than merely substitute for labor. Second, in the event this is verified, mechanization should be channeled through rental programs available to all farm sizes, if the government is concerned about preventing increased rural inequality. Third, simpler, intermediate mechanical improvements should be encouraged, as opposed to tractor or combine mechanization. Fourth, prices reflecting true factor scarcities should replace the common artificially low principal and interest prices for farm machinery in order to improve the chances for avoiding premature mechanization.

NOTES

1. Cf. Income Distribution in Latin America (New York: United Nations, 1971).
2. A more detailed description of these types of governmental strategies is given in Keith Griffin, "Policy Options for Rural Development," Oxford Bulletin of Economics and Statistics (November 1973), pp. 239-274.
3. The history of Mexican land reform and the formation of ejidos is documented in Folke Dovring, "Land Reform in Mexico," in Land Reform in Brazil, Cuba, Guatemala and Mexico (Washington: Agency for International Development, Spring Review of Land Reform, 1970).

4. Eduardo Venezian and William Gamble, The Agricultural Development of Mexico—Its Structure and Growth since 1950 (New York: Praeger Publishers, 1969), pp. 105-107. A detailed description of the nature of the so-called Green Revolution is given in Sudhir Sen, A Richer Harvest (Maryknoll, N.Y.: Orbis Books, 1974).

5. Donald Freebairn, "The Dichotomy of Prosperity and Poverty in Mexican Agriculture," Land Economics (March 1969), p. 36.

6. "Population and Development: Interdependent Phenomena," Review of the Economic Situation of Mexico (May 1973), p. 169.

7. Keith Griffin, The Political Economy of Agrarian Change (Cambridge: Harvard University Press, 1974), p. 194.

8. Banco Nacional de Mexico, S.A., Review of the Economic Situation of Mexico (various issues).

9. Banco de Mexico, Department of Industry and Commerce, and Direccion General de Estadistica, "Ingresos y Egresos de las Familias en la Republica Mexicana," mimeographed (1969-70).

10. Cf. John Ross, The Economic System of Mexico (Stanford: The California Institute of International Studies, 1971), chap. 1.

11. Cf. Frank C. Child and Hiromitsu Kanada, "Links to the Green Revolution: A Study of Small Scale Agriculturally Related Industry in the Pakistan Punjab," Economic Development and Cultural Change (January 1975); and Bruce F. Johnston and Peter Kilby, Agricultural Strategies, Rural-Urban Interactions and the Expansion of Income Opportunities (Paris: Organization for Economic Cooperation and Development, Development Center, 1973), chap. 4.

12. G. Edward Schuh, The Agricultural Development of Brazil (New York: Praeger Publishers, 1970), chaps. 5, 6, 7.

13. Herman Daly, "The Political Economy of Population," in H. Jon Rosenbaum and William G. Tyler, eds., Contemporary Brazil: Issues in Economic and Political Development (New York: Praeger Publishers, 1972), pp. 376-377.

14. A good survey of the development of land reform legislation (particularly land taxes) is given in Ben-Hur Raposo, Reforma Agraria Paro o Brazil (Rio de Janeiro: Ed. Fundo da Cultura, 1965); see specifically Estados Unidos do Brazil, Estatuto da Terra: Lei No. 4504 de 30 de Novembro de 1964 (Rio de Janeiro: Departamento de Imprensa Nacional, 1965).

15. Solon Barraclough, Agrarian Structure in Latin America (Lexington, Mass.: Lexington Books, 1973), pp. 81-83.

16. Ibid.

17. Figures are calculated from preliminary data in A Estrutura Agraria Brasileira, Dados Preliminares, vol. 1 (Rio de Janeiro: Institute Brasileiro de Reforma Agraria, 1967).

18. William Cline, Economic Consequences of a Land Reform in Brazil (Amsterdam: North-Holland Publishing Company, 1970), pp. 175-181.

19. Cf. Kenneth B. Platt, "Land Reform in Iran," Land Reform in Iran, Iraq, Pakistan, Turkey and Indonesia (Washington: Agency for International Development, 1970), pp. 38-55.

20. The Law for Establishment of Companies for Utilization of Lands Downstream (Teheran: Iranian Ministry of Water and Power, n.d.), p. 2. An excellent case study of the evolution of farming structures in Iran is given in Okazaki Shoko, The Development of Large Scale Farming in Iran—The Case of the Province of Gorgan (Tokyo: Maruzen, 1968).

21. Ibid.

22. Quarterly Economic Review—Iran Annual Supplement (London: The Economist Intelligence Unit, 1974), p. 9.

23. Figures are computed from 1969 Rural and Urban Household Budget Survey (Teheran: Iranian Statistical Institute, 1970). See also Robert Looney, The Economic Development of Iran: A Recent Survey with Projections to 1981 (New York: Praeger Publishers, 1973), chap. 1.

24. Cf. Bank Markazi Iran, Annual Household Budget Survey (Teheran: Bank Markazi, various issues); and Annual Report and Balance Sheet (Teheran: Bank Markazi Iran, various issues).

25. S. Thomas Stickley and Bahaoldin Majafi, "The Effectiveness of Farm Corporations in Iran," Tahqiqat e Eqtesadi (Winter 1971), pp. 19-25.

26. Cf. Deepak Lal, "On Estimating Income Distribution Weights for Project Analysis," Economic Staff Working Paper No. 130, International Bank for Reconstruction and Development, 1972; and V.C. Nwaneri, "Income Distribution and Project Selection," Finance and Development (September 1973).

27. Oh Young-Kyun, "Agrarian Reform and Economic Development: A Case Study of Korean Agriculture," Koreana Quarterly (1969), p. 99.

28. South Korea, Agriculture in Korea (Seoul: Ministry of Agriculture and Forestry, 1970), pp. 5-17.

29. James Shaffer et al., "Review of Organization and Performance of the Agricultural Marketing System in Korea," Korean Agricultural Sector Study (East Lansing: Michigan State University, Agricultural Sector Study Team, 1969), pp. 5-11.

30. United States Operations Mission to Korea, Rural Development Program Evaluation Report, Agency for International Development (Washington, 1967) p. 91.

31. Gilbert Brown, Korean Pricing Policies and Economic Development in the 1960s (Baltimore: Johns Hopkins Press, 1973), p. 127.

32. The theoretical discussion of these issues is given in Bruce Johnston, "Criteria for the Design of Agricultural Development

Strategies," <u>Food Research Institute Studies in Agricultural Economics, Trade, and Development</u> (1972), pp. 27-58.

33. Ibid., p. 53.

CHAPTER

6

THE EFFECT OF GOVERNMENT INDUSTRIAL POLICIES ON INCOME DISTRIBUTION

It would be hard to name a newly industrializing country in which political leaders and development planners do not express concern about issues that are variously referred to as stagnation of industrial demand and employment creation and as decentralization of industry. They pose questions along these lines: "What can be done to curb the excessive growth of consumer durables in the metropolis (usually the capital city)? How do we get industry to take hold in the provinces? How can we foster industry in villages and towns so as to absorb rural underemployment and to bring modernization to the countryside?"

Most officials have approached these problems by following the same set of policies that created the problems in the first place, that is, placing emphasis on establishing industries that cater primarily to the domestic market—a market which was previously supplied by imports. These policies entail usually substantial deficit financing by the government accompanied by inflation and an increasingly overvalued exchange rate; quantitative restrictions on imports, which are usually preferred to tariffs; and credit rationing at interest rates lower than those that would prevail under free market conditions. In fact, these policies are intended to displace competitive markets rather than work through them.[1]

However, the use of these policies to stimulate investment in import replacing industries is likely to be highly inefficient since, in practice, the price of industrial goods is usually pegged high relative to that of agricultural goods; capital goods are often priced low relative to consumer goods, both because imports are undervalued and the interest rate is kept artificially low. For these reasons industrial production is likely to be capital- and import-intensive in spite of the presence of cheap, abundant labor. The allocation of resources is thus such that the potential rate of growth is reduced through preventing resources from being used in areas where their productivity is highest.

Since these policies are designed in large part to provide windfall profits for industrialists—on the presumption that this will stimulate their rate of investment in the new industries—they have a number of implications for income distribution and employment.

To examine the effect of these policies on income distribution, we shall concentrate on a particular aspect of their influence on the industrialization process in each country in our study: regional integration (Mexico); stagnation of demand (Brazil); overexpansion of consumer goods (Iran); exports of manufactures (Korea); capital-labor substitution (Mexico); and financial reform (Korea).

MEXICO

Every tourist in Mexico, however brief his visit, will see that there is a pressing problem in the country connected with the regional distribution of economic activity. One may visit Mexico City, one of the world's leading cities, which appears to be prosperous and quite up-to-date in its buildings and services and in the sophistication of its population. On the way to the ancient Aztec ruins one may also inevitably see farmers in fields using tools similar to those designed by their ancient ancestors, poorly dressed peasants standing before their mud huts, the absence of machinery, the grinding poverty.

Admittedly, the disparities in income between various regions in Mexico are not exclusively the product of recent industrialization; they also reflect imbalances that existed before this growth began. Certain areas in the country have had natural advantages since the country's independence. These include a favorable location for trade, communication, and agricultural production.[2] Given the existing population patterns, particularly the high density of population in the Federal District, there is no doubt that industrialization would have been attracted to these areas in any case. However, the industrial policies used by the government in Mexico have tended to reinforce this natural pattern of industrial location. The problem of regional development in Mexico at the present time is to efficiently bring about some balance between the living standards of the different regions in the country.

Government Policies Toward Industrialization

Government policies have generally favored certain regions in an effort to stimulate industrial growth. For example the government has structured railway freight charges so as to encourage industry to move toward the central region, and in particular to the Federal District. By setting low rates for transport of most raw materials, and particularly minerals (while simultaneously establishing high rates for finished products) the government has induced industrialists to locate their plants close to markets[3] (principally Mexico City) regardless of how far away the raw materials may be—a situation that has limited the development of a number of areas with abundant natural resources. Government charges for electricity have also tended to favor the central region, where the average price of power per kilowatt hour is generally equal to or less than that charged in other regions of the country, even though the cost of producing electricity in these areas is often less than that in the capital. Of even more importance in influencing industrial location is the reliable provision of this power. Again, the government has influenced industrial location by expanding generating capacity in the Federal District much more rapidly than in the rest of the country.[4]

Further evidence of the government's policy in focusing on certain regions for industrial growth is the distribution of credit. The federal government has not taken any substantive measures to control the geographic allocation of loans by the commercial banking sector. As reported by the National Banking Commission, credit in Mexico has been highly concentrated in two areas—the central region and the six northern states (dominated in most cases by Nuevo Leon). In most years the central region has received about 50 percent of the mortgage loans; in 1966, the two areas together received about 95 percent. The northern area has received 25-to-40 percent of the loans, with Nuevo Leon the major recipient. At least for the five-year period from 1962 to 1966, the distribution of loans shows that the two geographic regions not only dominated the market for these loans, but also the major part of industrial production.

In general these two areas alone usually account for approximately 80 percent of the loans granted by the country's commercial banks. In contrast the regional distribution of commercial bank deposits has a completely different composition, with the rest of Mexico accounting for a higher percentage of deposits than these two areas. Thus there exists a pronounced flow of savings from the rest of Mexico to the central region and the six northern states.[5] This outflow of savings has hindered the development of local industries, yet the Mexican government has done little to alter the geographical flow of funds.

Thus the Mexican government, while officially stating that it desires the spread of industries to all parts of the country, has in practice undertaken policies which have done the opposite. Through its transportation and electricity rates, and (lack of) control over commercial bank lending patterns, it has contributed to the increased industrial concentration in the two most rapidly growing areas of the country. The private banking system, if not regulated, will undoubtedly continue siphoning off savings from the poorer regions and transferring them to the richer.

An additional factor contributing to the concentration of industry in the more prosperous regions of the country is the government's policy of establishing industrial training centers in these regions to the detriment of the less developed areas. Of the ten training centers existing in 1965, four were in the Federal District and one in each of the prosperous northern states: Jalisco, Nuevo Leon, Guanajuato, Coahuila, Puebla, and Veracruz.[6]

Effect of Government Policies on Income Distribution

Eight states contributed 82 percent of the industrial output in 1965. The Federal District accounted for 38 percent, or 48 percent if the district's entire metropolitan area is considered.

Industrial activity scattered throughout the rest of the country is characterized by small enterprises emerging from handicraft industries and by orientation of their production to small local markets. These territorial units, which cover 41 percent of the country and contain 27 percent of its total population, are the site of 7 percent of the manufacturing industry.[7] Consequently in approximately one-half of the country, modern industrial development and its associated high levels of income have not yet begun.

The development in areas other than the northern and central regions has been deteriorating since 1960; not only have they had a smaller share in total national production but, at 1950 prices, the value of their manufacturing production has diminished.[8] Furthermore, a comparison of industrial production (and incomes) per worker indicates that the productivity of the northern region is twice as great as that of the other regions. In other words, industrial growth in all parts of the country except the northern and central regions has lagged behind population growth and is relatively stagnant in comparison with the growth of those two regions. In sum, the pattern of geographical distribution of industry has resulted in large differentials in incomes of the various regions.

The process of industrial concentration and associated regional income distribution pattern has been cumulative. The central region's market has always been the largest in the country, and has undergone a process of continuous expansion—the result of three factors: an increase in population from 10 million in 1930 to 21 million in 1965; an increase in incomes faster than the national average; and an increase in the share of this income spent on products produced by the domestic industrial sector. This combination of factors has been a prime consideration in the decision of industry to locate in the Federal District (the most populous state in the central region) and particularly in the metropolitan area of Mexico City.

Not only has industrial production become more concentrated, but since 1940 all categories of income (wages and salaries, self-employed income, rent, and interest) have declined as a percentage of GNP, with the highest loss (27 percent) experienced in wages and salaries. This decline in wages and salaries was reflected in the percentage gain in profits, whose share of GNP increased from 29 percent in 1940 to 34 percent in 1966. Although their percentage share of GNP declined during this period, real wages in manufacturing still grew by 23 percent, while output per worker increased by 64 percent. Accordingly, labor cost per unit of manufacturing output fell by 26 percent.[9] It is clear therefore that the increase in profits as a percentage of GNP was a result of industrialists keeping most of the gains in productivity, instead of sharing this gain in real income with their workers. This process accounts for a major part of the shift in the distribution of income during this period.

Additional government policies affecting the pattern of industrial growth include tariffs, quotas, and exchange controls. All have provided protection from foreign competitors by making the entry of these goods into Mexico too expensive or, in some cases, prohibitive. As a consequence, Mexican entrepreneurs have begun the production of a great number of goods previously imported. But because the government lacked a coherent regional development strategy, these policies were simply a patchwork of incentives to aid local industrialists irrespective of their location.

Since most of the protection granted by the government was for consumer goods and little or none was given for the intermediate and capital goods used in their production, Mexico City and the northern areas have become import enclaves. Instead of purchasing their inputs from other regions of the country these industries have imported most of their inputs. This occurred in spite of the low freight rates for many of these inputs from the rest of the country.

The government's discretionary power also involved establishing criteria for selecting those activities to grant protection to and which imports to allow. One criterion most commonly used was whether or not there was an adequate market for an additional domestic producer. In practice the government considered the new firm's probable effect on the prices and utilization rates of existing firms in the industry. If these effects were undesirable from the standpoint of existing producers (because their profits would be lowered) new applications would be rejected.[10] Such an approach meant that the incentive often offered to new industries was not only protection from imports, but also protection from domestic competition. It is evident that such an incentive provided guaranteed profits without providing any inducements for the firm to search for labor-intensive processes or regions that might have a comparative advantage in production.

The effect of government policies toward industry are reflected in a number of trends during the early 1960s. During this period, manufacturing employment increased at an annual rate of 7.3 percent, while manufacturing real value added increased at a rate of 14.8 percent, gross domestic product at a rate of 5.8 percent, urban population by 4.9 percent, and nonagricultural labor by 3.8 percent. Also, capital per worker increased at an annual rate of almost 2 percent, while money earnings per worker increased at 6.7 percent, and real earnings per worker at 4.8 percent.[11]

These trends in wages, output, and employment can be explained by the concept of the elasticity of substitution. The elasticity of substitution is the ability of firms to substitute one factor of production (for example, labor for capital) as a result of a change in relative prices of these productive inputs. A slower rate of employment than manufacturing growth, while the capital per worker and money earnings per worker increased, indicates that the elasticity of substitution of capital for labor must have been less than unity.[12] (See Appendix B.) This interpretation of the income and employment trends during the early 1960s is a bit shaky since there was an increase in the elasticity of substitution for a number of industries during this period. In fact for a number of industries the elasticity of substitution assumed values greater than one.[13] This change in the elasticity would have theoretically caused the share of labor income to increase at the expense of capital remuneration, that is, an increase in the elasticity of substitution would allow the firm to adopt productive methods using more labor (the faster growing and thus the relatively cheaper factor in the Mexican economy) than capital. Since the distribution of income did not show any marked shift in favor of labor's share (the reverse was the case of GNP during this period, factors other than the relative prices of capital and labor must have been more important in determining the capital intensity of the production processes selected by the industrial sector.

The explanation is as follows. During the 1960s a number of mergers took place in Mexican industry. These tended to consolidate production in a few large firms. These were also industries where the level of protection was higher than for most manufacturing. These industries enjoyed high profit rates, a high capacity of self-financing, and an easier access to capital markets than most firms in the country. It was primarily these industries that experienced increases in the elasticity of substitution to values over unity.[14]

The decrease in competition (through mergers and their insulation from market forces) reduced the incentive for firms in these industries to search for cost reducing measures in order to maintain high profit rates. As a result, increases in the wage rate relative to the return on capital had little effect on the choice of production processes in these industries. Lack of competition therefore explains why, in spite of an elasticity of substitution of labor for capital greater than unity, there was not a larger amount of employment creation, and thus a more equitable distribution of income.

Further, government policies have resulted in a widening of the productivity gap between modern industries and the more traditional (particularly rural) industries. By facing different factor prices modern and traditional industries have adopted production techniques using different capital/labor combinations. Protected modern firms have adopted processes using relatively large amounts of capital, while the reverse is true for the more traditional firms. The introduction of a modern sector in the economy, and the widening productivity gap between it and the traditional sector explain the growing inequality in the income distribution. This increase in inequality has taken the form of a reduction in the income share of the lower five income deciles rather than an increase in the share of the very highest income brackets. The major beneficiaries of such income changes are the members of the seventh through ninth deciles (counting from the bottom.)

This need not have happened. Government policies forcing the modern industrial sector to face strong competition could have assured that firms in these industries would pass on their productivity gains in lower prices, rather than higher profits and incomes for a limited number of workers. Instead, the decline in competition in industries with an elasticity of substitution greater than one (thus having the potential to undertake large substitutions of labor for capital) and the heavy use of capital (subsidized by the government) have resulted in a concentration of incomes in the upper income brackets rather than an expansion of employment opportunities and income in the middle and lower brackets. Lack of broadly based increases in employment and wages have produced an income distribution in Mexico where the average income in the upper one-half of the distribution is 5 1/2 times as great as in the lower one-half.

To summarize, there is great inequality in the top half of the distribution of income in Mexico. The greater inequality begins in the seventh decile, and from the seventh through the ninth deciles, incomes rise about 40 percent from one decile to the next.[15] Part of the explanation is that the modern sector occupies a relatively small proportion of the labor force in Mexico and the rapid growth has been concentrated in the expansion of this sector. This has taken place through the availability of cheap imports (equipment) to encourage the use of capital-intensive techniques, with very high productivity and incomes for the limited number of persons employed. Instead of creating incentives for firms to expand through labor using techniques, government policies encouraged the importation of foreign technology designed to conserve the use of labor. The government subsidies to stimulate investment have simply gone to finance idle capacity (around 25 percent).

Industrial strategies in Mexico have unfortunately focused on the relief of perceived scarcities (such as capital), not on the utilization of obvious surpluses (labor). But subsidies to capital have encouraged investment in capital-intensive processes or wasteful investment, so that the factor in surplus (labor), instead of being increasingly drawn into the growth of modern industry, has been displaced.

Conclusions

In the future regional industrial development in Mexico will depend on how both the private and public sectors respond to changing prices and market incentives. Unless there is a marked change in the government's industrial policy, private entrepreneurs will continue to favor plant sites in the already concentrated areas. The process of concentration will remain cumulative due to the continuing concentration of effective demand in these locations—a result of the relatively high wages paid by modern industry. In fact the market in the Federal District is already three times as high for many industrial products as that of the other 34 state capitals combined. The result of this development pattern has been that in Mexico the traditional distinction between plant sites chosen by firms to be near customers and those chosen for their proximity to sources of raw materials has lost much of its meaning. Now the national core region (particularly the Federal District) provides both supplies of inputs and demand for products at the same point. This greatly reduces the possibilities of industrial, productivity, and employment development in other sections of the country.

Recommendations

To overcome this process of regional industrial concentration the government should instigate a strategy of regional self-financing, coupled with mutual support among the lower-income regions. This should take place through a planned expansion of their joint markets.[16] This strategy is necessary since the underdevelopment of many regions in the country persists because absolute cost advantages, rather than comparative advantage based on local factor endowments, has become the basis of regional trade in Mexico. Given their low cost advantage (in large part created by government policies), the developed areas remain the most profitable sites for private industrial development.

To stop the centralization of development in Mexico and the drain of savings from lower- to higher-income regions, the government should prevent flows of capital between regions. The point is that the government should stimulate transformation in the rural sector, which will orient people individually and collectively toward growth—a process that will gradually yield the necessary capital required for the expansion of an economic base capable of sustaining growth.

One of the means by which the government could accomplish this end is to take advantage of the Green Revolution, since this has the potential for increasing rural employment incomes, industrialization, and savings through industry's interaction with agriculture. First, agricultural growth can generate a demand for output of the domestic manufacturing sector, and conversely, the supply of agricultural inputs can be the basis for rural rejuvenation. Second, this rural industry can be truly small in scale and a vehicle for marshaling indigenous funds for local investment. Finally, the development of the industry can occur spontaneously with no subsidies, no tax concessions or special credit arrangements, no technical assistance, and even no recognition by official agencies.

For example, tube-well equipment, moderately priced, is within the reach of all but the most humble farmers. Similarly, rudimentary capital equipment is all that is necessary and this is within the financial capability of the vast majority of farmers. The methods of production would remain small in scale and labor intensive and would require only a modest departure from current agricultural practice. In short, there could be a substantial backward linkage from agricultural to domestic industry if Mexico would emphasize a technology based on improved agricultural implements and machinery which could be produced by an indigenous small-scale engineering industry. Both the small independent farmer and the small engineering firm would not only survive but would thrive, enabling them to generate their own savings for local investment projects.

BRAZIL

Economic growth and socioeconomic development are not necessarily synonymous. Many developing nations have experienced relatively high growth rates, accompanied by unemployment and underemployment, and a worsening of the income distribution pattern. Brazil's experience, particularly that leading up to the 1964 revolution, offers a clear example of such economic growth without development. The key issue facing the country now is whether economic growth can be sustained without attention to underlying economic and social problems.

Government Policies toward Industry

Government policies in Brazil have been largely concerned with encouraging industrialization for the domestic market. Import policies have been the major instruments used to achieve this goal, and have evolved from quantitative controls implemented by an import licensing system (1947-53) to quantitative controls implemented by a multiple-category exchange-auction system (1953-57), to a modified exchange-auction-ad valorem tariff system (1957-64).[17]

Since 1964 the government policies toward industrialization have relied more on market forces than on trade controls. The government has intervened by giving tax incentives and other cost reducing inducements to industrialists, particularly private foreign investors.

In 1964 the government developed an action program,[18] largely to alter the distribution of income in favor of those groups that would purchase consumer durables. This involved concentrating income in the upper-income groups, particularly the top 5 percent. This program was intended to create sufficient demand to eliminate the excess capacity in such industries as automobiles, appliances, and residential construction. The major method used to concentrate income in the upper levels was the government's wage policies. These were intended to (1) maintain but not allow increases in the share of wage earners in the national income; (2) prevent excessive salary adjustments from reinforcing the inflationary process; and (3) correct wage distortions, particularly in the Federal Public Service.

EFFECT OF INDUSTRIAL POLICIES

To ensure comparability among wage levels and adjustments, the government established a National Wage Policy Council with authority to approve or reject all wage changes. Initially, the principles were applied only to the minimum wage rate, public sector salaries, and salaries in firms subsidized by the government. To ensure compliance with these principles in the adjustment of wages, the government approved a formula which included three criteria or coefficients: a coefficient for restoring the average real wage of the previous two years; a coefficient for increases in productivity; and a coefficient for the inflationary residual. The inflationary residual was determined by the National Monetary Council on the basis of planned expansion of the money supply.

Under the formula and because of the continuous underestimation of the rate of inflation on the part of the government, the differences between the projected and actual rates of inflation resulted in a decline in average real wages. The decline was noted by the government economists but, believing that industrial wages were above the value of the contribution of the workers to production and determined to force a deep cut in inflation, they held the wage formula virtually unchanged until 1968, when they added a productivity coefficient of 2 percent. Again however in 1968 real wages, due to the nature of the government's formula, declined as the inflation continued at three times the projected inflationary residual.[19]

By 1968, due to the transfer of income to the upper-income groups, demand had become sufficient to utilize most of the capacity in industry. There was therefore no longer any reason to further concentrate income. A series of wage allowances since 1968 has provided for slight increases in real wages.[20]

Effect of Government Policies on Income Distribution

The government, through its wage and pricing policies, has been a fundamental factor in the deterioration of the distribution of income in Brazil between 1960 and 1970. During that period, of the total gain in per capita income, the richest 10 percent of the population appropriated almost three-fourths, the poorest 50 percent less than a tenth. Every decile of the population except the highest experienced a relative decline in income. Urban incomes, which were already higher than rural earnings, grew more rapidly than did those in rural areas. Those with university education experienced a rise in income of 52 percent, while the half of the population with some primary education received 1970 incomes only 14 percent greater than those in 1960. Persons aged 40 to 49 obtained the largest gain of any age group; all below 30 years of age suffered relative declines. Of the six main geographical regions, only the richest, the state of Sao Paulo, registered an above-average increase in income.[21]

In addition to the government's direct role in the deterioration of the distribution of income, its policies had an indirect effect on income distribution due to the fact that although there were many workers who were paid the minimum wage, or whose salary bore a fixed relation to it, the degree of compliance with minimum wage laws was far from perfect. More importantly, the majority of the Brazilian labor force was not covered. This benefited the high-income workers, since those workers earning more than the minimum wage or who were not covered by the minimum wage laws could obtain wage increases greater than the periodic adjustments in the minimum wage. In particular those with relatively high levels of education could expect better settlements, or at least not worse. On the average this meant that the income dispersion increased.

Since the government stabilization policies caused wages to decline relative to increases in industrial productivity, profits in manufacturing increased rapidly during this period. Pressure on firms to minimize their costs was therefore lessened. In practice firms used their extra profits to distribute part of the income transferred from the lowest paid workers (those whose incomes were controlled by minimum wages) to those receiving the highest wages (those whose incomes were not controlled by minimum wages).

To live with inflation that was around 14 percent in 1973, and may have doubled in 1974, the Brazilian government has introduced a system of adjustments in prices, that is, indexing, under which wages, rents, bank interest, loans, and mortgages are permitted to rise each year according to a formula based on the wholesale price index.[22] For example: if a Brazilian receives 4 percent interest on a bond and the inflation rate for a particular year is 15 percent, then the interest paid to the bondholder that year would be increased to reflect the 15 percent inflation.

This has allowed those in the middle class to preserve their savings. But indexing probably has reduced the purchasing power of the urban working class, since the constant devaluations made necessary by inflation have increased the price of imports. Indexing has simply taken the pressure off the government to stop the inflation.

Conclusions

The most controversial aspect of Brazilian economic policies is the approach taken by the government toward income distribution.

Unfortunately, the government had little alternative in following the strategy of intentionally concentrating the distribution of income if it was to break out of the vicious cycle of import replacement without, in the short run, sacrificing long-run growth.

The government's rationale for increasing demand was based on the fact that accumulation of productive capacity is a much simpler process than the decumulation of existing capacity. To be decumulated, any industrial installation in Brazil had to be effectively used until all its parts became scrap. This would take some time, much longer than the original installation. Nor would the sale or destruction of an industrial installation at a great loss represent decumulation in real terms. Brazil was simply not rich enough to afford the correction of its industrial imbalance by these means. Besides, the production capacity for consumer durables was excessive only relative to its present real per capita income. Through concentrating this income in high-income categories, the government could make existing capital stock compatible with the new structure of demand.[23]

This economic reality is based on the fact that in Brazil, as in most countries, a commodity is included in the budget of an individual only after his real income has exceeded a certain level. All commodities can be divided into wage-goods—those consumed ordinarily by the workers and low-income earners—and consumer durables. The result of any increase in the income of upper classes in Brazil was usually confined to an increase in the demand for consumer durables.

The mechanism of demand creation was as follows. With real wages held down for stabilization purposes, increases in demand for manufactured goods consumed primarily by low-income groups could come only from an increase in employment. However, employment increases in lower-income groups were incapable of generating a level of demand capable of eliminating the excess capacity in the consumer durable industries. Obviously, since the real incomes of the great majority of workers in Brazil were such that they could not afford an automobile, the creation of additional jobs with the same wage could not increase the demand for vehicles.

In addition, since individual real wages are as low as they are in Brazil, individual demand for industrial (for example, textile) wage-goods was small. Therefore a government policy of equalizing the distribution of income and thus increasing the demand for the type of manufactured goods consumed by the lower-income groups would not be sufficient to induce high rates of investment in this sector or in the consumer durable industries.

Not only did this imbalance of the economy make additional investment in industry difficult, but it created an environment that was likely to defeat any attempt at decreasing the rate of inflation through the use of harsh monetary policies (due to falling sales many companies were dependent on short-term credit for meeting salaries and other variable costs). On the other hand, to follow a policy of continued high rates of credit expansion would perpetuate the high rate of inflation and the associated industrial stagnation. The government was therefore faced with a dilemma. Given the conditions in 1964, short-run growth with equity was impossible. Fortunately, there was not an equity-growth conflict in the long run, only a period of approximately five years during which time market forces began correcting the imbalances in the industrial structure which had been caused by the import policies prior to 1964.

Increases in overall output were 9 percent in 1970, 11 percent in 1971, 14 percent in 1972, and 15 percent in 1973. The government recognizes, however, that sustained growth at these levels will be possible only if new investment takes place, because at the end of 1973, 90 percent of installed capacity was in use. Expansion of plants and capacity has enabled production in the motor vehicle industry to rise. In 1972 output reached 608,895 units and in 1973, 729,135 vehicles. Current growth in Brazil is fragile. Its maintenance still depends in large part on the state's ability to manipulate the income distribution to maintain high levels of domestic demand. Left to itself, the economy would not be self-sustaining. In fact, a curious paradox has developed in Brazil. Both protectionist policies of the 1950s and early 1960s and the market-oriented policies of the late 1960s and early 1970s increased inequalities, the former policies because they strengthened domestic market imperfections and monopolies and reduced the demand for labor-intensive processes, the latter policies because the market rewarded mostly those factors that are relatively scarce (capital, management, professional skills) and penalized those in abundant supply (labor).

Recommendations

If Brazil is to emerge in the ranks of the great powers and secure a decent standard of living for the bulk of its inhabitants, the government will have to restructure its industry along lines commensurate with the country's factor endowments, incomes, and comparative advantage.[24]

In fact, the only solution for correcting the unbalanced structure of the economy and setting it on the right track of balanced development is to deemphasize gradually the growth of the consumer durable industries and to develop industries more oriented toward the demand profile of growing lower- and middle-income groups. This pattern of industry has provided the largest and the most solid basis for the development of the more advanced economies.

While government wage and price policies have aggravated the income distribution in Brazil, wages are still low primarily because the productivity of labor is also low. The most long-lasting approach to an improvement in income distribution is through labor productivity and that can only be accomplished through improvements in education and training programs that are consistent with the requirements of a modern industrial society. Not only is continuing improvement in the quality of the labor force probably a necessary concomitant of sustained growth, but it should have the beneficial by-product of contributing to a redistribution of income in a more egalitarian direction.

IRAN

Intensive industrialization in Iran, which began in the late 1950s is still continuing. It has had the twofold purpose of reducing the economy's dependence on exports of primary goods and of increasing the rate of economic growth. Because a demand existed in the country for imported manufactured products, the government believed that the internalization of this demand through various protective measures would act as an incentive to establish industries both foreign and domestically owned. Except for the building of the necessary complementary infrastructure, few changes were attempted in the traditional sectors of the economy, since it was assumed by the government that the process of establishing industries producing for the domestic market would in itself generate sufficient demand to sustain the initial momentum of growth it had created.[25]

Government Policies toward Industry

The government has fostered industrial development by tax and duty concessions; by creating a sheltered domestic market as a result of quantitative restrictions of imports and high tariff rates; by making financing available through special credit institutions; by establishing an export guarantee fund; and by providing official training schools and other technical assistance facilities. It has also instituted policies that require new industries to purchase 65 percent of raw materials from domestic sources and contribute to industry at least 40 percent of value added in their production.

The government has further influenced the pattern of industrial development and income distribution through its wage and price policies. Government wage and price policy in Iran operates through the wage level it sets for its own employees. Since government enterprises employ a considerable share, often 20-to-40 percent, of the workers in the modern sector, their salary scale frequently sets wage standards for private firms in this sector.

Statistics supplied by the Iranian Ministry of Labor indicate that in 1971 the average daily wage for skilled and semiskilled workers in manufacturing in Teheran (the city where wages are highest) was about 170 rials, plus 19 percent in overtime pay and a sum of 17 rials resulting from profit sharing, making a total of 220 rials a day or 66,000 rials ($180) a year. In executive positions in labor, in private firms, or in the upper range of government service, annual salaries of over 1 million rials ($12,000) a year are common.

Since minimum wages are set above the price that would equate supply and demand for labor, they determine the earnings of low-skilled labor. Given this kind of split-level wage structure, it seems likely that because of population pressure the earnings gap between the modern and traditional sectors will widen. An important consideration here is that the value added per worker in the modern sector is likely to rise quite rapidly over time—partly through on-the-job training, both for workers and managers, and partly through other types of technical progress.

The Iranian law on profit sharing, of 1963, was passed in order both that workers could share in profits and a mechanism could be effected by which wage increases could be granted in line with rising labor productivity. The law charges management and labor with concluding agreements that provide for wage increases consistent with a share in the reduction of costs, reduction of waste, or increases in net profits. If workers and management cannot settle on the division of profits, the government has the power to distribute up to 20 percent of a company's yearly net profits as wage increases. After the sum paid into the profit sharing account is determined, that sum is distributed within two months among the workers. The law on profit sharing, coupled with effective price stabilization policies, particularly for food, is intended to help improve the real wages of workers in industry.[26]

An effect of the law is that under the conditions governing the termination of employment, it has reduced the number of workers hired in the modern sector, because of its provisions to allow workers to claim additional compensation for termination of employment. This is in addition to the 15 days' wages for each year of service which a worker receives automatically. This means that, in practice, a worker may obtain a termination grant corresponding to three years' wages after three months of service. (Data obtained from the Teheran Labor Office covering 1,004 cases of termination of employment show that the average indemnity initially granted corresponds to the wages for 204 days and is reduced to an average of 101 days on appeal.) It is therefore understandable that employers reduce their employment of labor to a minimum.

Additional government policies include direct controls over consumer prices such as those on agro-industrial products, meat, and pharmaceuticals.

Effect of Government Policies on Income Distribution

In spite of the fact that the government has shown little interest in small-scale manufacturing, a trend has been taking place in Iran toward more absorption of the population from agriculture into small-scale manufacturing, employment in which it grew at a rate of 11.8 percent annually between 1964 and 1967 in comparison with 9.2 percent for the same period in large firms. Of the labor employed in manufacturing in 1969, nearly 61 percent was concentrated in the fields of food, tobacco, textiles, and clothing—industries consisting of predominately small firms.

Most of the employment increases have taken place in small industries where many of the government's wage laws are not enforced, and in which the firms do not receive the special protective and credit treatment granted to the large modern firms.

During the period 1963-69, additional employment in newly established large-scale industries amounted to just over 35,000 or about 16 percent of the increase in the total number of industrial workers.[27] The remaining 183,750 or 84 percent were employed by firms of less than ten workers.

In conjunction with the employment situation are the inequalities of income distribution, as indicated by the results from the Central Bank's Urban Budget Survey. Since lower-income groups spend a higher proportion of their incomes on food than do high-income groups, movements in the food/consumption ratio can be used to infer general movements in the distribution of income.

The Central Bank's Urban Budget Survey shows that the fraction of total expenditures spent on food declined from 49 percent in 1959 to 39 percent in 1969. This implies that urban average incomes rose substantially during the decade. In contrast, the fraction of total expenditures for the rural areas declined from 71 percent in 1964 to 60 percent in 1966, but then rose steadily each year to 67 percent in 1969. The evidence indicates therefore that the income distribution became more equal up to 1966 but more unequal after 1966. On the other hand, the rise in the rural consumption percentage indicates an absolute decline in rural family income, probably due to the decline in the price of agricultural products compared to that of manufactures, resulting from the government's import replacement policy. The result has been a widening in the gap between the rural and urban areas since 1966, which again is likely to be the major source of national inequality.

Despite the relatively high incomes of urban workers, government policies toward the industrial sector have reduced those real incomes from the levels they would have achieved under free market conditions. Statistically, the magnitude of this loss is impossible to determine. However, the mechanism of income transfer from workers to industrialists is well established. For example, if the protected firms are almost as efficient as their world-market competitors, yet the government continues to allow tariffs to remain, an income transfer will occur through workers paying higher prices while the industrialists' costs are the same—the difference is pure profit for the manufacturer at the expense of the consumer.

The government's policies have also concentrated income geographically.[28] For industry as a whole, including crafts, 36.2 percent of the employment, 63.3 percent of value added (market prices) and 21.1 percent of establishments are concentrated in the Central Ostan Province (primarily in the Teheran metropolitan area).

The heavier concentration of industry in the Teheran area is confined in large part to the relatively "modern" heavy industries, in which minimum-scale requirements, because of technological conditions, are of decisive importance. Because of limited demand in their local markets the products of these firms must be sold nationally in utilization of their plant and capacity. Light consumer goods industries, especially those that are material-oriented or of a handicraft nature, are more evenly distributed among the various regions of the country. Isfahan-Yazd is the only other region of significant concentration, particularly in the textile industries which in 1968 generated 33 percent of value added in industry.

The degree of regional concentration is even more striking when it is seen that in 1968 four cities—Teheran, Isfahan, Tabriz, and Mashad—accounted for 45 percent of the urban establishments and 50 percent of the industrial employment in the country. Teheran alone accounted for 27 percent of the industrial establishments and 31 percent of the manufacturing work force in the country.

The market (74.6 percent of the wholesale market in the country is in Teheran), however, has not been the sole determinant of industrial location in Iran; an appreciable correlation exists between regional concentration of Iranian industry and the cost structure of the

TABLE 6.1

Iran: Material Inputs and Spatial Variation, 1967

Product Group	Ranking CSV*	Material Inputs (percent)	Ranking
Food	13	85.38	16
Beverages	8	78.96	15
Tobacco	1	25.79	1
Textiles	11	59.68	11
Apparel	9	71.06	12
Leather	5	78.79	14
Furniture	17	48.82	5
Rubber	4	57.47	8
Paper and printing	2	52.58	7
Chemicals	3	51.45	6
Nonmetallic minerals	16	46.00	4
Basic metals	12	71.37	13
Metal products	18	44.27	3
Machinery	7	26.61	2
Transport equipment	14	59.20	10
Other	15	57.49	9

*Coefficient of Spatial Variation.
Source: Compiled by the author.

various industrial groups. The relative importance of production expenditure on material inputs is shown to be inversely related to the concentration of industrial activity, as measured by the coefficient of spatial variation. (See Tables 6.1 and 6.2.) The strength of this relationship is particularly significant when one considers the countervailing influence of other noneconomic factors. It is evident that raw material-oriented industries show a rather satisfactory degree of dispersion, or at least a tendency to locate outside the greater Teheran area. Such industries with low location quotients for the Central Ostan are those engaged in food processing and textiles, which use large quantities of local agricultural materials.

By contrast, industries in which labor costs count heavily tend to be market-oriented and thus to concentrate in a few urban centers, particularly the Teheran area. This shows that the size of the market, economies of scale, economies of localization, and economies of organization (agglomeration) have become more dominant as attracting forces in all industries, other than those heavily dependent on Iranian agricultural or mineral products. Market orientation is therefore

TABLE 6.2

Iran: Cost Structure of Production, 1965
(percentages)

Product Group	Domestic Goods and Services	Imports	Material Inputs	Wages and Salaries	Rent Profit and Interest
Food	81.85	3.53	85.38	4.27	6.98
Beverages	78.22	.74	78.96	7.89	8.63
Tobacco	24.44	1.35	25.79	13.17	46.69
Textiles	51.58	8.10	59.68	8.07	25.53
Apparel	62.18	8.88	71.06	5.05	21.33
Leather	66.67	12.12	78.79	2.20	16.06
Furniture	41.13	7.69	48.82	9.30	33.65
Rubber	40.14	17.33	57.47	7.31	10.58
Paper and printing	23.30	29.27	52.58	11.84	19.69
Chemicals	18.34	33.11	51.45	5.95	21.65
Nonmetallic minerals	42.53	3.47	46.00	13.37	32.61
Basic metals	71.37	—	71.37	7.77	18.42
Metal products	16.14	28.13	44.27	9.99	25.41
Machinery	14.93	11.68	26.61	28.22	27.00
Transport equipment	33.76	25.44	59.20	5.65	26.01
Other	15.60	41.89	57.49	1.39	27.53

	Depreciation	Value Added (Factor Cost)	Indirect Taxes	Value Added (Market Prices)	Value of Output
Food	2.18	13.43	1.18	14.62	100.0
Beverages	4.39	20.60	.44	21.04	100.0
Tobacco	14.18	74.04	.17	74.21	100.0
Textiles	2.98	36.59	1.17	40.32	100.0
Apparel	2.00	28.38	.56	28.94	100.0
Leather	1.97	20.23	.98	21.21	100.0
Furniture	3.39	46.35	4.83	51.18	100.0
Rubber	9.25	27.13	15.39	42.53	100.0
Paper and printing	3.66	35.19	12.23	47.42	100.0
Chemicals	3.28	30.87	17.68	48.55	100.0
Nonmetallic minerals	5.24	51.22	2.78	54.00	100.0
Basic metals	2.33	28.52	.11	28.63	100.0
Metal products	2.33	37.73	17.99	55.73	100.0
Machinery	5.22	60.43	12.96	73.39	100.0
Transport equipment	2.28	33.94	6.86	40.60	100.0
Other	.62	29.54	12.97	42.51	100.0

Source: Iran, Ministry of Economy, 1965.

the primary attracting factor in the distribution of Iranian manufacturing activity in Iran.

In short, the Central Ostan, particularly metropolitan Teheran, was able to grow during the 1950s and 1960s because, first, it was the seat of government administration. The income generated was mainly spent in this region, thus stimulating further growth; it contributed to the expansion of a major urban center, development of new markets for new products, extension of the region's social infrastructure (public and private capital), increases of skilled labor and service institutions. These phenomena, in turn, enhanced the attractiveness of the area because of the resulting lower real costs of production. In addition, increases in income and the resulting change in demand patterns that occurred during the 1950s made rapid growth possible in the region because it possessed income levels required by the new composition of demand, as well as the mutual reinforcement of linkage and multiplier effects.

Because many of the new industries locating in Teheran during the latter 1960s were consumer durables whose demand increased faster than did the rate of increase in income, the region was thus able to maintain the momentum built up during the 1950s. The Teheran region was able to attract these industries because its market was at the same time at the core of the national market, and because external economies were obtained from the agglomeration of industries and social overhead investment. Both factors provided this region with the economic environment most conducive to becoming a pole of attraction. If Iran had adopted an industrial strategy based on the importation of nondurable consumer goods and the stimulation of exports, the effect on regional growth would have been different. Growth in the Teheran region would have been much less dynamic, because its industry mix would have been based on goods with inelastic demand (essentially foodstuffs, textiles, and other light consumer items), while development would have taken place in those regions with resource endowments well adapted to satisfy a newly created foreign demand. Instead, the government's strategy of import replacement further concentrated production in the Teheran region by encouraging the production of commodities which catered to the high-income groups in the area and had high income elasticities of demand.

Conclusions

Trends in national and regional growth of income and in the types of new industrial ventures will continue to be influenced by the policies toward industrialization adopted by the government. If incentives are given to the production of capital and intermediate goods, regions rich in natural resources and raw materials will have an advantage over Teheran (there is little agricultural land or high-quality mineral deposits in the immediate vicinity of the city). Continued emphasis on import replacement of consumer durables will however enable Teheran to temporarily continue its dominance, since it has the only domestic market large enough to attract these industries.

However, a continuation of the government's current industrialization policies would be unwise since the growth in output in certain lines of consumer durable production was declining in the late 1960s—most of these products were produced only in Teheran. For example during 1969, there was a contraction in the production of the following commodities: buses, refrigerators, water heaters, stoves, electric heaters, and electric lamps.

The slackening of demand for these products can be explained by the fact that, as import replacement moved from simpler consumer goods to more sophisticated consumer durables, the amount of capital per unit of labor and output increased. This substitution of capital for labor took place in spite of the fact that the rate of unemployment increased quite rapidly during this period. Competition for jobs tended to hold real wages down. Capital-intensive methods were adopted because the government subsidized the importation of sophisticated equipment. With real wages nearly constant during this period, and the lack of competition due to high levels of protection, increases in productivity associated with the new machinery resulted in higher profits for the industrialists. The concentration of income in a limited number of capitalist families prevented the development of large mass markets in the country. This was the chief cause of the slackening of demand for consumer durables. Stagnation was prevented only by the windfall increase in oil revenues in the early 1970s which thus allowed the government to increase its expenditures sufficiently to maintain high levels of aggregate and industrial demand.

Agriculture has not been an important market because the masses of agricultural workers are at subsistent income levels, that is, the agricultural purchasing power is in the hands of the landlords. The question therefore in Iran is not necessarily one of quantitative lack of demand but of its composition. Also, the demand coming from the industrial profit recipients themselves is not adequate enough to pick up the slack.

As a result of these factors, the growth process and its effect on income distribution has limited the possibilities for increased diversification of demand. The imbalances that have characterized sectoral development during the 1960s mean that incomes in rural areas, incomes in small cities, and the incomes of the unskilled in manufacturing and services have lagged behind. Differential rates of income growth between lower and upper groups have reduced the growth potential of the market for a number of important manufactured goods. For durables, the problem is more complex: There are cutoff points on the income scale, that is, points at which expenditures on an item rise suddenly from zero or some negligible sum to relatively significant amounts. In other words, the market is restricted to the high-income group. The income elasticity is zero before the cutoff point, extremely high at the point, and much flatter beyond it. The major determinant of market expansion is the rate at which people pass the cutoff point.

The high differential levels of income between low- and high-income groups in the country result in an index of inequality over 0.5. At the early stage of industrialization, this may be beneficial for durables, since even at low levels of national income, enough families would have incomes sufficient to create a market for these products. Still, with time, the upper-income groups will move well beyond the cutoff points and with them their high rates of demand. Thus the rate of passage through the cutoff point will fall. Another important limitation to growth in Iran is a consequence of the relative neglect of agriculture by the government. This neglect restricts the prospects of expanding the production of intermediate goods for that sector. It may well be that many of these goods present advantages over many of the consumer durable goods currently being produced.

The rapid rates of nonoil growth observed in the 1960s may therefore slow down due to lack of purchasing power in the lower-income groups. It is true that there is evidence of borrowing in the lower-income deciles but, of course, households cannot borrow continuously. An income inequality of 0.6 or 0.7 (as in Iran) implies that lower-income groups will fall increasingly into debt and the higher-income groups will be increasing savings, further increasing the disparity in the ownership of wealth. This in turn will contribute further to growing income inequality. Such a situation is inconsistent with sustained (or long-run) growth rates of national product of the order of magnitude of 10 percent per year (over a period of two decades). The reason is that sustained inequality will soon lead to stagnation of purchasing power for many industrial products.

In short, the nonoil economy is currently caught in a vicious circle. The existence of a sizable surplus of labor, together with an industrial sector that adopts techniques causing a rapid increase in the capital-labor ratio, gives rise to a pattern of income distribution that seems to affect the allocation of productive resources in such a way as to reduce economic efficiency and to concentrate income still further.

The longer that redistribution steps are delayed, the larger the proportion of resources—enterprise, skilled manpower, capital equipment, foreign exchange—that will have congealed in industries catering to the demands of the rich in Teheran, and therefore the more difficult it will be to reorient the pattern of industrial production. In this context, the process of industrialization in Iran which has occurred in a setting where there have been relatively few other basic changes is likely to result in the establishment of an industrial productive capacity for which eventually there will be no adequate demand. The process will be self-terminating, since it neither generates sufficient income nor distributes it by income group or region in such a manner as to create sufficient demand to utilize the new capacity fully and keep it expanding.[29] New sources of demand and a means of dispersing economic activity are vitally needed for continued self-sustaining growth. Fortunately there are a number of steps available to accomplish this change in strategy.

Recommendations

The inequality in consumers' incomes, created by government-sanctioned industrial monopolies, could be corrected by obliging the firms to repay the government, out of their profits, such amounts as reflect the costs borne by the consumers during the period in which the firms enjoyed their years of protection (the infant industry tariff). Thus if a firm enjoyed 25 percent protection for an initial period of five years, it would be required to pay back to the government an amount equal to 25 percent of the value of its first five years' sales, this to be repaid in sums consisting of, say, one-third of its profits until such time as the full amount has been repaid. In effect, the sacrifice borne by Iranian consumers in the early years of an industry's existence could then be viewed simply as a loan.

The country should, instead of using indiscriminate industrialization to create employment opportunities, resort to a general principle of economic policy which states that the most efficient way to stimulate a given action on the part of the private economy is to tie the incentives in question as closely as possible to the objectives being sought. The application of this principle to Iran's unemployment problem suggests that if incentives are introduced with the aim of reducing urban unemployment, they should be structured explicitly for the purpose of increasing employment of workers by business firms. Equally it suggests that, given the concentration of unemployment in the low-skilled and unskilled range of the labor force, incentives should be designed which are focused in these specific categories.

Such an incentive scheme might allow as a tax credit (that is, a deduction from the tax due) a certain amount, say, per man-day, for the employment of workers. This plan would reduce the wage rates paid by employers by a corresponding amount, and thus give all employers, old firms and new, foreign and domestic, the incentive to hire more labor of the affected type. It would also contain a built-in incentive toward greater employment outside the metropolitan area, because since wage rates are substantially lower there—probably little more than half those prevailing in the urban areas—the percentage reduction in labor cost implied by a flat tax credit per man-day would be correspondingly greater.

Iran should recognize that modern industry has a limited ability to absorb labor to a large degree. Even if its industries could operate profitably on a highly labor-intensive basis, it does not follow that the urban unemployment problem would be any less severe, since rural migrants would continue to flow into the industrial sector. In such a case, neither the objective of rapid growth nor that of low urban unemployment is likely to be achieved satisfactorily. Small-scale rural industry, however, offers possibilities not only for increased employment, but for a widely dispersed pattern of development which would tend to lessen migration and would at the same time improve the personal and geographic distribution of income. The government should seek to assist small-scale industries to improve their productivity and growth so that they may play a greater role in employment creation and industrialization. This change in policy orientation would require the following steps:

1. The elimination of inadvertent discrimination against small-scale industries. This would involve the restructuring of production more in line with the country's resources and would end discrimination against intermediate and capital goods vis-a-vis consumer goods, both by the rearrangement of those duties and the ending of exemptions of import duties. The ending of the exemptions on capital equipment would help small industries develop their own technology.
2. The ending of licensing, at least for small-scale industries.
3. The provision of credit facilities for fixed and working capital for small-scale firms, with some provision for credit on concessional terms for "infant" firms.
4. The establishment of small-scale industry organizations to assist small-scale industries with their technical, production scheduling, quality standard, purchasing, sales, and accounting problems in order for them to become more efficient. The aim of these policies should be to increase small-scale industrial productivity. Continued production would only encourage the maintenance of low productivity in small-scale industries. On the contrary, a major objective should be to enable small

firms to meet such competition, and for this purpose small-scale industry requires not only adequate financial support but appropriate recognition of its importance in the public service.
5. Small-scale industries have particular difficulties in entering export markets because of the complexity of the commercial transactions involved. Experience in many developing countries, however, suggests that small industries can make substantial contributions in labor-intensive products, including parts and components, provided that they are given appropriate assistance in finding markets, in establishing and maintaining production standards, and credit facilities.

A very important factor in a long-term strategy of employment creation and improvement in the distribution of income in Iran is the development of a domestic capital goods industry. This is necessary not only for an extension of the internal market, but also for the stimulation of a technology more in tune with the country's factor proportions and to prepare the country for self-sufficiency when its oil reserves are depleted.

Although the expansion of engineering and machine tools industries is often thought to cause a deterioration in the distribution of income because of their assumed capital-intensive nature, these industries are in fact one of the more labor-intensive industrial branches. This phenomenon lies in the nature of the machine-producing technology which is usually not amenable to mass production methods. In semi-industrialized countries production of capital goods must take place in response to specific orders embodying differing specifications. This production requires small shops and highly flexible labor adaptation in the face of rapidly changing demand. Not only is the machinery branch not a heavy user of capital, but it offers the advantage of small-scale production that may be relatively efficient. The absence of substantial economies of scale is the result of the specialized, non-mass production nature of the industry.

Given the future demand for these goods when the Green Revolution spreads to Iran, the country may well be competitive even in the production of the most modern capital goods. Moreover, apart from the advantages to be derived from the production of efficient labor-intensive machines, other benefits would certainly be significant. Despite the oil boom, foreign exchange shortages frequently have interrupted development programs and resulted in either an interruption in the investment program or a reduction in the current rate of employment creation and production, since imports of capital goods had to be cut back. The development process and income distribution were adversely affected because of foreign exchange shortages rather than a deficiency

EFFECT OF INDUSTRIAL POLICIES   139

of domestic savings. The existence of domestic capital-producing
capacity would therefore eliminate an important constraint on growth
and employment creation.

It is only when the Iranian people are able to make their own tools
and other equipment that genuine economic development can take
place.[30] In a healthy society which employs an appropriate technology,
the argument that unemployment cannot be conquered for want of capital could never be true, because there would always be the possibility
of turning unused labor into the production of capital goods.

KOREA

Korea was chosen for study because (1) the country has experienced spectacular economic growth; (2) it has pursued an industrialization strategy which, since it is export-oriented, avoids some of the
negative income distribution consequences associated with import
replacement; (3) it has fostered a program that utilizes the human
resources of its country in the most efficient manner possible; and
(4) the rapid expansion of industry took place after a series of government policies had made the distribution of wealth and income quite
equitable. In short, Korea provides a favorable test case for the
proposition that rapid growth is not inconsistent with equity, if a
proper set of government policies are implemented.

Government Policies toward Industrialization

In the aftermath of war, Korea in the early 1950s turned toward
fairly conventional import replacing policies, which tended to favor
industry through foreign exchange controls and an increasingly overvalued exchange rate. As a consequence, relative prices were not
effective in propagating growth, the distribution of income, or the
efficient allocation of capital and labor; the growth rate in GNP was
just about high enough to keep up with population rates, and savings
rates were negligible, and for some years even negative.

By 1964 the choices facing Korea were (1) to carry import replacement further, especially in intermediate and heavy industries (the
capital-intensive path adopted by most other countries) or (2) to
emphasize export expansion in labor-intensive consumer nondurables.
Korea chose the latter strategy, since that offered the most rapid
growth prospects consistent with the country's comparative advantages
in labor skills.[31]

Consequently, in late 1964, the government introduced, first, interest rate reform, which had the effect of greatly reducing the wage-to-capital ratio and, second, a package of trade liberalization measures which enabled the economy to concentrate on the production of manufactured goods for export. Together, these changes permitted the economy to pursue a growth strategy more nearly in line with the country's labor-abundant and capital-scarce factor endowment.

Further, the government doubled the commercial bank interest rate for both savings accounts and deposits to almost 30 percent in real terms.[32] As a result of the relative costs of capital, the labor intensiveness of the manufacturing sector declined. The interest rate reform also resulted in an increase in savings, making larger domestic sources available for investment.

Interest rates on savings deposits doubled and deposits responded by rising by more than 700 percent by September 1968. To indicate that this was not simply a shift from one form of savings to another, the overall savings rate, which had been negative in the 1958-62 period and had stood at only 6 percent as late as 1962-64, reached 13 percent in 1968 and was over 15 percent by 1970.

Further, the government devalued the won by 50 percent and introduced a number of export incentives and export promotion mechanisms. It granted exemptions on customs duties, imported materials, and capital equipment used in the production of export commodities, on business activities, and on commodity taxes. It reduced income taxes on profits earned from exports by 50 percent and granted export credits and loans for the purchase of raw materials and equipment at preferential rates. It introduced an export-import linkage system enabling exporters to import goods on the prohibited list for their own use or for resale. And it granted a high wastage allowance on raw materials imported for use in exports, and preferential electricity and transportation rates, to encourage production of industrial goods for world markets.

Effect of Government Policies on Income Distribution

The policy changes resulted in (1) a phenomenally rapid expansion of exports and GNP (at average annual rates of 38 percent and 11 percent in constant prices, respectively, between 1964 and 1970) and (2) a rise in nonfarm employment of 1.6 million accompanied by a drop in unemployment from 7.7 percent to 4.5 percent of the labor force (over the same period). The increase in exports was almost exclusively in labor-intensive industries; indeed, between 1966 and 1970 nearly one-half (320,000) of the overall increase in the labor force was absorbed directly into export-related employment.[33] This large labor absorption occurred despite some evidence that between 1968 and 1970 overall production became more efficient in its use of labor.

The increase in exports has had diverse effects on the composition of the large increase in employment. First, it has created jobs for workers who are engaged directly in production of the export commodities (direct effect). Second, since raw materials and machinery used in such production are supplied from the home market, more labor has been required. At the same time, new jobs have been created in supporting service industries, for example, electricity and water supplies, transport, storage, and commerce (linkage effect). Third, the enhanced purchasing power of the workers who have found jobs as a result of these effects has created more effective demand for various goods and services. The result has been to create additional employment (multiplier effect). Fourth, since foreign exchange shortages set a ceiling to the amount of raw materials and machinery that can be imported, increased foreign earnings by exports have raised the potential rate of growth and thus increased employment.

Estimates indicate that during the 1960s every $1 million increase in exports of Korean manufacturers created in the short term (approximately a year) jobs for some 500 workers in export industries, about 150 jobs in their supporting industries, and another 150 in consumer goods and service industries. In the longer run, the total effect has been much larger, partly owing to the cumulative nature of the various employment effects and partly because of the employment made possible by capital investment and related construction works that were needed to facilitate the export expansion.[34]

Rural industrialization has also been stimulated by government reforms. There has been an expansion of employment opportunities in the countryside, along with a trend toward balancing production geographically and raising agricultural productivity generally.

To summarize, financial and trade reforms contributed greatly to the growth in income and employment in the Korean economy by utilizing the country's abundant resource—that is, labor—and by enabling the country to economize in its use of capital; by permitting the use of large-scale production methods and encouraging technical improvements in export industries; and by creating demand for domestic materials, raising incomes, and augmenting the availability of imports.

The direct effects of these policies on income distribution can only be inferred since a number of other factors, such as continuing educational development, were also simultaneously occurring. Nevertheless, in 1964 the distribution of income in Korea was among the best in the developing countries and remained so in 1970.

Importers (and possibly farmers in 1965) appear to be the only identifiable groups that suffered from the stabilization program and new development strategy and even then probably only in the short run. For importers, the liberalization of imports meant lower incomes at least in 1964 when the volume of imports and their profit margins fell (because of the effects on demand of higher costs of imported goods relative to domestic goods, and the end of previous speculative demand based on expectations of devaluation); however, the greatly increased volume of imports after 1965 would appear to have been sufficiently adequate to offset largely any initial loss in incomes.

Though some firms might have suffered from the liberalization of imports and their loss of monopolistic position, industry overall clearly gained from the increased incentives for export expansion and from the considerably greater availability of imports. Consumers almost certainly benefited from liberalization of imports by increased real incomes due to the lower prices of imported goods. Farmers may have suffered temporarily because of the 75 percent increase in the price of fertilizer (at that time mostly imported) as a result of devaluation between 1963 and 1965. Agriculture's domestic terms of trade declined by 15 percent between 1964 and 1966, but only after having risen by 40 percent between 1960 and 1964. The previous rise had been so sharp, brought about by 1962 and 1963 crop failures, that it was almost inevitable that good crops in 1964 and subsequent years would lower agricultural prices relative to nonagricultural prices.

Although the relative distribution of income changed little during the rapid growth phase of the Korean economy, it is likely that the real incomes of the poorest 20 percent more than doubled. Between 1964 and 1970, real wage rates of production workers in manufacturing rose by over 85 percent and those of wage earners in agriculture doubled. The real incomes of the poorest income groups of farm households increased by 15 percent.[35] These wage changes were the result of market forces only, since unionization of labor played no role. Agricultural incomes rose, however, aided by the government's fixing of a high price for rice.[36]

Conclusions

By requiring more efficiency for economic success, government policies toward industry have been partly responsible for the high labor-capital and output-capital ratios in Korean export industries. For example the devaluation of the won made the import of capital equipment more expensive. The resulting greater labor intensity of export production has had important income distribution effects in reducing unemployment and thereby contributing to higher wages. Also, it has shifted a significant segment of the labor force to a higher-income sector (manufacturing) from lower-income sectors (agriculture and services).

It is quite likely that Korea can continue its growth rate of over 10 percent per annum it is experiencing today (1975). This will be facilitated by the fact that, with an index of income disparity of less than 0.4, the volume of purchasing power of households in the middle-income groups—which comprise one-third of the total purchasing power in Korea—is rising rapidly enough both to buy the products of modern industries and to supply the savings for the expansion of modern industries. At the same time, the purchasing power of the lowest income groups is rising rapidly enough to purchase the products of agriculture and of both traditional and some of the modern industries.

The end product of the Korean development strategy has therefore been to lay the framework for self-sustaining growth with equity.

CONCLUSIONS FOR THE FOUR COUNTRIES

The experiences of Mexico, Brazil, and Iran have shown that the labor-saving effect of imported technology, and a growing surplus of labor, may result in downward pressure on the wage rate, so that there will be a trend toward the concentration of national income. The result of such a trend will be that the benefits of accumulation of capital will accrue to small groups who buy a large part of their consumption goods abroad. Their demand for highly capital-intensive durable goods industries will (if accompanied by government protection) stimulate investment in these areas. Owing to the smallness of the market created by the privileged minority, such an allocation of resources tends to foster even more concentration of income, and the country may be caught in a vicious cycle of growth and eventually stagnation without equity.

The fact that the acceleration of economic growth per se (as in the cases of Iran, Mexico, and Brazil) will not solve the employment problems indicates that a strategy of development must be formulated that emphasizes the true scarcity of labor, capital, and foreign exchange necessary for financial and price reforms. As the case of Korea illustrates, these reforms can increase employment, achieve a more equal income distribution, and maintain a high rate of growth of GNP. The crucial element in preventing income equalization from taking place in Mexico, Iran, and Brazil is their lack of financial reform and capital market development.

The following general observations can be made regarding this situation:

1. Financial markets in Iran, Mexico, and Brazil are relatively undeveloped.
2. One of the consequences of financial market underdevelopment is that the middle- and lower-middle classes have virtually no access to financial instruments in which to invest their savings. In addition, credit for purchases of consumer durables (houses, cars, electrical appliances) is in short supply and expensive.
3. The development of financial markets should open up related liquid financial investment possibilities for the middle- and lower-middle classes. This in turn should give an incentive to these groups to increase savings and, in the longer run, obtain some income from capital in addition to labor.
4. Financial market development should have favorable effects on the availability of credit and the rate of interest at which these groups can borrow for the purchase of houses, cars, and electrical appliances.
5. Financial market development would stimulate the expansion of small and middle-size enterprises in all sectors of the economy. This in turn, together with the increased availability of credit and capital, would in all likelihood induce the creation of new ventures by potential middle-class entrepreneurs.
6. Although the development of financial markets would have the same general effects on the upper-income groups as those described for the middle- and lower-income groups, there are important differences. On the one hand, upper-income groups, through their involvement in business and easy access to international markets, have already ample and profitable investment opportunities. They would have to share some of these opportunities if financial markets were more developed. On the other hand, credit and its costs for purchases of consumer durables are relatively insignificant as a proportion of upper-class family income.
7. For short periods of time, rapid economic development can occur in Iran without the presence of efficient economical markets. In fact in Iran, where the role of government and private securities has been negligible, it is apparent that efficient financial markets are not a necessary condition for economic development, since there are alternative means of financing fixed investment. One alternative is financial intermediation, particularly by institutions that attract long-term deposits with adequate interest yields and that allocate long-term loans by competitive loan interest rates.

EFFECT OF INDUSTRIAL POLICIES   145

   8. The relationship of capital market development to distribution of income is sometimes questioned. In the early stages of that development, it is likely that the benefits may accrue more to the upper classes than to the lower. But in later stages, when stocks and shares have widespread appeal, capital market institutions can play an important role in encouraging savings and in affording greater public participation in the profits of industrialization and more rapid growth.
   9. Finally, the development of freely working financial markets is likely to equalize income distribution primarily through a number of indirect effects. For example research indicates that there is no technical reason why the use of more labor rather than capital is not possible. In this case, a rise in interest rates and foreign exchange rates relative to wage rates may both raise employment and increase the wage share of income.

                                   NOTES

   1. For a more detailed discussion of these policies and their impact on all facets of the economy see Ian Little, Tibor Scitovsky, and Maurice Scott, Industry and Trade in Some Developing Countries (London: Oxford University Press, 1970).
   2. Cf. Charles Nash Myers, Education and National Development in Mexico (Princeton: Industrial Relations Section, Department of Economics, Princeton University, 1965), chap. 2.
   3. P.L. Yates, El Desarrollo Regional de Mexico (Mexico City: Banco Nacional de Mexico, 1961), p. 171.
   4. R. Carrillo Arronte, An Empirical Test on Interregional Planning (Rotterdam: Rotterdam University Press, 1970), p. 52.
   5. Robert Aubey, "In the Private Sector: Regional Credit and the Mexican Financial System," Growth and Change (October 1971), pp. 25-33.
   6. A complete geographical breakdown of educational facilities is given in Myers, op. cit., chap. 5.
   7. Banco Nacional de Mexico, "Industrial Decentralization," Review of the Economic Situation of Mexico (August 1972), p. 267.
   8. Eliseo Mendoza-Berrueto, "Regional Implications of Mexico's Economic Growth," Weltwirtschaftliches Archiv (1968), pp. 101-104.
   9. Ariel Buira, "Development and Price Stability in Mexico," Weltwirtschaftliches Archiv (1968), pp. 58-63.
   10. The complete list of governmental policies toward the industrial sector is contained in Timothy King, Mexico: Industrialization

and Trade Policies Since 1940 (London: Oxford University Press, 1970).

11. Banco Nacional de Mexico, Review of the Economic Situation of Mexico (various issues).

12. See Charles Ferguson, The Neoclassical Theory of Production and Distribution (Cambridge: Cambridge University Press, 1971), part II.

13. Data are based on estimates in Juventino Balderas-Moreno, "Production Functions, Technology and Functional Income Distribution of Income in Mexico: A Cross-Section Analysis of the Manufacturing Sector in 1960 and 1965" (Ph.D. diss., University of Colorado, 1973), chap. II.

14. Ibid.

15. See Income Distribution in Latin America (New York: United Nations, 1971), pp. 61-68, for a description of the concentration of income in the upper-income brackets.

16. In part these ideas stem from T. Vietorisz, "The Planned Interregional Location of Industry: Argument in Favor of a 'Trade-Not-Aid' Approach," in Industrial Location and Regional Development: Proceedings of Interregional Seminar Minsk, 14-26 August 1968 (New York: United Nations, 1971), pp. 63-115. It should be noted that the author of this study disagrees with many of Vietorisz's ideas concerning regional development.

17. Cf. Joel Bergsman, Industrialization and Trade Policies in Brazil (London: Oxford University Press, 1970), chaps. 3 and 4.

18. Ministerio do Planejamento e Coordenacao Economica, Program de Acao Economica do Governo, 1964-1966 (Rio de Janeiro, 1964). This document outlines the specific stabilization procedures used.

19. The stabilization policies of the government are described and analyzed in Howard Ellis, "Corrective Inflation in Brazil, 1964-1966," in The Economy of Brazil, ed. Howard Ellis (Berkeley: University of California Press, 1969); and Alexandre Kafka, "The Brazilian Stabilization Program, 1964-66," Journal of Political Economy (August 1967). Both authors defend the gradual nature of the disinflationary strategy adopted by the government.

20. The Economist Intelligence Unit, Brazil: Quarterly Economic Review (various issues).

21. Cf. Albert Fishlow, "Brazilian Size Distribution of Income," American Economic Review (May 1972), pp. 391-402; and Carlos Langoni, "Distribuicao da Renta e Desenvolvimento Economico do Brazil," Estudos Economicos (1972), pp. 5-88.

22. Ronald Krieger, "Inflation and the 'Brazilian Solution'," Challenge (September/October 1974), pp. 43-52.

23. See Georgescu-Roegen, "Structural Inflation-Lock and Balanced Growth," Economies et Societies (March 1970).

24. For a description of increased flexibility in foreign exchange markets see Juergen Donges, Brazil's Trotting Peg: A New Approach to Greater Exchange Rate Flexibility in Less Developed Countries (Washington: American Enterprise Institute, 1971).

25. A more extensive description of these policies is given in Robert Looney, The Economic Development of Iran: A Recent Survey with Projections to 1981 (New York: Praeger Publishers, 1973), chaps. 6, 7, and 8.

26. For a description of Iran's series of income policies see International Labor Office, Employment and Income Policies for Iran (Geneva, 1973), especially chap. 7.

27. Iranian Ministry of Economy, Annual Industrial Survey (Teheran, various issues).

28. This section is based on Robert Looney, "Industrial Decentralization in Iran," University of Santa Clara Business Review (1973).

29. For variations on this idea see Celso Furtado, "Marx's Model in the Analysis of the Underdeveloped Economic Structures," Yale University Economic Growth Center, reprint 164, 1970; J. F. Fweyemamu, "A Model of Perverse Capitalist Industrial Development," East African Economic Review (1972), pp. 21-40; and Werner Baer and Andrea Maneschi, "Import-Substitution, Stagnation, and Structural Change: An Interpretation of the Brazilian Case," The Journal of Developing Areas (January 1971), pp. 177-192.

30. This is based on the idea that an "intermediate technology" will allow a more intensive use of local resources, and enable the country to become more flexible in meeting the needs of low income families; cf. E. F. Schumacher, "Industrialization Through 'Intermediate Technology'," in Ronald Robinson, Developing the Third World: The Experience of the Nineteen Sixties (Cambridge: Cambridge University Press, 1971), pp. 86-88.

31. The rationale for this strategy is given in Bela Balassa, "Industrial Policies in Taiwan and Korea," Weltwirtschaftliches Archiv (1971).

32. National Income Statistics Yearbook (Seoul: Bank of Korea, various issues).

33. Statistical Yearbook, 1969 (New York: United Nations, 1970).

34. Ibid. For an analysis of the Korean interest reforms see particularly Ronald McKinnon, Money and Capital in Economic Development (Washington: The Brookings Institution, 1973); and Edward Shaw, Financial Deepening in Economic Development (New York: Oxford University Press, 1973). Shaw was instrumental in designing the strategy of financial liberalization in Korea.

35. South Korea, Annual Report on the Family Income and Expenditure Survey, 1970 (Seoul: Bureau of Statistics, Economic Planning Board, 1971).

36. South Korea, Report on the Results of Farm Household Economy Survey of Agricultural Products (Seoul: Bureau of Statistics, Economic Planning Board, 1971).

CHAPTER

7

THE TOTAL EFFECT OF GOVERNMENT POLICIES ON INCOME DISTRIBUTION

This book grew out of the belief that a theory capable of explaining the effect on income distribution of policies under government control in semiindustrialized countries is lacking and is vitally needed. The book can therefore be viewed as an attempt to derive a framework for examining the impact of government policies on the income distribution patterns in these countries. The basic point is that the governments of those countries (with the possible exception of Korea) have lacked a clear understanding of the interrelationships between the objectives, priorities, strategy, and budgeting necessary for a coordinated set of policies which would improve their economy's income distribution, without sacrificing overall economic growth.

The approach taken here differs from the conventional orthodoxy used for government policy decision making in that it emphasizes three beliefs often neglected by economists and government officials: first, that economic theory is of fundamental importance since it is the prerequisite for any consistent set of policies; second, that economic theory is irrelevant unless set in an empirical context; and third, that in the absence of evidence to the contrary, free market forces (as exist in Korea) yield a distribution of income more equitable than that resulting from the structure of production created by the government-controlled price regimes in Brazil (prior to 1964), Mexico, and Iran. To explain the failure of these government policies in obtaining a more equitable distribution it is necessary to define their deficiencies.

MAJOR DEFICIENCIES IN GOVERNMENT POLICY TOWARD INCOME DISTRIBUTION

The failure to use government policy effectively in improving the income distribution in the selected countries can be traced to deficiencies in two major areas of government decision making: failure of concept and failure of policy. Failure of concept has occurred when the authorities have not comprehended or identified the basic mechanisms of economic growth that exist in their countries during the time policy decisions are being made. The result has been that nearly any policy they undertook to improve income distribution has been doomed from the start. Failure of policy on the other hand has arisen when an incorrect policy (perhaps because of political pressures or corruption) was chosen by the government even though the authorities' understanding of the economic forces currently at work in their countries may have been correct.

Failure of Concept

By far the greatest deficiency in government decision making in Brazil, Mexico, and Iran has been the failure of concept. This is evidenced by the policy makers' continued reliance on Keynesian economic theory as a basis for decision making. The appeal of Keynesian theory to these governments has lain in the hope it gives for relatively rapid advancement. Through providing a scientific basis for policy making, Keynesian theory implies that the failure of an economy to perform satisfactorily is simply a result of governmental mismanagement. Economic performance therefore can be easily improved by the application of scientific intelligence. Keynes himself looked to the intelligent use of general fiscal and monetary policies to provide a higher level of employment income and security. Keynes felt these goals could be accomplished by a country while it simultaneously eliminated many other economic and social injustices.

Policy making in these countries has been influenced in large part by these fundamental propositions of Keynesian thought. Keynesian theory, however, is based on a set of assumptions relevant only for advanced economies during times of recession or depression.[1] In addition Keynesian theory is of a short-run nature (probably three or four years). These characteristics make the theory a poor guide for policy in our sample countries. Specifically Keynes was theorizing about an advanced economy in which both modern machinery and the skilled labor required to operate it were present in adequate supply for high levels of output, but were idled by lack of demand. In this situation policy makers' attention naturally focused on the existence and plight of unemployed labor. In advanced economies the Keynesian policy prescription was to raise aggregate demand sufficiently to draw this labor back to manning the capital equipment it was trained to operate. This could be accomplished rather quickly, according to Keynes, through the use of expansionary fiscal and monetary policy to stimulate increases in real consumption and investment. Also in the short-run context of his theory investment was simply regarded as a source of demand for final output. It was not viewed by Keynes as a means of providing additional productive capacity for the economy as a whole.

Keynesian theory has proved to be a dangerously misleading guide to development policy in semiindustrialized countries because it stresses four concepts that have proved, in the light of experience, to have relatively little empirical or theoretical foundation in this environment. First, the Keynesian assumption of the existence of mass unemployment (or employment in lower-grade jobs than those for which workers were qualified), while valid for advanced countries during recessionary periods, has little meaning in semiindustrialized countries. Not recognizing this, policy makers have diverted their attention from the problem of training the labor force in modern industrial skills—an essential part of the process of achieving a more equitable distribution of income—to that of employment creation in modern industry irrespective of the skill level of the labor force.

Second, Keynesian theory gave major emphasis to the level of capital investment as the determinant of the level of income and employment. Policy makers in semiindustrialized countries have converted the Keynesian short-run stabilization theory into a long-run growth model by making the rate of growth dependent on the proportion of income saved and the incremental effect of investment in machinery dependent on productive capacity. This stress on capital formation has also led to the neglect of developing labor skills and has in large part caused the deterioration of the distribution of income.

Third, the Keynesian framework does not give an accurate account of how savings and investment decisions are made in semiindustrialized countries. Using Keynesian theory, policy makers in these countries have operated on the spurious thesis that savings decisions are made quite independently of investment decisions. Admittedly, in the advanced countries, savers as a group are, by and large, different from investors as a group. Therefore the decision on the part of one individual to save is not necessarily sufficient to induce another individual to invest. In such situations, Keynesian theory is correct in asserting that the government should undertake policies to ensure that a decision to save does lead to a decision to invest, either by giving incentives to investors or by using private savings to undertake public sector projects.

However, in semiindustrialized countries a different saving-investment mechanism exists. A decision to save in Iran, for example, is also largely a decision to invest because in Iran savers are usually the individuals who actually carry out the process of investment.[2] Most of this investment is carried out by small owner-investors who do not make their consumption decisions independently of savings decisions. In fact, they first determine their investment policy on the basis of investment opportunities, and then determine their consumption as a residual. Since the mid-1950s, through a system of irrational controls, the government of Iran has frustrated the small investor. Through its system of incentives (not available to local firms) for foreign investment, the government has allowed U.S. and Western European firms to preempt markets that local firms could have supplied. When this has happened local entrepreneurs have had no alternative (due to lack of efficient capital markets) but to use their savings for consumption. This consumption has at times led to inflation. The government, largely because of political reasons, has repressed this inflation through price controls.

In practice these controls have only diverted goods and services into flourishing black markets. Open or suppressed inflation is usually condoned by policy makers not only in Iran but in Mexico and Brazil because of Keynesian assertions that inflation has few harmful effects on the saving and investment process. Keynes's cynical reference to the "euthanasia of the retainer" however is hardly applicable to conditions in developed countries, let alone semiindustrialized ones. Inflation either open or repressed has been responsible for a number of distortions in the income distribution and social relationships in these countries. Inflation has (1) penalized those whose actions have in no sense been responsible for its initiation (those classes which loathe the idea of striking or threatening to strike—the salaried middle classes, the thrifty retainers, the learned and charitable institutions that have relied upon interest on endowments, and pensioners); (2) encouraged a sordid scramble on the part of each organized group to get more for itself out of the total sum of income created during a given time period; (3) destroyed the motive to give one's best in the common social task, particularly at the entrepreneurial level; (4) weakened the rewards for ingenuity, enterprise, and effort; (5) sapped the incentive for thrift and growth; (6) discouraged individual responsibility toward one's own future and that of one's dependents (through destruction of efficient capital markets; (7) encouraged the squandering of the community's capital; (8) created a need for the multitude of officials and controllers with delegated judicial and legislative powers

TOTAL EFFECT OF GOVERNMENT POLICIES 153

able to arbitrarily make or destroy fortunes; and (9) created a tendency toward the degeneration of representative government into a system of vote buying.

Finally, the fundamental assumption underlying Keynesian theory, for example, that free market forces associated with the capitalist system were the root cause of the depression in the 1930s was interpreted by political leaders in semiindustrialized countries as proof that growth in their countries was readily accessible. All that was needed was for the economy to throw off the shackles of the free market, adopt price controls, accumulate physical capital, invest in modern industry, and eliminate its dependence on agricultural and raw mineral production.

Keynesian ideas are obviously congenial to political and economic nationalism. They make backwardness and stagnation in semiindustrialized countries a consequence of free market forces, and make development a condition that can be achieved in a relatively short period of time. Further, the Keynesian assumptions make it appear possible for development to be achieved along with the implementation of social, cultural, and equalitarian restrictions on the freedom of competition through the practice of widespread government intervention, particularly in the process of industrialization.

In short the attractiveness of Keynesian theory as a guide to policy in semiindustrialized countries is the promise it gives of having one's cake and eating it too—that there exists some mysterious source of untapped economic energy which, if liberated by government policy, can provide for development and the simultaneous fulfillment of numerous social goals.

Needless to say, previous chapters have shown that a number of policies and controls derived from Keynesian theory have not led to development, but rather only widespread economic waste and a general tendency for development programs to produce disappointing results in terms of employment creation and income distribution. Keynesian policies of inflationary finance and associated price controls have consistently worked against lower-income groups. By destroying or preventing the development of capital markets through inflationary finance these countries have selected the worst possible policy orientation in terms of income distribution. Inability to borrow has prevented small-scale farmers, industrialists, and other low-income groups from investing either human (education) or physical capital. Due to credit rationing, opportunities for investment have been limited to only a select few.

In as much as education is one of the major sources of growth (not physical capital), Keynesian policies not only have resulted in poorer income distributions than those usually generated under free market conditions, but have also have prevented these countries from achieving their full growth potential.

The Need for an Alternative Framework
For Policy Making

What is needed to overcome the failure of concept is a new theory more capable than Keynesian theory in explaining the economic forces in semiindustrialized countries. This framework should consider not only the short-run effect on demand (Keynesian theory) for domestic products resulting from government policies, but should also indicate the precise fashion by which government policies affect supply (the long-run growth of the economy), and the generation of factor income over time resulting from the increase in supply.

This theory must also be capable of identifying the interrelationships between different sectors over time, and of explaining how these interrelationships result in a modification of the initial income distribution created by a particular set of government policies. The importance of these interrelationships in explaining patterns of income distribution cannot be overemphasized. This can be illustrated by the case of an increase in minimum wages. Normally one would expect higher wages to result in a deterioration of the income distribution since fewer workers would be employed. It is possible however that higher minimum wages might increase employment and improve the distribution of income. The reasoning for this is based on the feedback of increased wages on demand. Laborers, receiving higher take-home pay, are able to increase aggregate demand for goods, since they consume most of their income. To meet this increased demand some firms may have to expand output. Since the demand for labor is dependent on the level of production, there will be an increased demand for labor. If the feedback mechanism from increases in demand is strong enough, it can offset completely the initial reduction in employment.

These feedback effects and their interrelationships are shown in Figure 7.1. The mechanisms involved can be illustrated with the present example. For instance since wage earners belong to the lower-income classes any increase in demand will be mostly reflected in demand for food. Therefore much of the impact may be only on the agricultural and consumption goods sectors. If agriculture is initially producing a surplus, the additional demand for labor may not be significant enough to offset the primary effect of increased wages on employment. If the agricultural sector is at full production, such feedback on demand will result in increased imports and balance-of-payments deficits. The resulting devaluation is likely to increase the income of rural landowners, if they export some of their surplus. The alternative to devaluation is an increase in the price of food. Inflation however would neutralize whatever gains are initially derived from

TABLE 7.1

Sources of Mexican Growth: Three Studies
(in percentages)

Author of Study	Period	Growth Rate in Gross Domestic Product	Annual Contribution to Growth Rate				
			Capital	Labor Force	Maintenance of Education Component	Improvement of Education	Hectares of Land Cultivated	Remainder
M. Selowsky[a]	1940-45	7.37	.71	.35	.52	-.13	—	5.92
	1945-50	5.84	2.73	.37	.55	.01	—	2.18
	1950-55	6.16	3.04	.37	.56	.21	—	1.98
	1955-60	6.31	3.28	.48	.71	.29	—	1.55
	1960-64	6.22	2.79	.58	.87	.51	—	1.47
M. Selowsky[b]	1940-45	7.37	.61	.42	.63	-.16	—	5.97
	1945-50	5.84	2.41	.45	.67	.01	—	2.30
	1950-55	6.16	2.60	.46	.69	.25	—	2.16
	1955-60	6.31	2.71	.59	.89	.36	—	1.76
	1960-64	6.22	2.31	.71	1.06	.63	—	1.51
Clark Reynolds[c]	1940-50	6.7	0.70	2.51	—	—	.18	3.3
	1950-60	6.1	1.37	2.17	—	—	.05	2.5
Manufacturing sector[d]	1940-50	8.0	5.3	2.5	—	—	—	0.2
	1950-60	7.3	4.4	2.2	—	—	—	0.7
Farm sector[e]	1939-49	5.2	1.7	.92	—	—	1.48	1.0
	1949-59	5.1	1.3	.96	—	—	.96	1.9
Henry Bruton[f]	1940-45	9.0	0.85	1.4	—	—	—	6.75
	1946-53	5.0	2.45	1.3	—	—	—	1.25
	1955-59	5.7	2.1	1.55	—	—	—	2.05
	1960-64	6.2	2.1	1.25	—	—	—	2.85

[a]Assumes capital participation in GDP as follows: 57.8 percent in 1940-45, 64.6 percent in 1945-50, 61 percent in 1950-55, 58.2 percent in 1955-60, and 56 percent in 1960-64.
[b]Assumes capital participation in GDP as follows: 49.2 percent in 1940-45, 56.9 percent in 1945-50, 52.2 percent in 1950-55, 48 percent in 1955-60, and 46.3 percent in 1960-64.
[c]Assumes participation in GDP of 25 percent for capital, 70 percent for labor, and 5 percent for land.
[d]Assumes capital participation in GDP as follows: 61 percent in 1940-50 and 54 percent in 1950-60.
[e]Assumes participation in GDP of 40 percent for labor, 20 percent for capital, and 40 percent for land.
[f]Assumes capital participation in GDP of 50 percent.

Note: Dash indicates no values were completed.
Sources: Compiled by the author.

increased wages. Legislation designed to uplift the poorer classes and therefore to give them more equity may at first be successful. However, the ultimate impact of policy may ironically lead to greater inequality.

The major policy instruments affecting income distribution should therefore be seen as interdependent—once they are applied they set into operation forces that operate simultaneously and in an iterative fashion. The eventual outcome cannot be predicted by use of the Keynesian framework.

A NEW FRAMEWORK FOR POLICY MAKING

The unique aspect of this study has been to establish a framework for examining these interrelationships. Eight sets of government policies are identified as having a significant effect on income distribution. As shown in Figure 7.1, each of these policies affect one of the major sources of growth of GNP. The income generated by this change in GNP, together with the government policies determine the composition of final demand for the increased output. The intersectoral relationships, identified by the country's input-output table, determine sectoral income, sectoral employment, and, together with the absolute size and distribution of wealth, the sectoral income distribution. This in turn determines the personal income distribution. Since each income group will have a different pattern of demand, the distribution of income initially produced will in turn change the composition of demand for goods and services. This change in final demand will again create, through the input-output relationships, a different sectoral income, employment, and personal income distribution. The important point here is that the distribution of income is created by the structure of production and in turn determines that structure. The process is cumulative and converges to a stable supply and demand equilibrium, the composition of which is determined by the government policy mix and the level and final distribution of income.

This framework indicates the difficulty of generalizing in areas of policy—things are not what they appear to be on the surface. Until government policy makers know the total effects on consumption and production in all areas influenced by their policies, they will remain unable to judge whether a given measure such as an increase in minimum wages improves, maintains, or worsens the distribution of income. One should not be surprised therefore that even a country such as Mexico whose constitution (1917) defines democracy as "not only a judicial structure and a political regime, but a way of life

FIGURE 7.1

Analytical Schema for Income Distribution

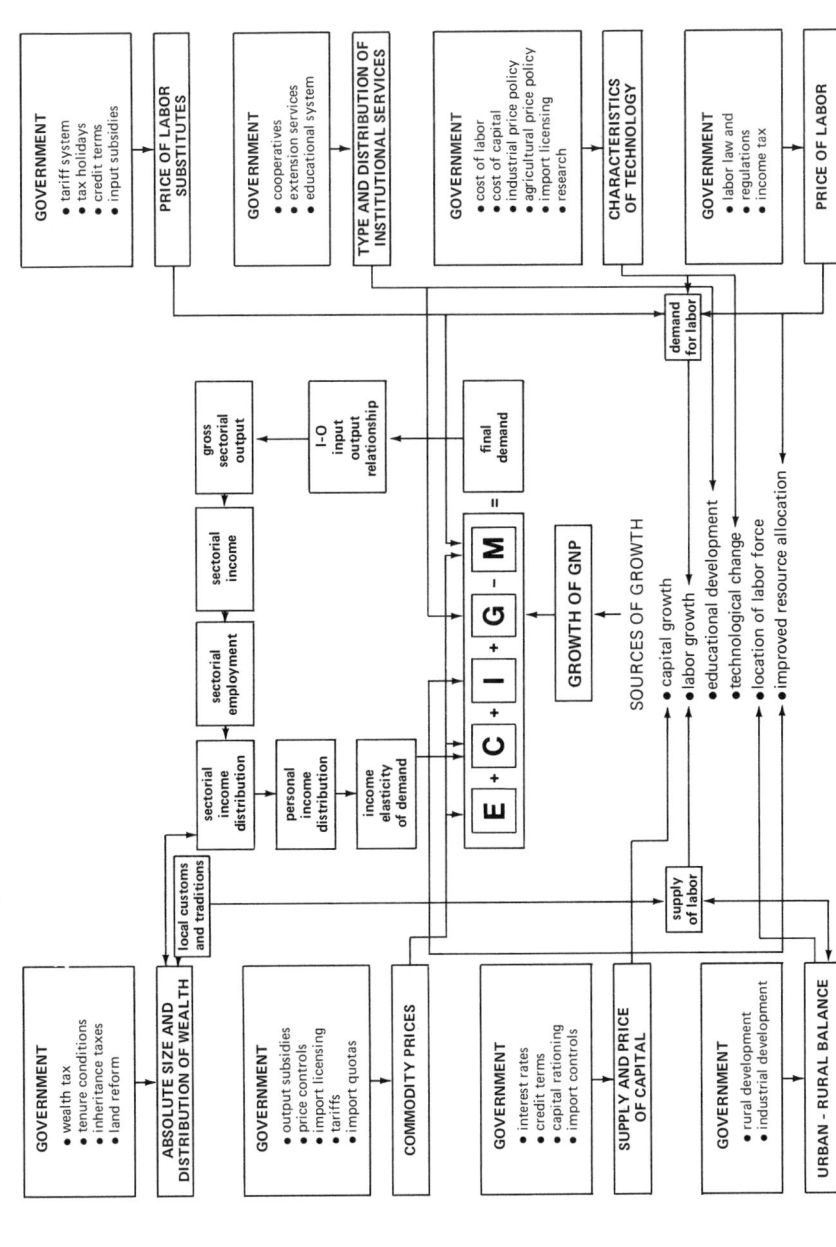

Legend: E- Exports; C–Consumption; I–Investment; G–Government Expenditures; M–Imports.

founded in the steady economic, social and cultural improvement of the people." The country has in fact seen its income distribution deteriorate.

This paradox can be explained by the government's use of Keynesian policies, the direct effect of these policies on income distribution, and the feedback mechanisms outlined in Figure 7.1. As illustrated, Mexico's major sources of growth are (1) changes in the amount of labor employed; (2) changes in the amount of capital employed; (3) changes in the average quality of the labor employed; (4) changes in the locational distribution of the labor force (migration); (5) changes in the country's terms of trade; (6) improvements in the allocation of resources (other than those produced by migration); and (7) improvements in technology.

The contribution of these factors to growth has been empirically estimated (see Table 7.2) and indicate that Mexico could expand more rapidly through quantitative and qualitative increases, brought about by increasing availability and utilization of physical capital and labor, and increasing the profitability of such resources through reallocating them among the major sectors of the economy, particularly in the agricultural sector.

An interesting result of the Mexican experience is that the contribution of capital formation to that country's growth seems to be more important than in the developed countries at similar stages of growth, and has been increasing. For example, that part of growth not caused by increases in the productive factors of labor and capital amounted to 6.75 percent a year in 1940-45, 1.25 percent in 1946-53, 2.05 percent in 1955-59, and 2.85 percent for 1960-64.[3]

The reasons for this tendency are a direct result of the policy mix used by the Mexican government, such as high tariffs on consumer durables and lower tariffs on capital and intermediate goods imports.

The process is as follows. During the war years, nonfactor inputs accounted for most of the growth in Mexico. During that period there was, of course, a high demand in the internal markets and for exports. Consequently, a great incentive existed to increase output. Yet it was virtually impossible for the country to import new plant and equipment, spare parts, and replacements needed for investment in order to increase output. The flow of many raw materials imports was irregular and unpredictable, and with foreign supplies of capital equipment difficult to obtain, firms were forced to find ways of using local resources more effectively. To do this they improvised and adapted their existing equipment to their domestic resources (particularly labor). Also, they developed through research and development technological innovations oriented toward improved methods and techniques capable of using the resources at hand more effectively.

TABLE 7.2

Long-run Impact of Economic Policy Instruments on Goals

Instrument	Growth Rate	Improved Income Distribution	Expanded Employment	Improvement in Balance of Payments on Current Allocation
Export promotion	+	+	+	+
Increase in governmental investment outlays	+	+	+	−
Increases in taxes on wealth and income	?	+	0	0
Reorientation of productive resources	+	+	+	+
Interest rate liberalization	+	+	+	+
Land reform	+	+	+	0
General impact of policy instruments on goals	+	+	+	+

Note: + = favorable impact; − = unfavorable impact; 0 = slight if any impact; ? = doubtful impact.
Source: Compiled by the author.

The innovative activity developed during that period therefore not only increased the use of domestic resources (labor of various skills and quality, raw material imports, and managerial ability), but also permitted efficient adaptation of production techniques to fit the country's market size and demand patterns.

This process resulted in capital formation being widely diffused throughout the economy, thus enabling the productivity and incomes of large numbers of workers to increase. Ironically, the process resulted in high rates of economic growth with small amounts of investment, so that capital formation was not a major constraint on growth during this period. Also, employment opportunities and the distribution of income in the country improved during this time.

After the war, capital goods imports were again available and, stimulated by windfall profits created by high tariff protection, accelerated large-scale industrialization. The nature of capital became more labor saving (since it was designed for relative scarcity of labor in the advanced countries from which it was imported and underpriced because of overvalued exchange rates). As a result, local entrepreneurs had little incentive to modify and adapt their production techniques to utilize the available labor. Indeed, the government created incentives which made it more profitable for local firms to meet demands for increased output by simply acquiring more capital from abroad rather than utilizing the resources at hand more efficiently.

During this time, in the agricultural sector the amount of GNP growth not accounted for by the increase in productive factors was comparatively much higher than in the industrial sector. For example, during the 1940-50 period only 0.2 percent of growth in the industrial sector can be attributed to factors other than labor and capital, while for 1950-60 only 0.7 percent was attributable to these causes. This compares with figures of about 1.2 percent and 1.9 percent in agriculture. In other words, greater competitive forces in agriculture than in industry caused farmers to search for better ways of using their resources most efficiently. This accounts for the higher percentage of nonfactor inputs to the contribution to growth in the farm sector.

If we adjust the labor force for improvements owing to education, another interesting conclusion emerges. The improvement in education has tended to increase steadily its weight as a factor in economic growth. Thus in 1945-50 improvement in education accounted for only 0.1 percent of the annual growth rate. Subsequently, in the 1950-55 period, it accounted for 0.21 percent per year, in 1955-60 for 0.20 percent, and in 1960-64 for 0.51 percent.

These results indicate that the need to increase profits of industrialists (on the assumption that the rate of saving out of profits is very high and the only way to increase savings is by making the income distribution more unequal) is totally erroneous, that is, it is based on the assumption that investment only comes from profits and is in turn the major source of growth. A number of studies have substantiated the fact that capital formation has never been an important source of income growth in countries where free market forces have allocated resources.[4] The apparent need for increased capital formation to enable high growth rates to take place in Mexico was therefore a facade, that is, it was simply a result of economic policies which have, through tariffs, controlled low rates of interest, and, through duty-free importation of machinery, artificially encouraged the use of capital. Since these measures suppressed the development of financial markets and the use of noncapital factors, the contribution to the growth of labor and technical innovation therefore appeared slight. The net result was a rate of growth that was lower than the economy's potential and one that could have been achieved with an improvement in the distribution of income.

However, if Mexico had oriented its economy in favor of agriculture by reallocating through free market prices private and public resources to these areas it would have stimulated an increase in the growth rate and employment. With these measures the country could have made better use of its comparative advantage. This would have been reflected directly in a more rapid rise in productivity, since the country's abundant labor and natural resources could have been utilized in activities where they were most productive. A policy of free market reorientation toward the agricultural sector would, in addition to increased productivity, also have a stimulating effect on the industrial sector on the demand side by providing a broad base of high income to rural inhabitants who have a high propensity to consume industrial goods.

A more efficient allocation of the investment resources channeled through the private sector of the economy requires however, as one necessary factor, a properly functioning financial market. Without this there may be potential investors who still fail to invest in areas of high return because they do not have the necessary financing and, in the same way, there may be others who use their surplus resources for investments of low productivity.

CONCLUSIONS

Each chapter of this book has laid down a comprehensive groundwork for a more complete study of the determinants of income distribution and the manner in which distribution has affected the rate of growth in four semiindustrialized countries. It has been useful to carry out this partial analysis in depth for each policy individually. It is clear, however, that proper policy measures can be worked out only if the related and interdependent aspects of the economy are analyzed simultaneously; that is, growth, income distribution, balance of payments, price level stability, and other similar objectives are in part competitive but also mutually reinforcing. Our conclusions on policy and goal relationships are quite tentative, even in a qualitative sense.

Methodologies that can give quantitative shape to these problems are only in the formulative stage. For example, the model we depicted in Figure 7.1 is not yet capable of incorporating financial price, market development, and technical changes adequately, and hence it does not treat adequately three of the basic elements for growth with equity. If these can be incorporated into this type of model, the determination of the mechanism of growth in an economy can be more precisely stipulated and appropriate policy implementation be more efficiently achieved.

One of the major reasons that this study was undertaken was to define logically both the problems that a country must overcome and the correct mix of policies that should be used in improving the distribution of income. Political leaders today appear totally lacking in comprehension of the interrelationships between policy, growth, income distribution, and demand that we have outlined in this chapter. To them, there are no feedbacks—if you want to help the poor you simply give them more money, cut their taxes, or give them some minimal amount of education. Even someone as devoted to clear thinking and articulation as George Orwell found this direct approach to policy attractive. Ironically, his life's work was an attempt to restore the meaning of words to prove that "good prose is like a window pane." "One ought to recognize that the present political chaos is connected with the decay of language, and that one can probably bring about some improvement by starting at the verbal end."[5] Therein lies Orwell's lasting power. He held out hope that ordinary citizens might see through bureaucracy and rhetoric, so that they might speak and write the truth to each other, and demand the truth from their leaders.[6]

The following remarks are typical of his direct attack on a seemingly simple problem:

> My thoughts turned towards the English working class. It was the first time that I had ever been really aware of the working class, and to begin with it supplied an analogy. They were the symbolic victims of injustice, playing the same part in England as the Burmese played in Burma. In Burma the issue had been quite simple. The whites were up and the blacks were down, and therefore as a matter of course one's sympathy was with the blacks. I now realised that there was no need to go as far as Burma to find tyranny and exploitation. Here in England, down under one's feet, were the submerged working class, suffering miseries with which in their different way were as bad as any oriental ever knows. The word 'unemployment' was on everyone's lips. That was more or less new to me, after Burma, but the drivel which the middle classes were still talking ('These unemployed are all unemployables,' etc., etc.) failed to deceive me. I often wonder whether that

kind of stuff deceives even the fools who utter it. On the other hand I had at that time no interest in Socialism or any other economic theory. It seems to me then—it sometimes seems to me now, for that matter—that economic injustice will stop the moment we want it to stop, and no sooner, and if we genuinely want it to stop the method adopted hardly matters.[7]

I agree with Orwell. Given the desire to eliminate inequalities in income, governments would have little difficulty achieving this goal. This study, however, has indicated that the methods used to accomplish this goal do matter. Unfortunately, politicians in many of the developing countries are more interested in rhetoric than in political courage, sound economic principles, or the harsh economic realities their countries are faced with.

NOTES

1. A critical evaluation of Keynesian theory is given in W.H. Hutt, Keynesianism—Retrospect and Prospect (Chicago: Henry Regnery Company, 1963).
2. See Richard Benedick, Industrial Finance in Iran (Boston: Division of Research, Graduate School of Business Administration, Harvard University, 1964), especially chap. 3.
3. Cf. M. Selowsky, "Education and Economic Growth: Some International Comparisons," University of Chicago (Ph.D diss., 1967); Clark Reynolds, The Mexican Economy (New Haven: Yale University Press, 1970), and Henry Bruton, "Productivity Growth in Latin America," American Economic Review (December 1967).
4. Cf. Robert Solow, "Technical Change and the Aggregate Production Function," Review of Economics and Statistics (August 1957), pp. 312-320; Edward Denison, The Sources of Growth in the United States (New York: Committee for Economic Development, 1962); and Richard Nelson, "Aggregate Production Functions and Medium Range Growth Projections," American Economic Review (September 1964), pp. 575-606.
5. Time, March 24, 1975. p. 77
6. Op. cit., p. 78.
7. George Orwell, The Road to Wigan Pier (New York: Harcourt Brace & World, 1958), pp. 180-181.

APPENDIX A

INCOME DISTRIBUTION AND ECONOMIC GROWTH

The literature of economic development is replete with assertions that an improvement in income distribution is in direct conflict with economic growth.[1] In other words, a transfer of money from the rich to the poor will reduce total savings, since the rich tend to save a higher percentage of an increment in their incomes than do the poor. These assertions are incorrect on both empirical and theoretical grounds; the facts are not what they are represented to be. First, only a linear Keynesian consumption function will yield reductions in saving as the result of an income transfer from high- to low-income groups. Empirically, there is little substantiation of this type of consumption function.[2]

In addition, there are two theoretical considerations that indicate that a trade-off between a more equitable income distribution and higher rates of economic growth is not necessarily in conflict. The first concerns the composition of demand resulting from a change in the distribution of income. It is quite probable that a change in the distribution of income toward more equality will reduce the demand for products that contain a high amount of those inputs (e.g., foreign exchange) which are scarce and whose deficiency has created a constraint preventing higher growth rates. Under these circumstances, an increase in the equality of income would allow an acceleration in the rate of growth of national income.[3]

The second consideration concerns the source from which the income redistribution is generated. If redistribution takes place through increasing the productivity of the lower-income groups of the economy—for example, by education, training programs, improved health care, or by absorbing the unemployed or underemployed so as to add to their productive contribution to the economy—there can be no conflict between redistribution of income by these measures and the strictly economic objective of adding to national output.[4]

SHORT-RUN REDISTRIBUTION EFFECTS

Several empirical studies illustrate these points. In one such study, William R. Cline examined the impact of savings on growth as

APPENDIX A

a result of simulating two alternative hypothetical income distributions in both Brazil and Mexico.[5] He defined the first distribution as one in which income has been taken from upper brackets to ensure a minimum income of one-half the total average family income to all lower brackets and the second, as a distribution equal to that currently existing in England. The English distribution of income (as of the late 1960s) is by all measures much more equal than that of either Brazil or Mexico. To arrive at these ends, he first estimated the proportion of income saved in each decile for Mexico, Brazil, and England. After converting the Mexican and Brazilian distributions to that of England, the savings in each decile were aggregated to obtain the implied change in savings for each country. Second, he converted these changes in savings into their effect on growth by using the relationship $\Delta Y/Y = S \frac{\Delta Y}{\Delta K}$ where $\Delta Y/Y$ is the rate of income growth, S is national savings and $\frac{\Delta Y}{\Delta K}$ is the productivity of capital. This assumes of course that all growth can be attributed exclusively to capital formation; education, technological change, and labor do not contribute at all. Cline found that these income redistributions would, at most, cost a sacrifice of about 1 percent annual growth in GNP.

Cline next examined the effect of income redistribution on growth via changes in the composition of demand through changes in the demand for imports. To do this, he calculated consumption by both industry and income bracket and then, using an input-output table, he calculated the direct and indirect effects on total imports of the two hypothetical income redistributions.

He found that these redistributions would result in negligible declines in imports (less than 2 percent). The major empirical conclusion of Cline's study is that the cost of income redistribution for growth is at most about one percent. However he rejected without empirical validation the possibility that income redistribution might have a positive effect on growth. This could quite likely come about as a result of the stimulating effect of increased equality on consumption and even investment.

Cline did not consider the effect of the shift in income redistribution on the likely change in demand from capital-intensive to labor-intensive sectors. This factor is important since there could be a net increase rather than decrease in growth rates if the resultant decline in the incremental capital-output ratio were significantly great. A lower capital-output ratio would reflect greater output per unit value of investment because of the more labor intensive nature of the investment, this would create the distinct possibility of higher total output as a direct result of income redistribution. This is quite possible because the capital-output ratio is nothing more than a weighted average of sectoral capital-output ratios. The weights are determined by the share of the sectors in the increment of total output. The sectoral ratios depend mostly on technology, being unrelated to the inequality level. The same assumption, however, is unacceptable with respect to the weights.[6]

Lafaiete de Padua Lopes also examined the effect of a change in the distribution on growth in Brazil.[7] In contrast to Cline his growth equation is given by $\Delta g/\Delta J = \frac{\Delta Y}{\Delta K} \cdot \frac{\Delta S}{\Delta J}$, where g stands for the rate of income growth ($\Delta Y/Y$ in Cline), S for the savings rate, J for the inequality index, and $\frac{\Delta Y}{\Delta K}$ for the productivity of capital (the Gini coefficient where values for J of zero indicate perfect equality and values approaching one indicate perfect inequality). Since $\Delta S/\Delta J$ is positive and since he assumed the inverse Keynesian relationship between income level and the marginal propensity to consume, he concluded that $\Delta g/\Delta J$ was also positive, i.e., inequality and growth are directly related. This, of course, implies that any equalization will have a cost in terms of growth reduction—the accepted doctrine on the relationship between inequality and growth.

His results show an insensitivity to the rate of growth of GNP as a result of equalization of the income distribution. In all simulations using alternative income distributions the maximum variation of this rate was less than two-tenths of a percentage point, for a range of shift in the Gini[8] coefficient of 28 percentage points (Gini = 0.48 to Gini = 0.20). Even considering the poor quality of the underlying data base it is possible to conclude therefore that changes in income distribution would not adversely affect the rate of growth.

These results for Brazil indicate that for that country the rate of growth of GNP turns out to be practically independent of the inequality level when the effect of the equalization of income distribution on the aggregate capital-output ratio is taken into account. In addition, if the government eliminates (through monetary and fiscal policy) the reduction in personal savings resulting from equalization, the rate of growth increases between five- and eight-tenths of a percentage point. In both cases, the results are substantially different from what conventional analysis would predict—there is, contrary to accepted doctrine, evidence to support the argument that an improvement in equality would actually accelerate national income growth rather than cause it to decline.

Samuel Morley and Jeffrey Smith in another study on Brazil tested the hypothesis that demand and growth patterns are sensitive to the distribution of income.[9] Their argument is that the effect of a change in the distribution of income may be direct, since it changes the consumption demand for the product, or it may be indirect, since it changes the output of some sector that supplies the inputs to produce

APPENDIX A
167

that product. Through use of an input-output table, they are able to determine the indirect backward linkages from final demand to each industry and thus obtain a more complete estimate of the relationship between change in income distribution, final demand, and changes in the structure of growth.

Their results indicate that the more regressive the distribution of income, the higher the industrial rate of growth, in part because of the importance of consumer durables, especially automobiles and the industries that supply them—rubber, machinery, metals, and fuels. This tends to support Brazil's policy of creating a more unequal distribution to maintain these industries at full capacity.

On the other hand, simulating the effect of the most progressive and the most regressive patterns of income distribution on growth, they found that the average growth of manufacturing increased by only 0.8 percent per year with the deterioration of income distribution. This indicates that the stabilization measures undertaken by the post 1964 governments were too extreme. High growth rates could have been achieved without the large increases in inequality brought about by government policies in the latter 1960s.

The relationship between income distribution and growth can be examined also in terms of functional (as opposed to personal) distribution of income.[10] The Mexican government in the 1940s, and even into the middle 1960s, assumed that a higher profit share (lower wage share) of national income would result in a higher savings rate. Their presumption was that profit recipients saved a higher proportion of their income than wage earners. The implication for income distribution strategy was clear: since the number of entrepreneurs was small relative to the number of workers, a general development strategy favoring a high profit share and the concentration of income in the entrepreneurial class would lead to higher rates of national income growth.

This strategy was followed in Mexico, in spite of the fact that the empirical link between the savings rate and the profit share in national income has never been estimated in a precise fashion. During the period from 1939 to 1963 the government followed a policy of holding down real wages to permit a redistribution of increased output to the entrepreneurial class, yet this reduction in labor costs and the increase in profits did little to finance greater investment. If we calculate the correlation between real wages in industry and gross capital formation expressed as a percentage of GDP, the following results are obtained:[11] for example, for 1939-53, r (the correlation coefficient) = -0.69; 1954-63, r = -0.22, while the correlation between private savings and real wages is -0.22, neither of which is significant.[12] This might be interpreted as indicating that the percentage of wages in the costs of firms is significantly small so that a reduction of labor costs by 30 percent has little effect in the level of profits. Alternatively, although profits increased, the increase did not mean increased capital formation, but simply higher levels of consumption on the part of entrepreneurs. The changes in personal income distribution over this period were not large enough to substantiate the first hypothesis. Therefore the second one would seem to be correct. This result is of great significance, for it would mean that government policies were used in Mexico simply to finance higher consumption of the higher-income groups with no increase in growth, and only made the income distribution more skewed.

A detailed study of the Korean economy using input-output analysis also found that changes in income distribution which affect demand would not reduce the rate of economic growth.[13] On the other hand, a number of government policies could be implemented so that income redistribution in the direction of increased equality would increase the rate of economic growth. In part, this results from the fact that a more equal income distribution would lower imports and lessen the foreign exchange constraint on growth.

These studies illustrate the simple short-run effects of income redistribution on growth as a result of taking income from high savers to presumed lower-saving groups—the most damaging argument against proposing a more equitable distribution. Even on these terms there is no reason to believe that a more equal distribution would have adverse effects on growth. But as noted above, if redistribution takes place over time through increasing the productivity of the lower income groups—for example, by education training programs and so on—there is no conflict between distribution of this type and the strictly economic objective of adding to national output. This can be illustrated by examining government expenditure patterns by region in Iran.

LONG-RUN REDISTRIBUTION EFFECTS

A number of countries similar to Iran have been strongly cautioned against spreading their scarce investment resources too thin by attempting to follow a policy of geographical decentralization of public investment.[14] It was argued that such a policy would, among other things, increase the aggregate capital-output ratio and thereby directly reduce the rate of growth. This is the strongest case that can be made for the concentration of investment in several already relatively high-income regions.

It should be noted that these arguments are usually based on a conceptual framework of resource allocation emphasizing the accumulation of capital and the productivity of this investment under a given technology—the assumptions most likely to give an equity trade-off result. The model developed below is designed to test the supposed regional efficiency (growth) and equity trade-off problem under very extreme conditions in Iran during its Fifth Five-Year Plan period (1972-77).

As a general set of guidelines, the author selected regional development objectives[15] that minimize regional income disparities and concurrently attain returns from the Fifth Plan's development programs to meet overall national targets. These goals are to be compatible with the following subobjectives: (1) accelerate rural and small- to medium-scale industry development, with the objective of increasing employment and reducing the income imbalance between rural migrant population and the rest of the country; (2) increase benefits from planned and existing national development programs through "local" programs; (3) raise the level of social services to minimum standards, thus reducing regional imbalances in social services currently being provided; (4) maximize local participation in the implementation of public sector development projects; and (5) strengthen and decentralize the regional planning machinery.

In order to implement the above objectives, we constructed a regional model to determine the allocation of national sectoral programs, in order to move more toward the equality of regional output than the preliminary Fifth Plan pattern as shown in Table A-1. (The regions are as follows: 1—Gilan, Mazandaran, Gorgan; 2—Azarbayejan; 3—Teheran, Semnan, Zanjan (the Central Region); 4—Khuzestan, Kuhkilluhen; 5—Hamaden, Lorestan; 6—Esfahan, Yazd; 7—Fars; 8—Sistan, Baluchestan, Kerman; 9—Khorassan; 10—Kermanshahan, Kordestan, Elam; and 11—Bandar-Abass, Bushehr.) The allocation of funds for fixed capital formation, and for other developmental expenditures, such as for education, vocational training, and public health, are key factors for meeting the plan objectives. These include the curbing of migrants to the overcongested urban areas by providing employment in rural areas and promoting increased mobility among skilled labor and management.

The model's investment requirements were structured to counterbalance the current inequality in regional well-being as measured by nonoil per capita output. This criterion was selected both because it meets the stated regional development objectives and for its operational convenience. All the regions were given targeted growth rates in per capita output greater than Region 3 (the central region) as compared to a projection of six of the ten regions growing slower than the central region.

The model gradually shifts investment to those regions that prove to be the more efficient for the production of each sector—or, in economic terms, those regions that have a relative comparative

TABLE A.1

Iran: Regional and Sectoral 1977 Output Levels Based on Plan Organization Fifth Plan Targets
(billions of 1972 rials)

Sector	1	2	3	4	5	6	7	8	9	10	11	National Total
Livestock	11.72	17.33	10.94	5.03	9.10	6.58	7.55	8.03	14.13	4.84	1.55	96.80
Crops	35.60	17.40	9.56	14.01	5.05	9.66	8.73	2.23	19.68	4.95	0.83	127.70
Forestry and fishing	4.96	0.30	0.02	0.10	0.10	0.02	0.10	0.02	0.10	0.10	0.78	6.60
Mining and quarrying	0.86	1.08	3.20	1.21	1.00	2.60	1.77	3.12	0.35	0.50	0.01	15.70
Oil and gas	—	—	—	—	—	—	—	—	—	—	—	—
Construction	2.43	3.15	54.00	4.68	4.68	13.23	3.60	0.54	2.25	0.54	0.90	90.90
Food and tobacco	4.06	2.63	30.02	2.48	0.84	4.77	2.25	0.51	2.75	2.24	0.45	53.00
Metals and metal products	2.51	4.45	40.51	6.01	4.24	10.50	0.93	1.05	3.02	1.54	0.94	75.70
Chemicals and petrochemicals	0.01	0.49	79.33	35.33	0.30	3.39	8.61	0.61	0.30	1.53	0.30	130.20
Nonmetallic minerals	1.34	0.96	21.60	0.68	1.79	2.70	1.40	0.70	1.42	1.06	0.35	34.00
Textiles and carpets	5.14	4.41	24.67	3.90	0.60	16.97	0.77	0.56	1.94	1.54	0.60	61.10
Other manufacturing	2.88	2.31	24.80	3.38	0.70	8.30	0.72	0.84	1.80	0.97	0.50	47.20
Transportation	4.19	5.33	30.10	4.62	4.12	11.36	3.05	1.35	4.33	1.56	0.99	71.00
Public utilities	3.11	3.66	24.60	17.15	3.18	6.84	1.87	3.46	2.28	2.00	0.95	69.10
Trade and commerce	38.47	30.43	218.55	30.00	16.06	31.70	15.64	9.61	17.02	10.14	5.08	422.70
Social services	6.95	6.65	16.40	4.02	3.95	6.46	5.02	2.72	4.52	3.32	1.39	61.40
Total	124.23	100.58	588.30	132.60	55.71	135.08	62.01	35.35	75.89	36.83	15.62	1,362.20
Per capita output (rials)	(30,102)	(19,913)	(83,081)	(50,844)	(18,891)	(39,313)	(26,614)	(20,143)	(21,590)	(15,930)	(18,142)	(37,800)
Percentage of Average annual growth rates per capita output (1972-77)	(5.5)	(6.1)	(7.5)	(9.1)	(7.4)	(10.3)	(6.8)	(6.9)	(5.6)	(8.4)	(12.2)	(7.59)

Note: Output is gross domestic product (excluding oil).

Source: Plan Organization, Preliminary Fifth Five-Year Plan, mimeographed (Teheran, 1973).

APPENDIX A

advantage in that sector within the targeted regional output constraint.[16] In mathematical form, the model reads

$$q_{irt} = \lambda_{irt} q_{it}$$

$$\text{with } \sum_r \lambda_{irt} = 1 \qquad \text{(A.1)}$$

where, first, q_{irt} = the output of sector i in region r in period t (1977). The sectoral outputs (the q_{it}'s) are derived from preliminary Fifth Plan targets by the Plan Organization (see Table A.2). They are assumed to be based primarily on the continuation of output trends. The regional output targets were set to reduce regional output disparities. And, second, λ_{irt} is the percentage of national output of sector i which is produced in region r in period t (1977). The production percentages for each region are, in turn, defined as

$$\lambda_{irt} = \alpha_{1i} \left(\frac{q_{irt-1}}{\sum_r q_{irt-1}} \right) + \alpha_{2i} \left(\frac{Y/P_{irt-1}}{\sum_r Y/P_{irt-1}} \right)$$

$$+ \alpha_{3i} \left[\frac{\left(\frac{\text{Value Added}}{\text{Input}} \right)_{irt}}{\left(\frac{\text{Value Added}}{\text{Input}} \right)_{\text{National}}} \right],$$

where q_{irt-1} is the output level in each region and sector in 1972; Y/P_{irt-1} is the per capita output in each sector and region in 1972, a term representing the equality considerations in our model—that is, welfare is measured in terms of per capita output; and $\left(\frac{\text{Value Added}}{\text{Input}} \right)_{irt}$ is the value added coefficient by sector and region in 1977.

This term represents the efficiency component in the model. In other words, it is argued that the larger the value added per unit of scarce inputs, the more efficient is region r at producing the products of sector i. This then becomes a proxy for comparative advantage, that is, for output at maximum efficiency, sectoral production should be relatively concentrated in regions which produce the greatest output per unit of input. Admittedly, profitability data, if available, would have been a more satisfactory proxy, but the conservation of scarce inputs is in line with plan objectives.

TABLE A.2

Iran: Regional and Sectoral 1977 Output Targets for the Regionalization of the Fifth Plan
(billions of 1972 rials)

Sector	Region											National Total
	1	2	3	4	5	6	7	8	9	10	11	
Livestock	11.69	16.34	10.83	6.00	8.85	7.33	7.63	7.12	12.57	5.43	2.83	96.62
Crops	30.23	16.55	10.69	12.53	6.79	9.96	8.74	4.24	18.13	6.17	3.18	127.21
Forestry and fishing	4.30	0.37	0.14	0.20	0.20	0.16	0.22	0.13	0.18	0.20	0.43	6.53
Mining and quarrying	0.84	1.10	3.36	1.65	1.04	1.68	1.62	2.64	0.64	0.74	0.38	15.69
Construction	4.04	4.85	45.01	5.34	5.42	9.96	4.36	2.40	3.64	2.47	2.20	89.69
Food and tobacco	3.91	3.92	25.09	3.32	2.07	3.94	2.47	1.54	2.79	3.41	1.05	53.51
Metals and metal products	3.63	4.19	39.94	5.22	4.33	6.86	2.56	2.16	1.20	3.19	1.44	74.72
Chemicals and petrochemicals	3.11	3.35	68.51	27.59	3.04	4.42	8.09	2.62	3.07	4.37	2.19	130.36
Nonmetallic minerals	1.78	1.49	18.87	1.36	1.83	2.31	1.91	0.89	1.42	1.30	0.78	33.94
Textiles and carpets	5.60	5.28	22.02	3.79	1.70	11.44	2.00	2.23	2.88	2.67	1.34	60.95
Other manufacturing	3.71	3.29	21.61	2.44	1.61	5.37	1.88	1.64	2.71	1.76	1.02	47.04
Transportation	4.79	5.61	26.58	4.89	4.64	9.11	3.69	2.40	4.49	2.73	1.82	70.75
Public utilities	3.87	4.13	21.14	15.83	3.40	6.04	2.52	3.95	3.32	2.96	2.09	69.25
Trade and commerce	38.63	33.44	194.95	27.90	22.37	25.91	18.81	15.30	20.92	16.06	9.93	422.22
Social services	6.82	6.72	14.57	3.94	4.37	6.37	4.31	2.98	4.86	3.51	1.77	60.22
Total	126.95	110.63	523.31	122.00	69.66	110.86	70.81	52.24	82.82	56.97	32.45	1,358.70
Per capita output (rials)	(30,750)	(21,901)	(73,905)	(46,771)	(23,550)	(32,264)	(30,391)	(29,777)	(23,562)	(24,641)	(37,677)	(37,700)
Percentage of Average annual growth rate of per capita output (1972-77)	(6.0)	(8.0)	(4.9)	(7.3)	(12.3)	(6.2)	(9.7)	(15.5)	(7.8)	(15.0)	(29.0)	(7.59)

Note: Output is gross domestic product (excluding oil).

Source: Compiled by the author.

APPENDIX A

The model is closed with the condition that

$$\alpha_{1i} + \alpha_{2i} + \alpha_{3i} = 1$$

For equity increases, α_{2i} must assume a negative value, since Y/P or per capita output is weighted heaviest for those regions most deficient in this respect.

It is readily apparent that q_{it}, or Plan Organization sectoral targets for the Fifth Plan, determined through past trend rates imply an increasing disparity of income. To counterbalance this, the regional model target was set by assigning a weight of .9 to the relative output term (α_{1i}), -.15 to the equity term α_{2i}, and .25 to the efficiency term α_{3i}. These sectoral output levels were allocated in a manner as described by the model above to yield the 1977 recommended regional pattern of output and growth, again based on Plan Organization Fifth Plan sectoral targets. It is apparent that the model shifts productive capacity away from Region 3 to the lagging and intermediate regions.

This is most dramatically shown by the acceleration of growth rates for Regions 11, 10, 8, and 5, which are the (relatively) more backward regions. In these areas, the average annual growth rates increase from 12.2, 8.4, 6.9, and 7.4 to 29.0, 15.0, 15.5, and 12.3 percent respectively, while the growth of Region 3 (the central region) declines from a 7.5 percent to a 4.9 percent average annual increase per capita output. The rather high growth rates for several of the more backward regions reflect the extremely low base from which growth in projected.

The results of the model further indicate that based on regional-sectoral capital value added estimates for 1977 the total investments required to meet Fifth Plan output targets, when regionally distributed, are less than those assumed to represent the National Fifth Plan requirements by 76.08 billion rials, or 4.1 percent (see Tables A.3 and A.4). This implies that some of the less advanced regions have a potential in certain sectors to produce more with lower capital requirements than do some of the advanced regions. The analysis can be made for all sectors between any regions by comparing the output target difference from Tables A.1 and A.2 with the investment requirement differences from Tables A.3 and A.4. This process can allow the planner to analyze selectively investment decisions between sectors and regions.

The proposed regional reallocation of investment shown in Table A.4 is not extreme. Region 3, with 19.12 percent of the 1972 population, still receives 36.14 percent of the total capital formation over the Fifth Five-Year Plan.

TABLE A.3

Iran: Regional and Sectoral Investment Implied by Plan Organization's National Fifth Plan Targets
(billions of 1972 rials)

Sector	Region											National Total
	1	2	3	4	5	6	7	8	9	10	11	
Livestock	9.21	14.28	11.57	4.20	5.22	2.96	5.01	3.81	9.88	2.70	0.69	69.53
Crops	14.24	7.86	4.44	6.78	1.36	6.89	5.76	1.31	10.07	2.25	0.17	61.13
Forestry and fishing	3.21	0.08	0.03	0.08	0.04	0.02	0.05	0.03	0.08	0.04	0.25	3.91
Mining and quarrying	0.41	0.17	0.97	0.11	0.73	3.06	1.17	2.21	0.18	0.13	0.01	9.15
Construction	0.79	1.02	54.37	3.09	2.20	17.72	1.75	0.33	1.40	0.26	0.42	83.35
Food and tobacco	6.60	4.17	60.77	2.08	0.90	13.23	4.86	0.69	7.27	1.66	1.32	103.55
Metal and metal products	3.97	4.73	39.15	11.44	5.07	25.87	1.80	1.52	12.03	1.28	1.35	108.21
Chemicals and petrochemicals	0.01	0.59	90.33	41.85	0.42	3.98	18.76	0.11	0.46	1.99	0.04	158.54
Nonmetallic minerals	0.96	0.99	22.49	7.53	2.54	2.42	0.86	0.70	1.92	0.79	0.48	41.68
Textiles and carpets	8.66	2.90	60.88	1.29	0.24	36.26	0.78	0.09	2.20	1.50	0.27	115.07
Other manufacturing	6.88	5.44	76.69	15.43	1.93	28.80	1.07	1.35	4.31	1.57	1.19	144.66
Transportation	3.14	4.20	35.12	4.45	4.12	14.35	2.64	0.94	5.06	1.72	0.84	76.58
Public utilities	30.68	32.29	165.82	141.43	15.00	55.96	19.94	22.97	13.39	10.47	5.55	513.51
Trade and commerce	28.71	19.28	169.24	24.09	9.94	29.97	11.48	6.00	15.89	7.68	4.36	326.64
Social services	6.32	4.70	10.54	3.28	4.03	2.98	4.19	1.47	5.15	3.39	0.83	46.88
Total	123.79	102.70	802.41	267.15	53.74	244.48	80.12	43.53	89.29	37.43	17.77	1,862.39

Source: Compiled by the author.

TABLE A.4

Iran: Regional Fifth Plan Investment Requirements
(billions of 1972 rials)

	Region											National Total
	1	2	3	4	5	6	7	8	9	10	11	
Livestock	9.52	12.75	11.37	5.74	5.05	3.63	5.10	2.96	7.81	3.34	1.82	69.09
Crops	10.18	7.15	5.40	5.48	2.20	7.25	5.77	3.58	8.64	3.38	0.84	59.87
Forestry and fishing	2.59	0.13	0.30	0.15	0.10	0.08	0.13	0.22	0.19	0.10	0.02	4.01
Mining and quarrying	0.40	0.17	1.10	0.25	0.76	1.73	1.04	1.64	0.43	0.23	0.19	7.94
Oil and gas	—	—	—	—	—	—	—	—	—	—	—	—
Construction	1.83	2.14	39.78	3.85	2.81	11.29	2.40	2.08	2.85	1.94	1.35	72.28
Food and tobacco	6.13	7.83	41.05	3.99	3.85	9.24	5.79	3.58	5.46	3.28	4.07	94.27
Metals and metal products	6.44	4.37	38.31	9.35	5.20	13.68	5.59	3.78	3.69	3.48	2.16	96.05
Chemicals and petrochemicals	6.58	5.31	72.38	29.02	5.23	5.42	17.31	0.64	5.18	7.53	0.33	154.93
Nonmetallic minerals	1.46	1.80	18.00	1.20	2.63	1.92	1.40	0.96	1.92	1.03	1.26	33.58
Textiles and carpets	10.21	4.11	49.47	1.25	1.14	18.28	3.09	0.72	4.15	4.24	0.79	97.45
Other manufacturing	10.28	9.31	62.21	9.98	6.81	15.23	5.86	3.53	8.02	3.99	2.96	138.18
Transportation	4.12	4.64	27.73	4.98	5.25	9.59	3.98	2.50	5.37	4.58	2.15	74.89
Public utilities	41.90	38.59	132.40	123.14	16.44	46.29	30.92	29.41	22.20	18.29	14.51	514.09
Trade and commerce	28.92	22.78	137.67	21.42	14.34	22.25	15.47	12.50	21.71	15.48	10.28	322.82
Social services	6.12	4.78	8.57	3.19	4.76	3.93	3.28	1.68	5.70	3.70	1.18	46.89
Total	146.68	125.86	645.74	222.99	76.59	169.82	107.12	69.70	103.33	74.58	43.91	1,786.31

Note: Data may not add to totals because of rounding.

Source: Compiled by the author.

Since the primary purpose of regional allocations is to bring the development experience to as many low-income people as possible, a more biased set of allocation weights assuring investment outside the central region could be selected.

NOTES

1. These are summarized in William R. Cline, Potential Effects of Income Redistribution on Economic Growth (New York: Praeger Publishers, 1973), chap. 2.

2. Cf. Thomas Mayer, Permanent Income, Wealth and Consumption (Berkeley: University of California Press, 1973). Professor Mayer has shown over a wide spectrum of countries and dates that a permanent income consumption function exists in modified form, that is, the strict permanent-income theory is wrong in asserting that the marginal propensity to consume is equal to the average propensity, but it is right in suggesting that the marginal propensity to consume permanent income is greater than the marginal propensity to consume measured income, though even for permanent income the marginal propensity is less than the average propensity. This result seriously casts doubt on any assumption that a redistribution of income would have any significant impact on national savings. In fact a good case can be made for the point that increased employment and consumption in lower-income categories could actually increase the total amount of national savings. With insufficient work, the families in the lower-income deciles usually have not only low incomes and large dissaving, but also low levels of consumption. With fuller employment, the members of lower-decile families must consume more in order to have the energy and other necessities required for work. But this need not lead to a rise in the rate of consumption because there is a large fixed overhead cost in human labor-costs in the form of consumption of food, clothing, housing and other necessities. For example, an adult completely unemployed must consume at least 1,500 calories of food, perhaps 40 grams of proteins, and so on, for maintaining basal metabolism. Full employment of an adult entails additions to consumption of necessities perhaps less than one-half of the income earned. The increase in the volume of consumption (mainly food and simple consumer goods produced locally) can be met by what appears to be fairly extensive underutilization of capacity in the small industries of our sample countries and in turn this will raise further the employment of household members in the lower-income deciles in these industries which are largely labor intensive. Since the rate of consumption may fall, the rate of savings may actually rise. Cf. Harry T.

APPENDIX A

Oshima, "Income Inequality and Economic Growth—The Postwar Experience of Asian Countries," The Malayan Economic Review (October 1970), pp. 33-34.

3. A description of the type of models used to identify constraints to national growth and the options (not involving income redistribution) to alleviate them are given in Jaroslav Vanek, Estimating Foreign Resource Needs for Economic Development (New York: McGraw-Hill, 1967), especially chap. 6. See also Laughlin Currie, "The Exchange Constraint on Development—A Partial Solution," The Economic Journal (December 1971), and Hiroshi Kitamura, "Trade and Capital Needs of Developing Countries and Foreign Assistance," Weltwirtschaftliches Archiv (1966).

4. This is based on the empirical work of Moses Abramovitz in "Resources and Output Trends in the U.S. Since 1870," American Economic Review (May 1956); Edward Denison, Sources of Economic Growth in the U.S. and the Alternatives Before Us (New York: Committee for Economic Development, 1962); Arnold Harber and M. Selowsky, "Key Factors in the Economic Growth of Chile: An Analysis of the Sources of Past Growth and of Prospects for 1965-70," mimeographed (1966); and Robert M. Solow, "Technological Change and the Aggregate Production Function," Review of Economics and Statistics (1957). These studies indicate that capital contributes a relatively small amount to national economic growth. On the other hand, the estimates of rates of return on educational expenditures in developing countries are quite high and therefore the contribution of improved levels of education of the labor force to the rate of national income growth is quite considerable. Finally, a large portion of the observed growth of most countries is unexplained by direct factor inputs (capital and labor) with improvements in productivity and technological change along with education accounting for most of the observed rates of GNP growth.

5. Cline, op. cit.

6. The limitations on using aggregate capital-output ratios for purposes of projecting economic growth are given in N. V. Gianaria, "International Differences in Capital-Output Ratios," American Economic Review (June 1970).

7. Francisco Lafaiete de Padua Lopes, Inequality and Growth: A Programming Model with Applications to Brazil (Cambridge, Massachusetts: Development Research Group, Center for International Affairs, Harvard University, 1973).

8. There has been much controversy on the "proper" way to measure personal income inequality; for an excellent discussion of the various measures and their limitations see A. B. Atkinson, "On the Measurement of Inequality," Journal of Economic Theory (September 1970), pp. 244-263.

9. Samuel Morley and Jeffrey Williamson, "Demand, Distribution, and Employment: The Case of Brazil," Economic Development and Cultural Change (October 1974). A slightly different result is presented in John Wells, Distribution of Earnings Growth and Structure of Demand in Brazil, 1959-1971 (Cambridge, Eng.: Center of Latin American Studies, University of Cambridge, 1972), p. 35. Through a careful examination of household budget surveys in Brazil, he concludes: "Nor do the budget survey results suggest that increasing concentration of income is the most rational way of sustaining demand; in fact, the reverse is true. If the present boom in production of finished durable goods is limited to the top 10 percent of the top 10 percent of the population, which was the only decile to increase its relative income share (after 1964), then the process is bound to be limited." The conflict between Wells and the study of Morley and Williamson is only an apparent one. Wells is using a longer time horizon, Morley and Smith a shorter one.

10. Cf. N. Kaldor, "Alternative Theories of Income Distribution," Review of Economic Studies (1955/66), pp. 83-100, and L. L. Pasinetti, "Rate of Profit and Income Distribution in Relation to the Rate of Economic Growth," Review of Economic Studies (October 1962), pp. 267-279.

11. The results are from Ariel Buira, "Development and Price Stability in Mexico," Weltwirtschaftliches Archiv (1968), pp. 61-62.

12. Cf. William Cole and Richard Sanders, "Income Distribution, Profits and Savings in the Recent Economic Experience of Mexico," Inter-American Economic Affairs (1973), for a similar result.

13. D. L. Chinn, "Effects of Income Redistribution on Economic Growth Constraints: Evidence from the Republic of Korea," Economic Bulletin for Asia and The Far East (1973), pp. 61-76.

14. W. Alonso, "The Location of Industry in Developing Countries," in Industrial Location and Regional Development (New York: United Nations, 1971), pp. 3-36, and Louis Lefeber and Mrinal Datta-Chaudhuri, Regional Development: Experiences and Prospects in South and South East Asia (The Hague: Mouton, 1971).

15. A complete description of Iranian regional objectives is given in Robert Looney, "Industrial Decentralization in Iran," Santa Clara Business Review (1973).

16. The model is somewhat similar in form to one developed by David Kendrick for transportation planning in Colombia; see Kendrick, "Mathematical Models for Regional Planning," Regional and Urban Economics (November 1971), pp. 281-284.

APPENDIX B

DISTRIBUTION AND EMPLOYMENT

The income effects associated with distributional and employment changes in the relative prices and the size of the elasticity of substitution are complex. In order simply to give an indication of some of the considerations that must be evaluated in order to predict changes in income distribution over time as a result of increases in productivity that occur independently of the level of investment, the following model is developed.

Suppose that all firms hire labor until the marginal product of labor equals a certain given wage rate. Suppose further that capital formation is determined autonomously, and that the following production function describes the modern manufacturing sector:

$$Y(t) = F(a(t) K(t), b(t) L(t)) \tag{B.1}$$

where Y is output
      a is the index of capital augmenting productivity growth
      b is the index of labor augmenting productivity growth
      L is labor
      K is capital
      t refers to time period.

Assume that this production function has constant returns to scale. Then the proportionate rate of growth of the demand for labor is

$$r_L = r_K + r_a - r_b + \frac{\sigma L}{Y - wL} [r_b - r_w] \tag{B.2}$$

where the r's identify proportionate rates of growth, for example, $\frac{dL}{dt} \frac{1}{dL}$, etc., w is the wage rate, and σ is the elasticity of substitution. Evidently, employment grows with capital formation and capital using productivity growth, and falls with labor using productivity growth. The most interesting component is the last, which tells us that labor using productivity growth, not matched by wage increases, will produce employment growth if the elasticity of substitution exceeds zero.

There are four points in particular to note about equation (B.2). First, if $r_a = r_b$ then employment will grow faster than r_k if $r_b > r_w$ and $\sigma > 0$. In that event the greater are σ and r_b (relative to r_w), the greater will be r_L; in order therefore for $r_k > r_L$, (1) r_b must exceed r_a and (2) $r_b \le r_w$ or (3) σ must equal zero. This suggests that considerations with respect to r_b, r_a, and σ are relevant in the income distribution problem. It may be noted that in almost all developing countries, capital's share is larger than in the more developed countries. Therefore with a given elasticity of substitution and a given difference between r_b and r_w, employment will expand more rapidly in the latter than in the former countries.

Second, if $r_w = r_a = 0$, then $r_L > r_K$ if

$$Y - wL - Y < 0$$
$$(1 - \sigma) < \frac{wL}{Y}$$
$$1 - \frac{wL}{Y} < \sigma$$

that is, if σ exceeds capital share. Evidently there is no reason to expect r_a and r_w to be equal.

Third, if $r_b = 0$, then $r_L > r_K$ if $r_a > \frac{\sigma Y}{Y - wL}[r_w]$. If $r_b = r_w = 0$, then $r_L = r_K = r_a$. In either case if $r_b = 0$, employment will grow more rapidly, the higher r_a is and the lower r_w is.

Fourth, the rate of growth of labor's share (with product prices assumed constant) can be shown to be[1]

$$r_{LS} = (\sigma - 1)[r_b - r_w] \ . \tag{B.3}$$

Labor's share will rise if r_b exceeds r_w and the elasticity of substitution exceeds unity. If wage rates are constant, and $\sigma > 1$, then labor's share will rise over time in this model. Above it was shown that employment will grow more rapidly, the greater is r_b relative to r_w and the greater is σ. Now from equation (B.3) it is evident that if σ exceeds unity, the greater it and r_b are, the more rapid will labor's share rise. With r_w equal to zero, the increase in labor's share is due entirely to increasing employment. In that event employment grows more rapidly than does output, and <u>observed</u> labor productivity falls. These circumstances would appear to produce the most favorable effect on low-end income groups as well as on the overall size of distribution (of income). If $\sigma > 1$, rising wage rates actually reduce the growth of labor's share by their penalizing of employment growth. It is also evident that if $r_w > r_b$, then a σ less than unity will produce a rising labor share, at the expense of a slow growth of employment.

In the model the elasticity of substitution plays a very important role in income distribution. The growth of wage rates is also crucial as is the rate of growth of productivity. This formulation also brings out the importance of different forms of productivity growth in both employment and income distribution, plus the fact that profit's increasing share is not a necessary condition for growth of employment, that is, certain circumstances will result in employment growth being great enough to produce an increase in labor's share. The general policy objective may therefore be defined as trying to foster the emergence of the conditions that produce these results.

The following are strategic elements in an analysis of the problem: productivity growth (magnitude and bias), wage rates, factor substitutability, and capital formulation (and hence profit rate). The question relating to income distribution then is how industrialization policies in general and trade policies in particular affect these several elements.

The model considered above places a heavy role on investment in modern manufacturing activities, but also on the condition that investment must take place in a manner consistent with the resource endowment of the economy. The investment must "fit" the economy, if it is to serve the income distribution objectives very objectively.

NOTE

1. Cf. Henry Bruton, "Industrialization and the Distribution of Income," mimeographed (Washington, 1974).

BIBLIOGRAPHY

Abramovitz, Moses. "Resources and Output Trends in the U.S. Since 1870." American Economic Review (May 1956).

Adleman, I., and C.T. Morris. An Anatomy of Patterns of Income Distribution in Developing Countries. Stanford: Stanford University Press, 1971.

Agency for International Development. Gross National Product—Growth Rates and Trend Data by Region and Country. Washington, D.C., various issues.

Alonso, William. "The Location of Industry in Developing Countries." In Industrial Location and Regional Development. New York: United Nations, 1971.

Amine-Zadeh, F. "Population Growth and Manpower Problems in Iran." In Symposium on Manpower Planning and Statistics. Teheran: Central Treaty Organization, 1969.

Amuzegar, Jahangir, and M. Ali Fekrat. Iran: Economic Development under Dualistic Conditions. Chicago: University of Chicago Press, 1971.

Arronte, R. Carrillo. An Empirical Test on Interregional Planning. Rotterdam: Rotterdam University Press, 1970.

Atkinson, A.B. "On the Measurement of Inequality." Journal of Economic Theory (September 1970).

Aubey, Robert. "In the Private Sector: Regional Credit and The Mexican Financial System." Growth and Change (October 1971).

Baer, Werner and Andrea Maneshi. "Import-Substitution, Stagnation, and Structural Change: An Interpretation of the Brazilian Case." The Journal of Developing Areas (January 1971).

Balassa, Bela. "Industrial Policies in Taiwan and Korea." Weltwirtschaftliches Archiv (1971).

BIBLIOGRAPHY

Balderas-Moreno, Juventino. "Production Functions, Technology and Functional Income Distribution of Income in Mexico: A Cross-Section Analysis of the Manufacturing Sector in 1960 and 1965." Ph.D. dissertation, University of Colorado, 1973.

Baldwin, G.B. Planning and Development in Iran. Baltimore: Johns Hopkins Press, 1967.

_____. "The Iranian Brain Drain." In Iran Faces the Seventies. Edited by Ehsan Yar-Shater. New York: Praeger Publishers, 1971.

Banco de Mexico. Encuesta Sobre Ingresos y Gastos Familiares 1968. Mexico City, 1972.

_____. Department of Industry and Commerce, and Direccion General de Estadistica, Ingresos y Egresos de las Familias en la Republica Mexicana. Mimeographed. Mexico City, 1969-70.

Banco Nacional de Comercio Exterior. Mexico. Mexico City, 1968.

Banco Nacional de Mexico, S.A. Review of the Economic Situation of Mexico. Mexico City, various issues.

Bank of Korea. National Income Statistics Yearbook. Seoul, various issues.

Bank Markazi Iran. Annual Report and Balance Sheet. Teheran, various issues.

_____. Annual Household Budget Survey. Teheran, various issues.

_____. Bulletin. Teheran, various issues.

Barraclough, Solon. Agrarian Structure in Latin America. Lexington, Mass.: Lexington Books, 1973.

Bartsch, W.H. "The Industrial Labor Force of Iran: Problems of Recruitment, Training and Productivity." Middle East Journal (Winter 1971).

Baster, Nancy. Distribution of Income and Economic Growth. Geneva: United Nations Research Institute for Social Development, 1970.

Bennett, Robert L. *The Financial Sector and Economic Development—The Mexican Case.* Baltimore: Johns Hopkins Press, 1965.

Bergsman, Joel. *Industrialization and Trade Policies in Brazil.* London: Oxford University Press, 1970.

Bird, Richard. *Taxing Agricultural Land in Developing Countries.* Cambridge: Harvard University Press, 1974.

Brown, Gilbert. *Korean Pricing Policies and Economic Development in the 1960s.* Baltimore: Johns Hopkins Press, 1973.

Bruton, Henry. "Industrialization and the Distribution of Income." Mimeographed. Washington, 1974.

Buira, Ariel. "Development and Price Stability in Mexico." *Weltwirtschaftliches Archiv,* 1968.

Bureau of Statistics, Economic Planning Board. *Annual Report on the Family Income and Expenditure Survey.* Seoul, 1970.

——. *Report on the Results of Farm Household Economy Survey of Agricultural Products.* Seoul, 1971.

——. *Annual Report on the Family Income and Expenditure Survey, 1970.* Seoul, 1971.

Campos, Roberto de Oliveria. "Facts and Fantasy in Brazilian Development." *Reflections on Latin American Development.* Austin: University of Texas Press, 1967.

Carnoy, M. "Rates of Return to Schooling in Latin America." *Journal of Human Resources* (Summer 1967).

Chenery, Hollis. *Redistribution with Growth.* London: Oxford University Press, 1974.

Child, Frank C., and Miromiteu Kanada. "Links to the Green Revolution: A Study of Small-Scale Agriculturally Related Industry in the Pakistan Punjab." *Economic Development and Cultural Change* (January 1975).

Chinn, D. L. "Effects of Income Redistribution on Economic Growth Constraints: Evidence from the Republic of Korea." *Economic Bulletin for Asia and The Far East* (1973).

BIBLIOGRAPHY

Cline, William R. Economic Consequences of a Land Reform in Brazil. Amsterdam: North-Holland Publishing Company, 1970.

_____. Potential Effects of Income Redistribution on Economic Growth. New York: Praeger Publishers, 1973.

Cole, William, and Richard Sanders. "Income Distribution, Profits and Savings in the Recent Economic Experience of Mexico." Inter-American Economic Affairs (1973).

Currie, Laughlin. "The Exchange Constraint on Development—A Partial Solution." The Economic Journal (December 1971).

_____. Accelerating Development—The Necessity and the Means. New York: McGraw-Hill, 1966.

Daly, Herman. "The Political Economy of Population." In H. Jon Rosenbaum and William G. Tyler, eds., Contemporary Brazil: Issues in Economic and Political Development. New York: Praeger Publishers, 1972.

de Alcantara, Cynthia Hewitt. "The Green Revolution as History: The Mexican Experience," Development and Change, no. 2 (1973-1974).

Denison, Edward. The Sources of Economic Growth in the United States and Alternatives Before Us. New York: Committee on Economic Development, 1962.

de Oliveria, Americo Barbosa, and Jose Zacarias Sa Carvalho. A Formacao de Pessoal de Nivel Superioe e o Desenvolvimento Economico. Rio de Janeiro: Campanha Nacional de Aperfeicoamento de Pessoal de Nivel Superior, 1970.

Departmento de Imprensa Nacional. Estados Unidos do Brazil. Estatuto da Terra: Lei No. 4504 de 30 de Novembro de 1964. Rio de Janeiro: 1965.

Diaz-Alejandro, C.F. Exchange Rate Devaluation in a Semi-Industrialized Country: The Experience of Argentina, 1955-1961. Cambridge: MIT Press, 1965.

Donges, J.B. Brazil's Trotting Peg: A New Approach to Greater Exchange Rate Flexibility in Less Developed Countries. Washington: American Enterprise Institute, 1971.

Dovring, Folke. "Land Reform in Mexico." In Land Reform in Brazil, Cuba, Guatemala and Mexico. Washington, D.C.: Agency for International Development, Spring Review of Land Reform, 1970.

Economist Intelligence Unit. Quarterly Economic Review—Iran, Annual Supplement. London, 1974.

_____. Brazil: Quarterly Economic Review. London, various issues.

Ellis, Howard. "Corrective Inflation in Brazil, 1964-1966," The Economy of Brazil. Edited by Howard Ellis. Berkeley: University of California Press, 1969.

Ferguson, Charles. The Neoclassical Theory of Production and Distribution. Cambridge: Cambridge University Press, 1971.

Fishlow, Albert. "Brazilian Distribution of Income." American Economic Review (May 1972).

Freebairn, Donald. "The Dichotomy of Prosperity and Poverty in Mexican Agriculture." Land Economics (March 1969).

Furtado, Celso. "Marx's Model in the Analysis of the Underdeveloped Economic Structures." Yale University Economic Growth Center, reprint 164 (1970).

Georgescu-Roegen. "Structural Inflation-Lock and Balanced Growth." Economies et Societies (March 1970).

Ghosh, A.P. Development Planning in South East Asia. Rotterdam: Rotterdam University Press, 1974.

Gianaria, N.V. "International Differences in Capital-Output Ratios." American Economic Review (June 1970).

Goldsmith, Raymond. The Financial Development of Mexico. Paris: Development Center of the Organization for Economic Cooperation and Development, 1966.

Goodman, Davis. "Industrial Development in the Brazilian Northeast: An Interim Assessment of the Tax Credit Scheme of Article 34/18." In Brazil in the Sixties. Edited by Riordan Roett. Nashville: Vanderbilt University Press, 1972.

BIBLIOGRAPHY 187

Gotsch, Carl. "Technical Change and the Distribution of Income in Rural Areas." Economic Development Report No. 205. Cambridge, Mass.: Development Research Group, Center for International Affairs, Harvard University.

Griffin, Keith. "Policy Options for Rural Development." Oxford Bulletin of Economics and Statistics (November 1973).

_____. The Political Economy of Agrarian Change. Cambridge: Harvard University Press, 1974.

Grove, Terence J. The Iranian Tax System. Teheran: The Industrial and Mining Development Bank of Iran, 1970.

Gurley, John; Hugh Patrick; and E.S. Shaw. The Financial Structure of Korea. Seoul: United States Operations Mission to Korea, 1965.

Hansen, Roger D. The Politics of Mexican Development. Baltimore: Johns Hopkins Press, 1971.

Harber, Arnold, and M. Selowsky. "Key Factors in the Economic Growth of Chile: An Analysis of the Sources of Past Growth and of Prospects for 1965-70." Mimeographed. 1966.

Harrell, William A. Educational Reform in Brazil. Washington, D.C.: Office of Education, U.S. Department of Health, Education and Welfare, 1968.

Hewlett, S.A. "Rate of Return Analysis: Its Role in Determining the Significance of Education in the Development of Brazil." Mimeographed. 1970.

Higgins, Benjamin. Economic Development—Problems, Principles and Policies. Rev. ed. New York: W.W. Norton, 1968.

Instituto Brasileiro de Reforma Agraria. A Estrutura Agraria Brasileira, Dados Preliminares, vol. 1. Rio de Janeiro, 1967.

Instituto de Investigaciones Sociales de la Universidad Nacional Automa de Mexico. El Perfil de Mexico, en 1980. Mexico City, 1970.

International Bank for Reconstruction and Development. The Current Economic Position and Prospects of Ecuador. Washington, D.C., 1973.

_____. The Current Economic Position and Prospects of Peru. Washington, D.C., 1973.

_____. Economic Growth of Colombia. Washington, 1972.

_____. Nigeria: Options for Long Term Development. Washington, D.C., 1974.

International Labor Office. Towards Full Employment: A Programme for Colombia. Geneva, 1970.

_____. Employment, Incomes and Equality: A Report on Kenya. Geneva, 1972.

_____. Matching Employment Opportunities and Expectations: A Programme of Action for Ceylon. Geneva, 1971.

_____. Employment and Income Policies for Iran. Geneva, 1973.

International Monetary Fund. Balance of Payments Yearbook. Washington, D.C., various volumes.

Iran Trade and Industry Publications. Echo of Iran, The Fifth Five Year Plan. Teheran, 1973.

Iranian Statistical Institute. 1969 Rural and Urban Household Budget Survey. Teheran: 1970.

Johnston, Bruce. "Criteria for the Design of Agricultural Development Strategies." Food Research Institute Studies in Agricultural Economics, Trade, and Development (1972).

Johnston, Bruce, and Peter Kilby. Agricultural Strategies, Rural-Urban Interactions and the Expansion of Income Opportunities. Paris: Organization for Economic Cooperation and Development, Development Center, 1973.

Kafka, Alexandre. "The Brazilian Stabilization Program, 1964-1967." Journal of Political Economy (August 1967).

Kaldor, N. "Alternative Theories of Income Distribution." Review of Economic Studies (1955/56).

Kanesa-Thasan, S. "Stabilizing an Economy—A Study of the Republic of Korea." International Monetary Fund Staff Papers (March 1969).

BIBLIOGRAPHY

Kendrick, David. "Mathematical Models for Regional Planning." Regional and Urban Economics (November 1971).

King, Timothy. Mexico: Industrialization and Trade Policies Since 1940. London: Oxford University Press, 1970.

Kitamura, Hiroshi. "Trade and Capital Needs of Developing Countries and Foreign Assistance." Weltwirtschaftliches Archiv (1966).

Krieger, Ronald. "Inflation and the 'Brazilian Solution'," Challenge (September/October 1974).

Ladman, Jerry. "A Model of Credit Applied to the Allocation of Resources in a Case Study of a Sample of Mexican Farms." Economic Development and Cultural Change (January, 1974).

Lal, D. "On Estimating Income Distribution Weights for Project Analysis." Economic Staff Working Paper No. 130. International Bank for Reconstruction and Development, 1972.

Langoni, C. Distribuicao da Renda e Desenvolvimento Economico do Brazil. Rio de Janeiro, 1973.

_____. "Distribuicao da Renta e Desenvolvimento Economico do Brazil," Estudos Economicos (1972).

Lefeber, Louis, and Mrinal Datta-Chaudhuri. Regional Development: Experiences and Prospects in South and South East Asia. The Hague: Mouton, 1971.

Little, Ian; Tibor Scitovsky; and Maurice Scott. Industry and Trade in Some Developing Countries. New York: Oxford University Press, 1970.

Looney, Robert. The Economic Development of Iran: A Recent Survey with Projections to 1981. New York: Praeger Publishers, 1973.

_____. "Industrial Decentralization in Iran." University of Santa Clara Business Review (1973).

Lopes, Francisco Lafaiete de Padua. Inequality and Growth: A Programming Model with Applications to Brazil. Cambridge: Development Research Group, Center for International Affairs, Harvard University, 1973.

Mayer, Thomas. Permanent Income, Wealth and Consumption. Berkeley: University of California Press, 1973.

McKinnon, Ronald I. Money and Capital in Economic Development. Washington, D.C.: The Brookings Institution, 1973.

Mendoza-Berrueto, E. "Regional Implications of Mexico's Economic Growth." Weltwirtschaftliches Archiv (September 1968).

Meyer, Richard L., et al. "Rural Capital Markets and Small Farmers in Brazil, 1960-1972." Washington, D.C.: Agency for International Development, Small Farmer Credit in South America, 1973.

Ministerio do Planejamento e Coordenacao Economica. Programa de Acao Economica do Governo, 1964-1966. Rio de Janeiro: 1964.

Ministry of Agriculture and Forestry. Agriculture in Korea. Seoul, 1970.

Ministry of Economy. Annual Industrial Survey. Teheran, various issues.

Ministry of Education. Educational Statistics in Iran. Teheran, 1963-71.

_____. Statistical Yearbook of Education. Seoul, various issues.

Ministry of Water and Power. The Law for Establishment of Companies for Utilization of Lands Downstream. Teheran, n.d.

Mobertson, H.M. "Alfred Marshall's Aims and Methods Illustrated from his Treatment of Distribution." History of Political Economy (Spring 1970).

Morawetz, D. "Employment Implications of Industrialization in Developing Countries." The Economic Journal (September 1974).

Morley, Samuel, and Jeffrey Williamson. "Demand, Distribution and Employment: The Case of Brazil." Economic Development and Cultural Change (October 1974).

Myers, Charles Nash. Education and National Development in Mexico. Princeton: Industrial Relations Section, Department of Economics, Princeton University, 1965.

BIBLIOGRAPHY

Nelson, Richard. "Aggregate Production Functions and Medium Range Growth Projections." American Economic Review (September 1964).

Nwaneri, V.C. "Income Distribution and Project Selection." Finance and Development (September 1973).

Ojha, P.D., and George Lent. "Sales Taxes in Countries of the Far East." International Monetary Fund Staff Papers (November 1969).

Orwell, George. The Road to Wigan Pier. New York: Harcourt, Brace and World. 1958.

Oshima, Harry T. "Income Inequality and Economic Growth—The Postwar Experience of Asian Countries." Malayan Economic Review (October 1970).

Pahlevi, H.I.M. Mohammad Riza Shah. Mission for My Country. New York: McGraw-Hill, 1961.

Pasinetti, L.L. "Rate of Profit and Income Distribution in Relation to the Rate of Economic Growth." Review of Economic Studies (October 1962).

Platt, Kenneth B. "Land Reform in Iran," Land Reform in Iran, Iraq, Pakistan, Turkey and Indonesia. Washington: Agency for International Development, 1970.

Politica Tributaria. Ministerio do Planejamento e Coordenacao Economica. Plano Decenal de Desenvolvimento Economico e Social, Tomo 2, Aspectos Macroeconomicos, vol. 1. Rio de Janeiro: 1967.

Raposo, Ben-Hur. Reforma Agraria Paro o Brazil. Rio de Janeiro: Ed. Fundo da Cultura, 1965.

Republic of Korea, Office of National Tax Administration. An Outline of Korean Taxation. Seoul, 1967; An Outline of Korean Taxation Seoul: 1968.

Review of the Economic Situation of Mexico (May 1974). "Austerity in Public Expenditure—A Weapon in the Fight Against Inflation."

Review of the Economic Situation of Mexico (August 1972). "Industrial Decentralization."

Review of the Economic Situation of Mexico (May 1973). "Population and Development: Interdependent Phenomena."

Reynolds, Clark. The Mexican Economy—Twentieth-Century Structure and Growth. New Haven: Yale University Press, 1970.

Ross, John. The Economic System of Mexico. Stanford: The California Institute of International Studies, 1971.

Rossmiller, Goerge, et al. Korean Agricultural Sector Analysis and Recommended Development Strategies, 1971-1985. East Lansing: Michigan State University, Department of Agricultural Economics, 1972.

Rweyemamu, J. F. "A Model of Perverse Capitalist Industrial Development," East African Economic Review (1972).

Schum, G. Edward. The Agricultural Development of Brazil. New York: Praeger Publishers, 1970.

Schumacher, E. F. "Industrialization Through 'Intermediate Technology,'" in Developing the Third World. Edited by Ronald Robinson. Cambridge: Cambridge University Press, 1971.

Sen, S. R. A Richer Harvest. Maryknoll, N. Y.: Orbis Books, 1974.

Shaffer, James, et al. "Review of Organization and Performance of the Agricultural Marketing System in Korea." Korean Agricultural Sector Study. East Lansing: Michigan State University Agricultural Sector Study Team, 1969.

Shaw, Edward. Financial Deepening in Economic Development. New York: Oxford University Press, 1973.

Shoko, Okazaki. The Development of Large-Scale Farming in Iran—The Case of the Province of Gorgan. Tokyo: Maruzen, 1968.

Shoup, Carl S. The Tax System of Brazil. Rio de Janeiro: Fundacao Getulio Vargas, 1965.

Solow, R. M. "Technical Change and the Aggregate Production Function." Review of Economics and Statistics (August 1957).

Stickley, S. Thomas, and Ebrahim Hosseini. "Small Farmer Credit in Iran—The Supervised Agricultural Credit Program of the

BIBLIOGRAPHY

Agricultural Cooperative Bank of Iran." Washington, D.C.: Agency for International Development Spring Review of Small Farmer Credit, vol. IX, 1973.

Stickley, S. Thomas, and Bahaoldin Majafi. "The Effectiveness of Farm Corporations in Iran." Tahqiqat-e Eqtesadi (Winter 1971).

Suk, Kim Kwang. "Rates of Return on Education in Korea." Mimeographed. Seoul, 1968.

Syvrud, Donald. Foundations of Brazilian Economic Growth. Stanford, Calif.: Hoover Institution Press, 1974.

Time. March 24, 1975.

United Nations. Yearbook of National Account Statistics. New York, various volumes.

_____. Income Distribution in Latin America. New York, 1971.

_____. Statistical Yearbook, 1969. New York, 1970.

_____. Economic Commission for Asia and the Far East. Intraregional Trade Projections, Effective Protection and Income Distribution. Bangkok, 1972.

United States Operations Mission to Korea. Rural Development Program Evaluation Report. Agency for International Development. Washington, D.C.: 1967.

Urquidi, V. L., and A. Lajous Vargas. Educacion Superior, Ciencia y Tecnologia en el Desarrollo Economico de Mexico. Mexico City, 1967.

Vanek, Jaroslav. Estimating Foreign Resource Needs for Economic Development. New York: McGraw-Hill, 1967.

Venezian, Eduardo, and William Gamble. The Agricultural Development of Mexico—Its Structure and Growth Since 1950. New York: Praeger Publishers, 1969.

Vietorisz, T. "The Planned Interregional Location of Industry: Argument in Favor of a 'Trade-Not-Aid' Approach," in Industrial Location and Regional Development: Proceedings of Interregional Seminar Minsk, 14-26 August 1968. New York: United Nations, 1971.

Wells, John. Distribution of Earnings Growth and Structure of Demand in Brazil, 1959-1971. Cambridge, Eng.: Center of Latin American Studies, University of Cambridge, 1972.

Whetten, N. L. Rural Mexico. Chicago: University of Chicago Press, 1948.

Wilkie, James W. The Mexican Revolution: Federal Expenditure and Social Change since 1910. Berkeley: University of California Press, 1970.

Williamson, Jeffrey. "Dimensions of Postwar Philippine Economic Progress." Quarterly Journal of Economics (February 1969).

World Bank. Trends in Developing Countries. Washington: 1973.

Yates, P. L. El Desarrollo Regional De Mexico. Mexico City: Bank of Mexico, 1961.

Young-Kyun, Oh. "Agrarian Reform and Economic Development: A Case Study of Korean Agriculture." Koreana Quarterly (1969)

Zahedani, Abdolhossain. "Iran: Evaluation of Agricultural Development Strategy 1962-1972." Ph.D. dissertation, University of California, Davis, 1974.

ABOUT THE AUTHOR

ROBERT E. LOONEY is Assistant Professor of Economics at the University of Santa Clara, and Senior Economist for Louis Berger International. Previously he was a lecturer in economics at the University of California, Davis, and a development economist at The Stanford Research Institute. He has traveled extensively in Iran, Latin America, and the Far East, during which time he gathered most of the material incorporated in the present study.

Dr. Looney received his B.S. degree in chemistry and Ph.D. in Economics from the University of California, Davis.

RELATED TITLES
Published by
Praeger Special Studies

BRAZILIAN ECONOMIC POLICY: An
Optimal Control Theory Analysis
        Gian Singh Sahota

DEVELOPMENT IN RICH AND POOR
COUNTRIES: A General Theory with
Statistical Analyses
        Thorkil Kristensen

THE ECONOMIC DEVELOPMENT OF IRAN:
A Recent Survey with Projections to 1981
        Robert E. Looney

ECONOMIC GROWTH IN DEVELOPING
COUNTRIES—MATERIAL AND HUMAN
RESOURCES: Proceedings of the Seventh
Rehovot Conference
        edited by Yohanan Ramati

INCOME DISTRIBUTION: A Comparative
Study of the United States, Sweden, West Germany,
East Germany, the United Kingdom, and Japan
        Martin Schnitzer

*PATTERNS OF POVERTY IN THE THIRD
WORLD: A Study of Social and Economic
Stratification
        Charles Elliott, assisted by
        Francoise de Morsier

*Also available as a Praeger Special Studies Student Edition.